White Self-Criticality
beyond Anti-racism

Philosophy of Race

Series Editor:
George Yancy, Duquesne University

The Philosophy of Race book series publishes interdisciplinary projects that center upon the concept of race, a concept that continues to have very profound contemporary implications. Philosophers and other scholars, more generally, are strongly encouraged to submit book projects that seriously address race and the process of racialization as a deeply embodied, existential, political, social, and historical phenomenon. The series is open to examine monographs, edited collections, and revised dissertations that critically engage the concept of race from multiple perspectives: sociopolitical, feminist, existential, phenomenological, theological, and historical.

White Self-Criticality beyond Anti-racism, edited by George Yancy

White Self-Criticality
beyond Anti-racism

How Does It Feel to Be a White Problem?

Edited by
George Yancy

LEXINGTON BOOKS
Lanham • Boulder • New York • London

Published by Lexington Books
An imprint of The Rowman & Littlefield Publishing Group, Inc.
4501 Forbes Boulevard, Suite 200, Lanham, Maryland 20706
www.rowman.com

16 Carlisle Street, London W1D 3BT, United Kingdom

British Library Cataloguing in Publication Information Available

Library of Congress Cataloging-in-Publication Data

White self-criticality beyond anti-racism : how does it feel to be a white problem? / edited by George
Yancy.
 pages cm. – (Philosophy of race)
 Includes bibliographical references and index.
 ISBN 978-0-7391-8949-8 (cloth : alk. paper) – ISBN 978-0-7391-8950-4 (ebook)
 1. Whites. 2. Whites–United States. 3. Racism. 4. Race relations. 5. United States–Race relations. I.
Yancy, George.
 HT1575.W47 2015
 305.809–dc23
 2014033100

♾™ The paper used in this publication meets the minimum requirements of American
National Standard for Information Sciences Permanence of Paper for Printed Library
Materials, ANSI/NISO Z39.48-1992.

Printed in the United States of America

In loving memory of both
my father, George Dewey Yancey, EL (1935–2014), and
philosopher and true friend, Joyce Mitchell Cook (1933–2014)

Contents

Acknowledgments

I would like to thank the contributors to this very important volume, especially for their commitment to fight against white supremacy and all the ways in which whiteness continues to function as a complex site of power, hegemony, and privilege. Thanks for being allies in the struggle to create a better world, one free from all forms of oppression.

I would like to thank Jana Hodges-Kluck, associate editor at Lexington Books. Jana is an absolute delight to work with. She has an astute sense of the mechanics of publishing and a very creative capacity to generate new ideas and to recognize and appreciate new projects. She also has her finger on the pulse of books that are designed to make a difference in our world. I would like to thank all of those who worked diligently toward the successful completion of this book: Natalie Mandziuk, Kari A. Waters, Lara Graham, and June Sawyers. Thanks for your professionalism and logistical help.

Thanks to James Swindal, professor of philosophy and dean of the McAnulty College of Liberal Arts. Jim has continued to respect my scholarship and has been a wonderful colleague and friend. Jim values fairness and embodies the mission of Duquesne University, which is to serve God by serving students. Thanks to Professor Fred Evans who has continued to be an intellectual partner, friend, and mentor.

Thanks to James Spady and the Marcus Garvey Foundation for their dedication to justice, nurturing young creative minds, and for the care that they demonstrated when I needed it most. Thanks to Charles Johnson for his support of my work and for his unconditional friendship. I am inspired by his humility and his incredible spirit to give of himself. There is so much to learn from him, ethically, spiritually, and intellectually. I would also like to thank Charles for the moving article that he sent to me when I needed it most.

Thanks to my student, Andy Mysliwiec, for creatively engaging James Baldwin's conception of a fixed star in terms of an analogy of being at sea. His navigational analogy was greatly appreciated within the context of thinking about white identity. Also, thanks to Tim Wood for taking, I believe, most of my philosophy courses. I wish him the best as he embarks upon his next challenge.

To the Yancy boys, please know that your dad refuses to settle for mediocrity. I expect that you will do the same. And know that I will always, always love you. To my mother and sister, you are always in my heart.

To Susan, you were there with me, together, as my dad continued to breathe, continued *to be with* us until he decided to be free. Thanks for being there with me during the most significant loss in my life to date.

Introduction

Un-Sutured

George Yancy

To be undone by another is a primary necessity, an anguish, to be sure, but also a chance—to be addressed, claimed, bound to what is not me, but also to be moved, to be prompted to act, to address myself elsewhere, and so to vacate the self-sufficient "I" as a kind of possession.—Judith Butler [1]

As a philosopher who thinks about and writes on themes within the areas of critical philosophy of race and critical whiteness studies, I aim to craft a style of writing where the *words become flesh*. The objective is to make words *do things* on the page. Often I am told by readers of my work that my style of writing captures the *lived* existential dynamics of race. Through the use of certain turns of phrase, the creative deployment of onomatopoeia, and the careful delineation of social encounters, along with their interstitial complexity, I am able to situate readers within the context of the thickness of various racial/racist real world encounters. For lack of a better expression, I defend what I call the "density project." The density project is an approach that emphasizes the importance of critically engaging the absolutely *messy* process of racialization as this process is *lived*. Hence, I describe and articulate the "dramaturgically" complex ways in which race is enacted or, more specifically, racialization is performed, within quotidian, embodied spaces of social transaction. These embodied spaces of social transaction are filled with rituals, spoken words, silences, grimaces, reactions, signs and symbols, body gestures, gazes, projections, denials, myths, and complex emotions. As I write, I attempt to dwell within the multifaceted landscape, as it were, of racial incidents, which are often so subtle that one might think there is nothing there of racial significance or consequence. My approach to writing about race is *not* inaugural. I am inspired by Frantz Fanon and his ability to *enflesh* the conceptual terrain vis-à-vis race as lived.

Within the context of this current volume, the density project locates the problem of whiteness within the context of its socio-political ontological constitution, its socio-historical embedded reality, and the implications of whiteness on the lives of black people or people of color. Hence, the density project, in relationship to the *desideratum* of white self-interrogation, emphasizes how white bodies are always already implicated in processes of racialization and racist complicity *ab initio.* The density project holds that the continued existence of white racism, its complex embodied expressions, is not simply the result of those who hold to the view that the concept of race does indeed *refer* to a state of affairs or a biological/genetic referent that is extra-conceptual. Rather, the density project holds that the concept of race— independently of the philosophical and scientific debates regarding its referential or non-referential status, and independently of questions of rational capacity—remains pregnant with real *qua* lived socio-ontological and psychological meaning that gets expressed behaviorally in the form of white racism. Indeed, the social, psychological, and phenomenological reality of race for whites is constituted through the intersubjective and interpersonal matrix in terms of which whites perform a shared mode of being-*raced*-in-the-world, a form of being-in-the-word that is marked as "benign" and "natural," but is nefariously oppressive and cunningly deceptive. Indeed, it is the seemingly unremarkable ways in which whiteness lives its social ontology that is fundamentally problematic. This distinction is important to make lest we only label those acts racist that are enacted by self-ascribed white racist individuals/groups. In short, then, specifically challenging anti-black white racism vis-à-vis its embodied lived reality for whites is not just a question of getting them to relinquish a false ontology or simply getting them to be more rational agents through the deployment of abstract ethical principles. Much more is required at the level of white *everyday practices* and the ways in which those white practices re-center white power or challenge white power. Such everyday practices consist of forms of life that are imbued with political, economic, social, imaginative, epistemic, aesthetic, axiological, and affective vectors. White self-interrogation, however, is a form of *striving*, etymologically, "to quarrel [*streiten*]" which means that one is committed to a life of danger and contestation, one which refuses to make peace with taken for granted "legitimating" white norms and practices that actually perpetuate racial injustice.

In this text, I have brought together a critical cadre of fourteen white scholars to address the question: "How does it feel to be a white problem?" Notice that the question asked is logically dissociable from the question regarding the ontological referential status of the concept of race. The question places these white scholars within the very heart of the lived, existential domain of a social ontology where whiteness is performed. Indeed, the question itself is a *relational* one as it implicates black bodies and bodies of color that suffer under the weight of the reality that whiteness is a problem, which means that *to be white* in white America is *to be a problem*. Each of the white scholars within this text is aware that he/she is not providing us with "unreflective confessions of badness, in this case the badness of participating in systemic racism."[2] All of the contributors are cognizant of the importance of practicing forms of epistemological humility that are necessary for white people to challenge whiteness as the transcendental norm that actually conditions their perception of themselves as not needing to undo anything at all. As the transcendental norm, whiteness actively militates against the recognition of itself as a problem. Each contributor is also deeply skeptical of any formulaic solution or easy fix to the problem of whiteness and white supremacy. And even as these white scholars are embedded within white racist forms of supremacy, they contest, though always already fallibly, the temptation for *uncritical* confessional expurgation, guilt, and shame, especially as these can easily function as forms of seeking shelter from doing something about the ongoing reality of white racism. What is required is one's activism against the prolongation of white racism. After all, after the publication of this book, white supremacy will continue and the contributors will remain white within its oppressive institutional structures. Indeed, "their experiences, beliefs, and behaviors [will continue to be] shaped by and contribute to a white-dominated world."[3] And the question will remain: "How does it feel to be a white problem?"

In *Black Bodies, White Gazes: The Continuing Significance of Race* (2008), I theorized the concept of ambush as a phenomenon that many well-intentioned white people undergo in the process of engaging in anti-racist activism, a process of which the scholars within this book are aware. I argued that whiteness is a master of disguise, but that whiteness is undone through profound irruptions that belie self-mastery. As I show in that book, etymologically, the word "insidious" (*insidiae*) means to *ambush*. An ambush experience is a profound and powerful metaphor as it brings to mind images and scenarios of being snared and trapped suddenly and unexpectedly. I argued that whiteness as a form of ambushing is not an anomaly and that the operations of whiteness are by no means completely transparent. This is partly what it means to say that whiteness is insidious, that is it not "fixable" through micro-management, though vigilance is indispensable. The moment that a white person claims to have "arrived," to be self-sufficient or self-grounded in their anti-racism, she often undergoes a surprise attack, a form of attack that points to how whiteness insidiously returns, how it ensnares, and how it is an iterative process that indicates the reality of white racist relational processes that exceed the white self. Hence, questions of temporality and historical constitution are essential ways of framing white identity formation, of theorizing the socio-ontological horizon within which white identity emerges and in terms of which the conditions for white ambush are more effectively explained.

In thinking through the importance of ambush as an expansion of the critical conceptual vocabulary for interrogating whiteness, I later came to link the concept of ambush to the concept of *dispossession*. Hence, in *Look, a White! Philosophical Essays on Whiteness* (2012) I connected the phenomenon of ambush vis-à-vis whiteness to what I began to recognize as indicative of a deeper *opaque* white racist self, one that is alien to itself, one that is a site of dispossession. On this score, the condition for ambush became explicitly linked to, and presupposed, a *relational* white self, one that has undergone processes of *arrival*. In short, arrival signifies that one has undergone social and psychological anterior processes of white subject formation that profoundly limit direct *epistemic* introspective access to aspects of the constituted white racist self. So, there was a progressive movement from theorizing whiteness as a site of ambush, of thinking through the conditions for white ambush, and then of theorizing those conditions in terms of how they are linked to the concept of white identity as a site of opacity and dispossession.

Given the above, I critiqued the concept of the white self as a site of self-possession or self-mastery vis-à-vis whiteness or white racism. The concept of white people undergoing processes of *crisis* and *losing their way* made sense given the ways in which I had hitherto mapped the psychic and socially embedded terrain of whiteness. Hence, in my co-edited book, *Exploring Race in Predominantly White Classrooms: Scholars of Color Reflect* (2014), I argued that it is important to cultivate spaces where white students, and whites more generally, can experience *crisis*. I argued that in therapeutic terms, "crisis" is typically something that we want to mitigate with alacrity. By crisis, however, I meant not only the sense of losing one's footing, of *losing one's way*, or a process of disorientation, but the etymological sense of the word (from the Greek *krisis*, that is, decision) where one is faced with the need to make *a decision* and where that decision has momentous implications. Within the context of having theorized whiteness as a site of ambush and as a site of dispossession in relationship to the fictive conception of the white self as a site of self-possession, my aim was to argue that a single action or intention does not "undo" whiteness. The concept of *deciding* denotes a life of commitment to "undo," to "trouble," over and over again, the complex psychic and socio-ontological ways in which one is embedded in whiteness. The decision is one that is made over and over again for the rest of one's life. Hence, the concept of crisis is suggestive of an iterative process that is to be reenacted.

Sustaining the process of being in crisis is demanding as it will require an iterative process of *losing one's way* vis-à-vis one's whiteness, especially as white social norms work against this process. Yet, I argued that one must *tarry* not only with the sense of loss, a form of tarrying that militates against centering whiteness in the form of a guilt-ridden and pitied white subject, but with the pain and suffering that people of color endure because of the effects of the historical sedimentation of white modes of being and their continued subtle and not so subtle manifestations. Therefore, one must be prepared to *linger*, to remain, with the truth about one's white self and the truth about how whiteness has structured and continues to structure forms of relationality that are oppressive to people of color. White people will typically flee such situations. They will seek a false sense of moral refuge by denying or eliding the various ways in which whiteness privileges them, infuses their being, their perception, and their affective and imaginative lives; indeed, the ways in which whiteness constitutes their embodiment, spatial motility, and "normalcy."

To expose white people to the idea that they *don't know who they are*, especially within a larger liberal ideological framework of intelligibility that reinforces the notion of "a radical creation of the self *ex nihilo*,"[4] that inculcates the *fabulous* (as in fable) Horatio Alger narrative, along with the doctrine of meritocracy, is to invite obfuscation, denial, anger, accusation, disbelief, aggression, violence, stereotyping, and name-calling. As James Baldwin says, while writing to his nephew about the terrors of whiteness and how black bodies are deemed worthless and how they are imprisoned within slums, "I know your [white] countrymen do not agree with me about this, and I hear them saying, 'You exaggerate'"[5] or they scream, "No! This is not true! How *bitter* you are!"[6] Yet, the accusation of exaggeration or of bitterness can function as another mode of seeking moral shelter, of what I refer to as a process of *suturing*.

Within the context of explicating whiteness, its ontological structure, suturing (from Latin *sutura*, meaning a "seam" or a "sewing together") is the process whereby whites install forms of closure, forms of protection from counter-white axiological and embodied iterations, epistemic fissure, and white normative disruption.[7] The process of suturing involves an effort—though I'm sure that for whites it is not recognized as an effort or as a site of active maintenance—to be "invulnerable," "untouched," "patched," "mended together," "complete," "whole," "sealed," and "closed off." To be sutured also implies a state of being free from a certain kind of "infection." In other words, within the context of critically engaging whiteness, the concept of suture functions as a site of *keeping pure*, preserving what is unsullied. Moreover, to be sutured within the context of white identity is indicative of "the narrative authority"[8] of the white self that occludes alterity. The process of suturing, then, is reflective of another fable: the white self as a site of self-possession and in absolute control of its own meaning, where such meaning is taken to be grounded within a larger white narrative history underwritten by a natural/metaphysical teleology. The white sutured self, along with its white sutured history, does not falter.[9] The sutured white self that tells the story of its own history and identity is not "stopped in the midst of the telling."[10] The sutured white self is not "called into question by its relation"[11] to heteronomous, *socially constructed* white norms and structures of power. The relationship of constitution and dependence is actively nullified. In other words, the sutured, white imperial self's narration of its own identity tells a story of absolute autonomy (a law unto itself). Heteronomy is too threatening as it renders visible the historically contingent struts of white normative and institutional power, which would call into question such a grand gesture of white self-creation "out of nothing." Such a grand gesture is a species of the epistemological "god-trick" critiqued by feminist epistemologists regarding another fable: that how we "know" the world is generally non-perspectival, a view from *nowhere*. Hence, the white self's non-relational narration of its own historical and ontological significance avoids relational processes that would function as "signs of its undoing."[12] In the telling, then, the white self is unexposed and thereby not "gripped and undone by"[13] white normative technologies that point to contingent relational hegemonic discursive and non-discursive realities that structure the nature of whiteness.

This suturing process can be conceptually linked to Fred Evans's conception of an oracle voice, "that is, a discourse that elevates itself above the others by presenting itself as universal and absolute."[14] Indeed, one might say that a sutured, oracular voice refuses to hear the "interplay among voices,"[15] refuses to come to terms with its own historical contingency and (*un-sutured)* openness to undergo modification or complete revision. As sutured, whiteness relegates other voices to meaningless chatter that is said to lack epistemological, political or moral authority—mere cyphers. This suturing process is also conceptually linked to what Peggy McIntosh refers to as a "single-system seeing," one which "is blind to its own cultural specificity. It cannot see itself. It mistakes its 'givens' for neutral, pre-conceptual ground rather than for distinctive cultural grounding."[16] To be un-sutured, which is linked to *losing one's way*, is dispositional and aspirational. As such, being un-sutured involves a continuous process of renewal and commitment. According to Baldwin, "To act is to be committed, and to be committed is to be in danger. In this case, the danger, in the minds of most white Americans, is the loss of their identity."[17] Hence, there is danger in becoming un-sutured. To reference Judith Butler's epigraph above, there is a sense of deep anguish in the process of un-suturing. It is also a *chance* not only to be touched and addressed through alterity but to rethink critically the ways in which the white self is not a site of self-sufficiency and self-possession but a site of dispossession whereby the constitution of the white self is found *at a great distance*. I will return to this concept shortly.

WAYS OF BEING SUTURED

I am very familiar with the responses of whites who are afraid to risk vulnerability, who avoid the epistemic and affective revelations made available to them by nurturing dispositions or encouraging practices of being un-sutured, which is a powerful process of being uncovered, open, and having the capacity, even if it waxes and wanes, to avoid narrative closure,[18] denial, and evasion. In short, I know many whites who do not make space for the question: "How does it feel to be a white problem?" Figuratively, there is a continuous process of encrustation, a scabbing over, as it were, of the white self that strives to remain un-sutured vis-à-vis the reality of white racism. This "scabbing over" can be theorized as the various ploys that whites use consciously or unconsciously to cover over the profound pain and distress caused from being palpably exposed. Being un-sutured, however, is not just to remain open to be wounded, but it is also to cultivate the practice of remaining with *the opened wound itself,* of tarrying with the pain of the *opening itself,* the incision, as it were. The somatic discourse is very rich, as it should be. Un-suturing is an embodied process, a somatic experience that opens the body to undergo moments of passion (etymologically, suffering), that suggests creating trouble at the level of the ontology of the body itself: *Where does this body end? Where does this body begin? Just how solid is this body? Just how porous or permeable?* Put differently, un-suturing is a deeply embodied phenomenon that enables whites to come to terms with the realization that their embodied existence and embodied identities are always already inextricably linked to a larger white racist social integument or skin which envelops who and what they are. Their white embodied lives have already been claimed; there is no white self that stands above the fray, atomic, hands clean.

As an example of suturing, I recently published a piece on Trayvon Martin in the *New York Times* in a section called *The Stone.* The article generated over 600 comments. A few were sent directly to my university email address. One read:

> Your stock in trade is white guilt. Your vision of justice is payback. Whitey is the cause of all your problems. You peddle your racial hatred, that makes you a racist, the very evil you accuse me of. I read your screed on a summer's eve, you write like one. There's a special place in hell for those that lead others astray. Say hi to Teddy Kennedy and Hitler when you get there.[19]

My sense is that the writer of the message failed to be vulnerable, failed to be un-sutured, failed to tarry, failed to linger, failed to be in crisis, failed to be undone. What I had to say about Trayvon Martin and the historical white demonization of black male bodies and the power of the white gaze as a mobile phenomenon left him insensitive and accusatory. Notice the personal and *ad hominem* nature of the attack. Notice the commentary about my writing. There is no argument advanced. And there ought to have been one, especially as I apparently "lead others astray." Why eternal damnation? He was not undone by my words; apparently there was no space in which "to be addressed, claimed, bound to what was not [him]."[20] He did not "vacate the self-sufficient 'I' as a kind of possession."[21] In short, he remained sutured. I realize that there are white responses/reactions that need not necessarily indicate responding from a place of white suturing, but my understanding of whiteness and my personal experience with white people (and critically thinking about and listening to the collective experiences of black people and people of color) have taught me to *trust* my *judgment*, to trust my own *testimony* even as they are not incorrigible. Many of the comments that appeared online deployed what has been referred to as "distancing strategies,"[22] which are ways that white people avoid being implicated in the perpetuation of white racism. I see this as another species of suturing. In this case, many of the writers wanted me to comment on the "real" problem, that is, black-on-black crime. More specifically, they argued that my critique of white racism and its narrative, historical, and structural importance in the killing of Trayvon Martin was secondary, perhaps even fruitless.[23] However, one writer wondered if the other writers had even read the same article that I had written. I, too, wondered about this. As I have written about this elsewhere, the article did not reject the reality of black-on-black crime but theorized the structural and ideological history of anti-black racism and its contemporary manifestations. There was an effort to shift the discussion, to blame the victims. "Black-on-black crime," however, is not an *institutional system* based upon white racist assemblages of "knowledge" and an entire ideological apparatus underwritten by white hegemonic material power. While this does not make "black-on-black crime" any less important, I think that it is a mistake to deploy the discourse of "black-on-black crime" as a way to obfuscate the magnitude and toxicity of white supremacy and its impact on black people.[24] Indeed, such discourse renders black people the cause of their own demise. The writers failed to listen, *to hear themselves called from elsewhere.* They failed to tarry with the gravitas of the reality of white supremacy vis-à-vis the racist stereotyping of black male bodies. "Genuine listening involves being open to hear something new, beyond recognition, but this also calls for a special type of vulnerability."[25] Un-suturing forms the condition for troubling Procrustean forms of recognition and installing open spaces for new ways of *re-cognizing*.

I will share some other examples of suturing that I have experienced within other contexts. Recently, I was asked to provide the keynote address at a conference whose members are predominantly white. It was organized by theologians and philosophers of a certain (again predominantly white)

Christian denomination. It was their first conference on race. I wasn't sure what to expect, but I knew that it was important that I speak about what it means to be black in white racist America, realizing, of course, the complexity of the issue. It was also during this conference that I decided to introduce for the first time, as I recall, the ways in which I was thinking about the concept of being sutured and un-sutured vis-à-vis white racism. After listening to the presentations, I was very impressed. The papers were especially notable in terms of engaging, for the most part, racism within the historical context of their denomination. Yet, the papers fell short in terms of explicitly calling out contemporary forms of white racism. Hence, my keynote opened a conceptual and affective space, a kind of un-suturing, which troubled what I saw as subtle forms of white self-congratulatory performances. My objective was to challenge their sense of themselves as "good whites" who can now say, with deep moral satisfaction, that they held a conference on race. Hence, my aim was to demonstrate how their white bodies are implicated within the continuous history of contemporary white supremacy and white privilege, to let them know that their *first* conference on race was not to be praised. In retrospect, my sense is that I wanted to communicate to them that they had failed to become un-sutured. They had, in effect, become sutured through their so-called good act of holding the conference. All of the questions, with the exception of one, which was really a powerful moment of un-suturing, pointed to distancing strategies, that is, suturing. During my talk I discussed what it feels like to find oneself, as a black philosopher, within the context of predominantly white academic spaces.

Philosopher #1: "I know what that's like. I've been in predominantly black spaces, and I have felt that sense of alienation too, of being alone." As I began to respond by pointing out how she conflated the two situations, and how she really didn't hear me at all, I witnessed a moment of re-cognition on her face and through her body language. One could see that she knew that she had failed to allow herself to be addressed from elsewhere. Her response was to collapse differences, but in doing so she occluded a form of re-constitution through an encounter with alterity.

During my talk, I had already critically discussed how black bodies undergo daily experiences of pain and suffering within an anti-black world, and how these forms of suffering result from white racist micro-aggressions. This response was an instance of such a micro-aggression.

Philosopher #2: "So, do *white* people even suffer?" His question was *not* about whether or not white people suffer under white supremacy. That would have been a great question. Rather, he wanted to know if white people suffer *as such* as I had only spoken about black pain and suffering under white supremacy. I was actually shocked by the question. What had I said about black people that would encourage that question? I said aloud that I had no idea how that question was relevant. I went on to say, yes, white people obviously suffer: they are vulnerable, they lose loved ones, and they undergo physical injuries like stubbing their toes in the middle of night. This last point actually garnered a bit of laughter. I went on to say to him, however, that white people *don't suffer* in ways that I had delineated black suffering under white supremacy. Had he been overwhelmed by my account of black suffering? Did he become defensive? Why would he interject the question of *white* suffering within a context where whites in that conference space were being told in no uncertain terms how black people suffer vis-à-vis whiteness? This was about black pain and suffering, not about white pain and suffering. My sense is that he remained sutured. He had to lay claim to (and remain sutured to) *white* pain and suffering as a way of reclaiming the white conference space, as a way of not losing himself, as a way of staying on the course of whiteness. Shannon Sullivan has warned of what she calls white ontological expansion where whites tend "to see all spaces—physical, cultural, and otherwise—as available for their legitimate inhabitation."[26] In some sense, he wanted to "inhabit" the narrative space of black pain and suffering that I had delineated. He wanted to consume, to colonize, the empathetic space that I was striving to create. For him, it was about *white* pain and suffering. He failed to critique the limits of a certain white ontological horizon. As Butler writes, "To make oneself in such a way that one exposes those limits is precisely to engage in an aesthetics of the self that maintains a critical relation to existing norms."[27]

Relying on the work of black theologian James Cone, I argued that whiteness is a form of *structural sin*,[28] that white people are embedded within a system that they did not choose. Yet, that system continues to hail them in ways that have violent implications for people of color.

Philosopher #3: "Yes. I agree that there is sin. We live in a sinful world." I immediately responded by saying that this was not my point. My point was that whiteness is a *specific* structural sin, a unique historical phenomenon for which whites are responsible. This form of suturing involved placing white supremacy, which was in no way historically necessary, under the rubric of the Christian narrative of the "fall of man." By doing so, the poignancy regarding my point about white supremacy, and by implication his white power and privilege, functioned to dismiss whiteness as a unique trajectory of structural sin. My point was to communicate, which I did, that this move lets whites off the proverbial hook by construing white supremacy as an unfortunate epiphenomenon of the "fall of man."

As the question-and-answer session was coming to a close, there was one additional hand up that I felt compelled to acknowledge. It was Wonil Kim, who is a specialist in Old Testament studies. He didn't have a question;

rather, he provided a powerful and unforgettable disclosure resulting from being addressed from elsewhere, from a place of alterity. If love can be described in the form of a profound risk, a self-effacing movement toward another in absolute honesty, even as there is no guarantee of reciprocity, then Kim displayed love that day. Kim began by openly sharing with me how he grew up in South Korea and that he was half Korean and half white. It was very powerful when he said that my keynote address functioned as an "epiphany and epistemological rupture" (his words) and that it encouraged him to think about his mixed race identity and how he thought about or imagined what it would have been like for him to have been half *black* and half Korean. He went on to explain that if he was going to experience being un-sutured he would need "to have a cut that would remain un-sutured." He shared his realization that he didn't know what that open wound would be like in the American experience of black and white people. In fact, he told me that he had planned to ask me how he could imaginatively connect to the experience of blackness, but that as he *listened* to me he changed his mind. One might say that he underwent a species of *kenosis* (emptying). Kim said that not only was it difficult to imagine what it would have been like to be half black and half Korean but that he did not want to imagine the black part of that experience. It was at this point that his voice cracked. Tears began to flow. A colleague near him had placed his arm around him. He later wrote to me: "After having heard you, I realized that I could not handle the experience of being black or half black; that my imaginative scenarios of being half black were naïvely romantic, nothing more than patronizing bullshit. No, I would not be able to handle the experience of being black, imaginatively or otherwise." He continued: "Even if I could do it in my head, I wouldn't be able to do it outside the intellectual playground; I wouldn't be able to handle it existentially." His message concluded: "Both of my adopted parents are long gone now, but their love for me was legendary and I loved them dearly. I still do. But I do wonder from time to time if they—or any Korean couple or person at that time—would have adopted me had I been half black and not half white. This is a very painful question for me, but this pain is nothing compared to the pain of being half black in Korea and here, the experience of which I have naïvely and romantically, and yes, patronizingly fantasized about from time to time."

In the other three responses above, each philosopher failed to tarry with what was said, failed to *listen*. There was no apparent recognition that they were white problems. There was no un-suturing, no exposure, only the attempt to conceal or to preserve. As Butler writes, "One seeks to preserve oneself against the injuriousness of the other, but if one were successful at walling oneself off from injury, one would become inhuman. In this sense, we make a mistake, unless we accordingly claim that the 'inhuman' is constitutive of the human."[29] Kim became undone at precisely the moment of realizing that what I described regarding the black experience could not be covered over, conflated with known terms of his own life experience or easily assimilated within the confines of his horizon of meaning. This, it seems to me, was an instantiation of being un-sutured; it was "a cut that would remain un-sutured" during his emotionally public disclosure of being unable to complete the line of questioning which would have implied a form of self-possession. Instead, the un-suturing was a site of dispossession that bound Kim to what was not himself; thus, revealing, in the process, the fable of narrative closure and demonstrating the power of relational constitution. After Kim's question, there was a deep silence. I said to the group, let's stop here. Everyone agreed. No more questions needed to be asked. Kim made his way up to the front where I eagerly awaited. Nothing was said. We embraced. When bearing witness to such rare and profound moments like this, I struggle with the weight of the responsibility that these encounters demand, which forces me in turn to interrogate my feelings of not being quite good enough in terms of a moral person to facilitate such a deep and beautiful encounter.

FINDING ONE'S WHITE SELF AT A GREAT DISTANCE

Recently, I have introduced my undergraduate students to the arguments set forth in my book, *Look, a White!* I laid out for them the argument that the white self is a site of white racist psychic opacity that does not know the limits of its own racism. I also introduced the idea that, as white, they are socially embedded within white racist structures that constitute who they are and that render them complicit with the operations of racial injustice. The first time that I introduced these ideas to them, there was great resistance. In one rare and yet powerful moment, one white female student raised her hand and said, "Though I feel like I'm choking, *I am a racist.*" I pointed out to the class that her use of the term "choking" was a figuratively demonstrable way of relating to the complexity and difficulty of admitting to the charge of racism *(her* racism) rooted within the conceptual framework presented. After delineating in greater detail the meaning of the terms psychic opacity vis-à-vis white racism and what it means to be embedded within a systemically white racist social matrix, I explained to my white students that this meant that they undergo processes of interpellation or hailing from within and from without.

The "race" of students aside, it is difficult for undergraduate students to be told that they are not what and who they think they are. It is even more threatening to white students' sense of moral self-certainty when they are asked to address the reality of their racism, especially within the context of a political ideology that emphasizes color blindness and that defines white racism as anomalous and something committed by those who are filled with racial hatred. I explained to them that at the heart of that day's lecture was the question: As white, who are you? Having recently come across one of Heraclitus's fragments, I explored the fragment within the context of the question about whiteness and identity. Heraclitus says, "I went in search of myself."[30] Within the context of the conception of the opaque white racist self and the socially embedded white racist self, I explained that if they were to go in search of who they are as white, they would find themselves at a great distance. That is, because they do not recognize the various ways that they have been constituted as white, which precede their emergence, it will require them to move far outside of what they know themselves to be in order to be aware of who they are as white and as a problem.

Many of my white students have come to think of the search for oneself as involving an introspective project. Yet, the white self that they are in search of outstrips introspection; indeed, it has the character of being "over there." After all, as they go in search of themselves they will come to realize that who and what they are as white is a site of dispossession. That is, who they think they are as white is constituted by history, white power, white epistemic regimes, repetitions of white norms, implicit white alliances, white axiological frames of reference, white communities of intelligibility, white modes of being-in-the-word, and so on. Hence, as one goes in search of one's white self, one has to relinquish the concept of the white self as a kind of self-possession or as a site of mastery. I explained to them that they have always already been claimed by whiteness, that they are already at a great distance from where they think they are, self-grounded in *this* moment. My aim is to get them to think critically about questions of the formation of the white self (*their white selves*); to encourage them to see that within the historical context of whiteness, and its discursive forces, there are implicit assumptions and consequences relative to the "setting of limits to what will be considered to be an intelligible formation of the [white] self."[31] Hence, I encourage them to understand that "there is no making of oneself (*poiesis*) outside of a mode of subjectivation (*assujettissement*)."[32] The white self that goes in search of itself will find itself at a great distance, having undergone processes of subjectivation. Yet, the searching presupposes an opening that allows for critically rethinking specific processes or configurations of subjectivation. Having come across the Heraclitus fragment when I did proved to be more pedagogically rewarding than I imagined. That semester, Tom Ball, a graduate philosophy student whose area is ancient philosophy, was my teaching assistant. Within the specific context of Heraclitus's aphoristic fragment, Ball suggests:

> That he (Heraclitus) would need to go in search of himself raises the question of where his self is to be found. It is plausible that his search for himself is not

a purely internal investigation. Instead, Heraclitus may be suggesting that one must go into the world to locate the self. If this is the case, one must search for oneself outside of, beyond, oneself. The self, then, is constructed through its engagement with the world and, more importantly, through its engagement with the polis. The self is constrained and informed by the beliefs and practices of the culture in which it develops. To understand the self, then, one cannot simply look within, as if the full extent of these influences will be immediately comprehensible. Instead, one must look to the culture and practices of the culture. One must learn to read the signs that these external forces have left upon oneself.[33]

In learning "to read the signs that these external forces have left upon oneself," the implication is that there is a critical opening of recognition, a critical relation to subjectivation. Indeed, there is the implication that those signs, while functioning as constraints, can be disrupted, re-signified, and varied. If there was no critical distance, no epistemic fissuring of some sort, there would be no possibility for reading those signs or for learning to read those signs. Indeed, perhaps with no epistemic fissuring there would be no signs to be read *as signs*; there would be no recognition that external forces have left any signs at all. If the white self was reduced to nothing more than forms of white subjectivation, it would be fruitless to encourage my white students to recognize that they will find themselves at a great distance. The white self that goes in search of itself at a great distance must *exceed* the conditions in terms of which it is already claimed as white. Perhaps this is what Ball is getting at when he said to me, "The self is known and unknown." Given my work on white racist opacity, however, this is precisely the reality of the white self. I have suggested to my white students that if it is true that who and what they are, within the context of a white racist society, is located at a great distance, then what is necessary is the indispensability of installing *anti-racist* forms of configured subjectivation, discursive practices, and regimes of intelligibility. If I owe myself to things that are not me (yet, paradoxically me), things that make me who I am as a problem, then I (the I which resists change, where that resistance implies a gap) need to change the conditions, and the repetitions that call/hail a different kind of subject—a different me. Although she theorizes this dynamic process in terms of habits, Sullivan argues, "A person cannot merely intellectualize a change of habit by telling herself that she will no longer think or behave in particular ways. The key to transformation is to find a way of disrupting a habit through environmental change and then hope that the changed environment will help produce an improved habit in its place."[34]

Part of coming to terms with one's white self *as a problem* is the critical recognition that one was never the imperial self that one assumed or the innocent white body just minding its own business while shopping, taking out a loan, renting an apartment, driving a car, falling in love with another white body, taking an evening stroll, and so forth. More importantly, I wanted to communicate to my white students, those who claim not to have a white racist bone in their bodies, that there is a fungible relationship between who they are *qua* white and those whites who consciously and actively express their white racist hatred toward black people and people of color. As they move through the world, having been claimed by whiteness, their lives are complicit with a white supremacist system of interpellation, a system that they help to perpetuate and, by extension, a system that diminishes the humanity of black people and people of color. Thus, "active racists" and "passive racists" are, if you will, still sitting at the front of the Jim Crow bus, and black bodies, by implication, are still being forced to sit at the back. Given this, the "active" and "passive" racism distinction loses its clarity of division.

Coming to re-cognize themselves as white problems, there is work *to be done*, a form of work, self-work, a socio-ontological project that will not conclude in the form of a *fait accompli*. It is through the search that one undergoes loss, a kind of death. "But this death, if it is a death," according to Butler, "is only the death of a certain kind of subject, one that was never possible to begin with, the death of a fantasy of impossible mastery, and so a loss of what one never had. In other words, it is a necessary grief."[35] I would like for my students to grieve, to mourn, to be un-sutured. Explaining to his nephew what it will be like when white people realize the loss of their identities, Baldwin writes, "Try to imagine how you would feel if you woke up one morning to find the sun shining and all the stars aflame. You would be frightened because it is out of the order of nature."[36] Striving to remain un-sutured, which is a continuous process, is about losing one's way; it is about creating a critical relation to those signs and forces that continue to operate within a larger white racist process of interpellation.

NOTES

1. Judith Butler, *Giving an Account of Oneself* (New York: Fordham University Press, 2005), 136.
2. Maureen H. O'Connell, "After White Supremacy? The Visibility of Virtue Ethics for Racial Justice," *Journal of Moral Theology*, Vol. 3, No. 1 (2014), 96.
3. Shannon Sullivan, *Good White People: The Problem with Middle-Class White Anti-Racism* (New York: SUNY Press, 2014), 2.
4. Judith Butler, *Giving an Account of Oneself* (New York: Fordham University Press, 2005), 17.
5. James Baldwin, *The Fire Next Time* (New York: The Modern Library, 1995), 7.
6. Baldwin, *The Fire Next Time* (New York: The Modern Library, 1995), 5.
7. Barbara Applebaum, in a personal correspondence (July 2, 2014), asked two very important questions. She wanted to know if my conceptualization of suture works to sustain white ignorance in Charles Mills's sense and if being un-sutured functions "to sustain another type of white ignorance that is constructive, an ignorance in which whites become aware of opacity in which they don't know who they are?" She notes that "there seems to be two types of ignorance implied—one problematic and one perhaps necessary for challenging whiteness and that may

involve understanding the white self as 'known and unknown.'" Regarding her first point, I would agree. For Mills, an epistemology of ignorance involves a constructed way of seeing the world falsely, a kind of cognitive dysfunction. It is a site of "knowing," which is really a site of not knowing that is supported, in this case, by whiteness as a system that has deep racist doxastic implications for maintaining power and sustaining a view of the world that *appears* true. So, I would argue that suturing functions as a way of *not* seeing the world correctly; a way of remaining covered, as it were, by the veneer of truth. This would function as a problematic form of ignorance. I also agree with Applebaum's other point. Being un-sutured does function "to sustain another type of white ignorance that is constructive." To be un-sutured is to remain in that *constructive* space of unknowing that allows for vulnerability, for being wounded. It is within this space that the reality of white opacity can be triggered, as it were, where white people come to recognize the reality of the limits of self-understanding vis-à-vis their racism. While I address this later in the introduction, the "known and unknown" indicates a dynamic space of movement. For more on Mills' conception of epistemology of ignorance, see Charles W. Mills, *The Racial Contract* (Ithaca, New York: Cornell University Press, 1997).

8. Judith Butler, *Giving an Account of Oneself* (New York: Fordham University Press, 2005), 37.

9. Judith Butler, *Precarious Life: The Powers of Mourning and Violence* (New York: Verso, 2006), 23.

10. Judith Butler, *Precarious Life: The Powers of Mourning and Violence* (New York: Verso, 2006), 23.

11. Judith Butler, *Precarious Life: The Powers of Mourning and Violence* (New York: Verso, 2006), 23.

12. Judith Butler, *Precarious Life: The Powers of Mourning and Violence* (New York: Verso, 2006), 23.

13. Judith Butler, *Precarious Life: The Powers of Mourning and Violence* (New York: Verso, 2006), 23.

14. Fred Evans, *The Multivoiced Body: Society and Communication in the Age of Diversity* (New York: Columbia University Press, 2008), 11.

15. Fred Evans, *The Multivoiced Body: Society and Communication in the Age of Diversity* (New York: Columbia University Press, 2008), 199.

16. Peggy McIntosh, "Interactive Phases of Curricular and Personal Re-Vision with Regard to Race" Working Paper #219, Wellesley College Center for Research on Women (now Wellesley Centers for Women, 1990), 1.

17. James Baldwin, *The Fire Next Time* (New York: The Modern Library, 1995), 8.

18. Judith Butler, *Giving an Account of Oneself* (New York: Fordham University Press, 2005), 64.

19. Anonymous communication.

20. Judith Butler, *Giving an Account of Oneself* (New York: Fordham University Press, 2005), 136.

21. Judith Butler, *Giving an Account of Oneself* (New York: Fordham University Press, 2005), 136.

22. Barbara Applebaum, "White Ignorance and Denials of Complicity: On the Possibility of Doing Philosophy in Good Faith" in George Yancy (ed.) *The Center Must Not Hold: White Women Philosophers on the Whiteness of Philosophy* (Lanham: MD: Lexington Books, 2010), 10.

23. The reader will note that this is not something exclusively claimed by white people.

24. For an elaboration on this point within the context of the killing of Trayvon Martin, see: George Yancy, E. Ethelbert Miller, and Charles Johnson, "Interpretative Profiles on Charles Johnson's Reflections on Trayvon Martin: A Dialogue between George Yancy, E. Ethelbert Miller, and Charles Johnson." *The Western Journal of Black Studies*, Vol. 38, No. 1, 2014: 3-14. Johnson is to be especially thanked for his profound reflections on Trayvon Martin, reflections that led to the creation of this very important article.

25. Barbara Applebaum, "White Ignorance and Denials of Complicity: On the Possibility of Doing Philosophy in Good Faith" in George Yancy (ed.) *The Center Must Not Hold: White*

Women Philosophers on the Whiteness of Philosophy (Lanham: MD: Lexington Books, 2010), 16.

26. Shannon Sullivan, *Revealing Whiteness: The Unconscious Habits of Racial Privilege.* (Bloomington, IN: Indiana University Press, 2006), 177.

27. Judith Butler, *Giving an Account of Oneself* (New York: Fordham University Press, 2005), 17.

28. For those interested in how I theorize the concept of whiteness within the context of white Christian identity, see my edited book, *Christology and Whiteness: What Would Jesus Do?* (New York, Routledge, 2012), especially the introduction, 1-18.

29. Judith Butler, *Giving an Account of Oneself* (New York: Fordham University Press, 2005), 103.

30. Charles H. Kuhn, *The Art and Thought of Heraclitus* (New York: Cambridge University Press, 1979), 41, 116.

31. Judith Butler, *Giving an Account of Oneself* (New York: Fordham University Press, 2005), 17.

32. Judith Butler, *Giving an Account of Oneself* (New York: Fordham University Press, 2005), 17.

33. Personal correspondence, December 3, 2013.

34. Shannon Sullivan, *Revealing Whiteness: The Unconscious Habits of Racial Privilege* (Bloomington, IN: Indiana University Press, 2006), 9.

35. Judith Butler, *Giving an Account of Oneself* (New York: Fordham University Press, 2005), 65.

36. James Baldwin, *The Fire Next Time* (New York: The Modern Library, 1995), 8.

Chapter One

Flipping the Script . . . and Still a Problem

Staying in the Anxiety of Being a Problem

Barbara Applebaum

> *All of my ways of knowing seemed to have failed me—my perception, my common sense, my good will, my anger, honor and affection, my intelligence and insight. Just as walking requires something fairly sturdy and firm under-foot, so being an actor in the world requires a foundation of ordinary moral and intellectual confidence. Without that, we don't know how to be or how to act . . . the commitment against racism becomes itself immobilizing. . . . If you want to be good and you don't know good from bad, you can't move.*
>
> —Marilyn Frye[1]

George Yancy's invitation to this edited volume proposes a thought-provoking challenge. Invoking W. E. B. Du Bois's question to those on the receiving end of racism who are *perceived* by whites to be problems, Yancy compels whites to "flip the script" and inquire what it means for whites to understand *themselves* to be the problem of racism. To pose this question in this way is already to assume that the one addressed acknowledges that whites *are* the problem. In fact, one of the most insidious impediments to continued anti-racist work is that whites not only refuse to acknowledge racism as a problem and that whiteness is the problem of racism but they also presume that they are "good" and beyond racist structures. Whites often deny any complicity in racism, something that has become especially resilient to contestation in contemporary United States where the election of its first black president emboldens a post-racial climate.

Even whites who are willing to acknowledge that whites are the problem of racism and who are sensitized to the ways that whiteness works through its

Barbara Applebaum

invisibility are not exempt from being implicated in racism. In writing this chapter that attempts to invert the white gaze on to itself, for instance, the danger is always present that in so many ways whiteness and white privilege will be re-centered and the trap of "white fetishism,"[2] a phenomenon that allows whites to take back the center, will not be avoided. The admission of this danger itself can function as a manifestation of complicity. How to live being this type of problem, and the resulting tensions, is part of the task that I believe Yancy is encouraging us to address.

This has been exceptionally and personally challenging for me. As the quote by Marilyn Frye above intimates, even progressive white feminists trying to deal with their racism and the seemingly fugitive nature of whiteness have to come to terms with the discomfort of not being able to rely on what one knows to be true and good. Frye explains that much has failed her—her common sense, her perception, her insights, and even her goodwill. She expresses grief at the inadequacy of her sincere efforts to be anti-racist. She concludes that white feminists need to find new ways of being. As I studied more about the relationship between racism and whiteness and my own complicity in racism, my own intuitions about "being good" have been severely challenged.

I understand the project of flipping the script and asking "what does it feel like to be a problem" as twofold. On the one hand, it can be a request to share stories about my own struggles as a white person *to acknowledge* my complicity in racism rather than deny it. Some white theorists have already taken on this project.[3] On the other hand, the nature of complicity is such that one can never feel like one has "arrived." Complicity is an intractable problem. Yancy, I believe, is prodding whites to reflect on how *staying in the anguish of being a problem* might be negotiated. How is the attendant discomfort to be navigated? Being explicit about how whites negotiate living in the problem of complicity would open up those negotiations to critique and challenge that can be a unique contribution to the field. In this chapter, therefore, I will focus on the question "How does one negotiate the intractable problem of being complicit?"

Given this understanding of the project, I will proceed by first briefly considering the unique type of problem that white complicity is. I will examine its intractability by exploring the desire for white innocence and the notion of white ignorance along with the white distancing strategies such ignorance supports. Then I turn to recent discussions around Judith Butler's work to help rearticulate what it means "to be a problem." Butler is best known for her work troubling our ideas of gender and sexuality. Although we can recognize that ethical concerns have always informed her work on subject formation and her concern with "livability," it is only recently that she has *explicitly* engaged in ethics offering new directions for rethinking responsibility on the basis of rather than despite the opacity of the self.

Butler's recent work and the secondary scholarship around it suggest important directions for considering how whites might go about negotiating complicity. Sara Rushing[4] hints at what I aim to glean from Butler's work when she maintains that Butler presents us with "a disposition of restraint that is not a 'quietism' in the face of real and pressing issues, but rather a part of a cultivated, insurrectionary practice of not-yet-doing, when traditional modes of 'doing' are immediate and often deeply satisfying regardless of their unintended consequences."[5] Finally, employing insights from Butler and the scholarship around her work, I will return to white complicity and try to respond to Yancy's question: "What does it feel like to be a white problem?"

COMPLICITY AS AN INTRACTABLE PROBLEM

The Desire for Innocence

> Of course race and racism are impossible to escape; of course a white person is always in a sticky web of privilege that permits only acts which reinforce ("reinscribe") racism.[6]

> Does being white make it impossible for me to be good?[7]

I am teaching a graduate course on race and racism. As an introductory exercise, I asked the students to tell us their names and to briefly explain why they took the course. Two white student nurses both noted that they wanted to understand "diversity" better so that they could enhance their care for their clients. This pronouncement of their benevolence was recalled throughout the course as both nurses resisted learning about their whiteness. After an intense discussion of Alison Jones's[8] article in which she argues that white students' empathetic desire to know the Other functions as a form of absolution and as a refusal to know, one of the white students proclaimed, "But I want to know, I want to help." To this one of the students of color responded, "Who asked you for your help?" Both white students stormed out of the class in tears.

In what might seem a paradox, white benevolence is an important site to interrogate the type of problem that white complicity is. White benevolence not only comes with implicit requisite demands but might also function to silence those upon whom benevolence is bestowed. Because benevolence is considered "good," the one who bestows benevolence has in effect secured his/her innocence and does not have to question his/her implication in injustice.

Damien Riggs[9] recounts how his white friend responded to a powerful quote that Riggs had stuck to his refrigerator. The quote by Lilla Watson, an indigenous scholar, states, "If you have come to help me, you are wasting your time, but if you have come because your liberation is bound up with mine, let's work together." Riggs's white friend remarked quite indignantly, "Well, she's a rude bitch!" When Riggs asked her to clarify what she meant, his friend said, "It was very ungrateful for the author to refuse help. Comments like that not only offend the people who want to help but will discourage them from helping in the future." As this case illustrates, the cost of a white person's benevolence often requires the silencing of the Other who might not find the white person's benevolence helpful and who may even believe that such benevolence usurps the Other's agency.

Being a "good" white might function to disguise white complicity in various other ways. For example, in his study of "racism without racists," Eduardo Bonila-Silva[10] explains how white people use the ideology of color ignorance in ways that maintain systemic racial injustice without themselves appearing racist. In fact, the ideology of color ignorance, the belief that race no longer matters in the United States and that racial inequality will disappear if we just stop referring to race, is often perceived by white people as a moral virtue. Yet the refusal to take notice of color when race clearly matters in our society prevents racist patterns of practices from being recognized and interrogated.

There are numerous other ways to demonstrate how the desire "to be good" might be implicated in racial injustice. As someone who is interested in how white people learn about their complicity, I will focus on scholarship in which even efforts to learn about complicity are implicated in what they claim to want to disrupt.

The dominant approach to teaching about whiteness in the United States, white privilege pedagogy, has been shown to unwittingly obscure its own complicity in protecting racial systems of injustice from being contested. For example, Peggy McIntosh's[11] seminal essay on the "knapsack of privilege" metaphor and the list of privileges that people of color do not enjoy often promotes naïve solutions such as how much privilege whites can give up or thinking that the remedy for racial injustice is to ensure that all people have the privileges that they enjoy. When white students read McIntosh's article in this way, it often functions to relieve them from considering how they have any direct and active involvement in the perpetuation of racism. Privilege is just something that is passively bestowed upon them and not something that they actively perpetuate.

Indeed, although McIntosh distinguishes between positive and negative privileges, white students frequently ignore that having white privilege can be a negative capacity that no one should have. As McIntosh emphasizes, some of the benefits of white privilege are undesirable. They give white people license to be ignorant, oblivious and arrogant without even knowing it. We will return to this in the next section.

Second, if the prime objective in teaching about whiteness through white privilege is making what was invisible visible, white students might be encouraged to assume that an individualistic psychologizing around privilege is sufficient to redeem them from complicity. The emphasis on personal awareness, therefore, overshadows the need for understanding and challenging the system of power that supports white privilege.

In other words, whites often assume that responsibility begins and ends with the awareness of privilege. By admitting to or confessing privilege, however, whites are actually able *to avoid* owning up to their complicity in systemic racism. In acknowledging privilege, whites often believe that they have "arrived" and that they do not have to worry anymore about how they are implicated in systemic racial injustice. Cynthia Levine-Rasky[12] explains that confessions of privilege serve as a "redemptive outlet" through which whites are able to perceive themselves as "good whites" in comparison to those "bad whites" who do not acknowledge privilege. The assumption is "that confessing to the inner working of whiteness in their lives would redeem them from their complicity with racism."[13]

Third, and relatedly, white students often neither perceive white privilege as connected to larger systems of power (although McIntosh explicitly states that privilege "confers dominance") nor do they comprehend how such privilege constitutes their own identities. They fail to consider how privilege is relational. Indeed, McIntosh brings to the foreground that whites are not being followed around in stores while people of color are. Yet, there is another relational aspect of privilege that often goes unnoticed. Privilege is not only about being able to walk through a store freely but also consists in the assumption prevalent in the social imaginary of white moral integrity that is contingent upon the co-constructions of black as morally suspect. Cynthia Kaufman[14] explicates this exceedingly well.

> The image of the black thief helps stabilize the image of the average good citizen (who of course is coded as white). When I walk into a store and the clerks look at me with respect and assumes that I am not going to steal anything, the trust that I receive is at least partially built upon the foundation of my distance from the image of the savage. When an African American walks into the store that unconscious material comes into play in the opposite way.[15]

White privilege protects and supports white moral standing, and this protective shield depends on there being an "abject other" that relationally constitutes whites as "good." White moral standing is a benefit of white privilege. In fact, as Zeus Leonardo[16] explains, all whites are responsible for white dominance since their "very being depends on it."[17]

Even the morality of the white critic of whiteness must be interrogated for whitely ways. Sara Ahmed[18] examines the discursive strategy of "confessing" one's whiteness. In declaring that one is white, or racist, or complicit, according to Ahmed, the declaration is doing something other than what they ostensibly claim to do. Ahmed is not saying that in their declarations of whiteness, white people *do not mean* what they say. Instead, her point is that such assertions do not *do* what they say. For instance, in *declaring* "I am racist" or "I am complicit," the white critic of whiteness actually implies the opposite: "I am not racist" or "I am not complicit." Somewhat like the person who declares, "I am modest" is clearly not a modest person, Ahmed cautions the white critic of whiteness that the assertion that "I am a bad white" can *indirectly* entail that "I am really a good white."

Fiona Probyn's[19] insight that "a white studying whiteness trying not to reinscribe whiteness" is a paradox was beginning to resonate with me tremendously. Whiteness is not only the object of the white critic's inquiry but also the subject and the obstacle to his/her project, especially when it obstructs the difficult task of being skeptical of the need to "have arrived somewhere."

White privilege, therefore, is something white people tend to assert even as they seek to challenge it. "Noble" declarations of whiteness must be probed for their desires for purity. Ahmed similarly cautions that the social conditions are not yet in place for white people to think that they can be non-racist[20] and she insists, "We need to consider the intimacy between privilege and the work we do, even in the work we do on privilege."[21]

What is personally so provocative about this scholarship is the realization that I can reproduce and maintain racism even when, and *especially when*, I believe myself to be morally good. My white student nurses are implicated in racism even when they claim to want to know the Other, even when they believe they care. "The most recalcitrant forms of racism"[22] involve well-intended white people for whom being morally good may not only *not* facilitate anti-racist initiatives but may actually frustrate them.

Audrey Thompson maintains that "There is no such thing as racial innocence; there is only racial responsibility or irresponsibility."[23] How does one negotiate the impossibility of racial innocence? What does responsibility look like under such conditions? The intractability of complicity is further complicated because whites can almost effortlessly flee from considering the problem and are socially sanctioned to do so.

WHITE IGNORANCE AND WHITE DISTANCING STRATEGIES

An ad campaign was at the heart of a huge controversy in Duluth, Minnesota, this past year that was titled "The Un-Fair campaign." The project was aimed to get the predominantly white population of Duluth to look at racism and their role in it and to encourage dialogues about the racism that exists in their city. An interactive website was set up (http://unfaircampaign.org/) that viewers were invited to engage with and that encouraged them to reflect on "how you may be part of the problem as well as part of the solution." As part of the campaign, a number of billboards were plastered along major roads with messages like, "It's hard to see racism when you're white." Many of the city's white residents complained loudly that the campaign and its messages were offensive, asserting that the ads implied that whites do not see racism and are to blame for it. Instead of engaging with the campaign, the message was denied and dismissed.

In the first chapter of his provocatively insightful book, *Black Bodies, White Gazes: The Continuing Significance of Race*, George Yancy[24] describes from the standpoint of a black man how his body is confiscated and blackened by a white woman's gaze in the quotidian space of an elevator.

> Well-dressed, I enter an elevator where a white woman waits to reach her floor. She "sees" my black body, though not the same one I have seen reflected back to me from the mirror on any number of occasions. Buying into the myth that one's dress says something about the person, one might think that the markers of my dress (suit and tie) should ease her tension. What is it that makes the markers of my dress inoperative?
> Over and above how my body is clothed, she "sees" a criminal, she sees me as threat . . .[25]

Yancy's description of the white woman's behavior and bodily comportment is grounded in the history of the experiences of many black men in elevators with white women. The white woman appears uncomfortable and she displays signs of apprehension. She clutches her purse as if to protect it, her eyes not daring to meet his. It appears as if these brief moments in the elevator, for her, are experienced as an eternity. She responds to Yancy not as an individual who occupies this space with her but through a complex, historically inflected white gaze that returns Yancy's body back to him without its subjectivity. Her comportment has "blackened" his body. As Yancy powerfully writes, "She performs her white body, ergo, I 'become' the predatory Black."[26]

Yancy underscores a crucial point. Not only is his body "blackened," but the white gaze also constitutively shapes and sustains the woman's white innocence! He notes that

> . . . not only does the white woman in the elevator ontologically freeze my "dark" embodied identity *but she also becomes ontologically frozen in her own embodied (white) identity*. . . . She "sees," but does not necessarily reflect upon, herself as normative, innocent, pure. Her performances reiterate the myth of the *proverbial white victim* at the hands of the Black predator.[27]

The white woman is co-constructed as "not threatening" and morally innocent all the while as she is, as bell hooks argues, "terrorizing."[28]

Not everyone, however, sees it this way, and it is all too easy for whites to
dismiss this interpretation of what happened in the elevator. Yancy relates
how a white student responded to his description of "the elevator effect" with
a confident outburst of "Bullshit!"[29] This quick and arrogant response seemingly appears as reasonable disagreement. Yet as Yancy notes, the student
"did not accuse me of having committed a non sequitur or having failed to
define my terms adequately."[30]

Nevertheless with her vitriolic response, she was able to position Yancy,
the professor, as the "bullshitter" and herself "as the discerner of bullshit and
so as one who ought to be believed."[31] As Yancy explains,

> "Bullshit" functioned as a form of erasure of the experiences of Black men
> who have indeed encountered the white gaze within the context of elevators
> and other social spaces. (The student) assumed no "responsibility to marginal-
> ized people and to the understanding developed from their lives." There was
> no suspension of her sense of self-certainty regarding the dynamics of race and
> racism and how Black men struggle daily to deal with issues of racism in their
> lives. She did not *listen* to me and did not take any steps toward conceding my
> understanding of the social world as legitimate.[32]

The white student has the privilege not to listen. The student has the privilege
to flee the discomfort of "difficult knowledge"[33] that challenges one's moral
integrity and that compels one to acknowledge one's role in the reproduction
of social injustice.

It is important to underscore that Yancy's point is not to prohibit critical
disagreement. Instead, he observes the certainty and alacrity with which the
student responded. There is a rush to avoid, a rush not to listen to what may
be uncomfortable and that may implicate one in the suffering of people of
color. In his latest book, *Look, a White!*, Yancy discusses a situation where a
black female student described how it felt to be called "the black girl" in an
all-white school. He notes how a white student *rushed* to remark that she
knew what that was like as she had been called "the white girl" in a black
neighborhood. As Yancy explains,

> She did not tarry with or allow herself to be addressed by the experience of the
> black student. . . . (she) did not hear what was being communicated. In fact,
> she became the hub of the discussion. Her feelings of white fragility became
> valorized at the expense of the black student's feelings.[34]

The white student in the above example did not allow herself to engage with
what the black student was saying and, in fact, failed to hear it.

Recent work in the epistemology of ignorance offers important insight into understanding how well-intended white people perpetuate racial injustice now, in the present, and continually through denials that sustain obliviousness, arrogance, and destructiveness. Epistemologies of ignorance around whiteness make a number of significant contributions to understanding whiteness.

First, white ignorance is not specifically about the ignorance of the overt racist that is often attributed to a deficiency of education. White ignorance refers to the type of not knowing prevalent in whites who are well-intended and "educated." It is the type of ignorance that Charles Mills[35] describes in his influential book, *The Racial Contract*. Mills contends that there is an unstated agreement on the part of the systemically privileged to "misinterpret the world" and to ignore or discredit any knowledge that would threaten their position of power within the social system. Thus, such not knowing is not merely a defect on the part of a particular knower but is actively and collectively produced and maintained. Put in another way, racism *requires* an active production and preservation of ignorance.

White ignorance must be continually conserved so that privilege and the system that supports it are shielded from critique. In her discussion of willful ignorance, Nancy Tuana[36] describes such not knowing as a form of self-deception on the part of those in positions of privilege "to actively ignor(e) the oppression of others and one's role in that exploitation."[37] White ignorance is an *active* state of unknowing in the sense that whites keep themselves from knowing something that would threaten the privileged system from which they/we benefits. Marilyn Frye[38] refers to this type of ignorance as "determined ignorance" highlighting the aspect of "to ignore" in the word "ignorance." White people, Frye maintains, *actively* refuse to pay attention to their complicity in racism. As Charles Mills astutely contends, ignorance is "the condition that ensures its continuance."[39]

Second, because such not knowing is socially sanctioned as knowing, it will *feel* like knowledge to those who benefit from the system. There is a *certainty* supporting such ignorance that poses as knowledge and involves a type of arrogance. In order to clarify how ignorance is an activity that is socially sanctioned as knowledge, it is important to understand white distancing strategies or white denials of complicity.

White ignorance fuels *a refusal to consider* that racism exists *and* that one might be morally complicit in its endurance. Denials of complicity are not perceived by those who perform them as "denials" because white ignorance masquerades as white racial common sense, logic or good intentions—for examples see some of the scholarship around "colorblindness"[40] and "meritocracy."[41] White denials have been extensively studied in two areas of scholarship: feminist studies and educational research. As a white educator teaching in a predominantly white institution of higher learning, I will focus on some of the research around white denials in the classroom.[42] Such denials involve discursive ways in which white students reject having any role to play in maintaining systemic racism and in which white students proclaim their white innocence.

Kim Case and Annette Hemmings[43] refer to "distancing strategies" to describe how white women preservice teachers avoid being positioned as racist or implicated in systemic oppression. They use these strategies to avoid acknowledging responsibility. Kathy Hytten and John Warren's outstanding ethnography of the rhetorical moves their white students performed in courses that attempt to teach about systemic oppression and privilege offers many examples of such tactics. Among the types of discursive strategies that Hytten and Warren discuss are: remaining silent, evading questions, resorting to the rhetoric of ignoring color, focusing on progress, victim blaming, and focusing on culture rather than race.

Hytten and Warren emphasize that these discursive moves are culturally sanctioned discourses of evasion that "were not original—that is, they are already available, already common forms of asserting dominance."[44] These rhetorical strategies work *to obstruct engagement* so that deliberations about one's complicity in systemic oppression can be avoided. Along similar lines, Alice McIntyre coined the phrase "white talk" to name discourse that functions to "insulate White people from examining their/our individual and collective role(s) in the perpetuation of racism."[45]

The point to be underscored is that white people have a variety of discursive mechanisms to avoid considering their complicity, to remain in the space of comfort, and these mechanisms are socially sanctioned. They have the privilege to avoid, evade, and ignore. Moreover, such evasions are socially sanctioned and thus extremely difficult to contest. When we want to escape too quickly, we may forfeit the opportunity to hear anything at all. How does one navigate the intractability of complicity, when privileged modes of existence are so readily available to protect one from such discomfort by preserving one's moral innocence?

VIGILANCE, CRITIQUE, AND STAYING WITH DISCOMFORT OF CRITIQUE

What might it mean to learn to live in the anxiety of that challenge, to feel the surety of one's epistemological and ontological anchor go, but to be willing, in the name of the human, to allow the human *to become something other than what it is traditionally assumed to be?*[46]

. . . by not pursuing satisfaction, we let the other live.[47]

Since whiteness "is deferred by the sheer complexity of the fact that one is never self-transparent, that one is ensconced within structural and material power racial hierarchies,"[48] George Yancy encourages whites to develop vigilance. Whiteness continuously "ensnares" and "ambushes" white people so that whiteness finds ways to hide "even as one attempts honest efforts to resist it."[49] Being an anti-racist white, therefore, is a project that always requires another step and does not end in a white person's having "'arrived' in the form of an idyllic anti-racist."[50] This should not lead to hopelessness, Yancy insists, but rather "one ought to exercise vigilance."[51] Vigilance, according to Yancy, involves the "*continuous* effort on the part of whites to forge new ways of seeing, knowing, and being."[52] I turn to Judith Butler's recent work to expand on what such vigilance looks like.

Best known for her work on troubling our ideas of gender and sexuality, Judith Butler has recently made an explicit turn to ethics. As scholars have noted, ethical concerns have always inflected her work. In contesting a fundamental distinction of feminist theory between "sex" as natural and "gender" as socially constructed, for instance, Butler attempts to uncover how norms of gender grounded in the male/female binary regulate which subjects are "intelligible" or "livable" and which are not. Her project has consistently been to expose what has been foreclosed by discursive formations and truth regimes.

In her recent work,[53] Butler develops an unconventional ethics based on the opacity of the subject to itself. In other words, she finds the development of ethical responsibility specifically at the point of the limits of self-knowledge. In this, she defends a position in which the "postulation of a subject who is not self-grounding, that is, whose conditions of emergence can never fully be accounted for not only does not undermine the possibility of ethics but is the source of ethical responsibility."[54] Moreover, she puts critique at the heart of ethics. As Butler puts it, "ethics undermines its own credibility when it does not become critique."[55] To understand how Butler can inform what "vigilance" requires, we must briefly examine her conception of subject formation, what she means by opacity and, finally, the type of critique she is advocating.

According to Butler, the "I" emerges from the "primary experience of having been given over from the start"[56] and is secured by the conceit of a self fully transparent to itself. Building on Foucault's notion that the subject is an effect of discourse, Butler contends that the presence of an addressee and the existence of social norms always mediate any account we give of ourselves. In her words, ". . . the very terms by which we give an account, by which we make ourselves intelligible to ourselves and to others, are not of our making."[57] The "I" comes into being through prior conditions and is dispossessed from the start. Moreover, we can give an account of ourselves only through regulatory, discursive norms that limit what the subject can be.

As Butler emphasizes, "It is only in dispossession that I can and do give any account of myself."[58]

Since, on Butler's account, one is always already given over to others and to the norms that constitute one as intelligible, one can never be totally transparent to oneself or to others, one is opaque to oneself. One will always be unknown to oneself.[59] Not only is it impossible to trace and account for how one has been addressed from the moment of birth but also there is a gap or excess between what might be and the limits of language and the norms that constitute us. I am a "girl" because there is a normative category that "girled" me and through which I am continually "girled." As Butler poignantly explains, "my body is and is not mine."[60] What aspects have been foreclosed for me? How would I know?

Any account of oneself, therefore, must fail because of the way available frameworks of intelligibility limit the subject. Since we come into being through language and norms that are outside of ourselves and not of our making, I am always dispossessed by these categories. Acknowledging that one is dispossessed and the limits of one's self-knowledge invites one to release one's presumption of an autonomous masterly self. It might be argued that relinquishing certainty about oneself and repudiating the sovereign subject would mark the end of ethical responsibility. Butler, however, insists that acknowledging opacity and breaking with the mastery of assuming a sovereign self encourages us to think critically about the conditions of our formation as subjects and thus forms the very basis of a new ethics. To understand her idea of ethics requires understanding the meaning and role of critique in such ethics.

By critique, Butler does not mean fault-finding or making judgments. Judgments attempt "to subsume a particular under an already constituted category."[61] Critique, in contrast, interrogates the occlusive constitutions of those categories themselves. Following Foucault, Butler maintains that critique is a practice that suspends judgment and "offers a new practice of values based on that very suspension."[62] Foucault defined critique as the practice of interrogating the truth of the "established order" which limits our understanding of what can be. Butler elaborates that the point of critique is not to evaluate whether something is good or bad, justified or not justified but instead to "bring into relief the very framework of evaluation itself" and to ask "To what extent is (any) certainty orchestrated by forms of knowledge precisely in order to foreclose the possibility of thinking otherwise?"[63] This disruption and unsettling opens up possibilities to ask what might "be" beyond our limited framework of intelligibility.

When one connects Butler's conception of subject formation with its focus on opacity to her understanding of critique it follows that calling into question the frameworks that constitute the subject risks calling into question one's own intelligibility as a subject. According to Butler,

> Critique is not merely of a given social practice or a certain horizon of intelligibility within which practices and institutions appear, it also implies that I come into question for myself . . . self-questioning of this sort involves putting oneself at risk, imperilling the very possibility of being recognized by others.[64]

Since the subject's intelligibility depends on this framework, by questioning these limits, the subject also risks its own being as intelligible and risks "a certain security within an available ontology."[65]

Yet at the same time, such a notion of critique makes a more expansive notion of the human possible. By exposing the limits of our frameworks of intelligibility, what is foreclosed by that framework can become visible. And here a space to form new subject possibilities that have been foreclosed by the framework opens up. Sara Rushing points to an important distinction when she clarifies that it is not that critique "makes the boundaries of the category stable but broader, it is that it troubles boundaries themselves *by showing solidarity with the as-of-yet-unintelligible.*"[66]

Butler recognizes that there is an impulse to avoid jeopardizing the intelligibility of one's being as a subject yet she counsels staying in the moment of uncertainty and resisting the impulse for comfort. She implores in the following, widely cited, quote that

> Ethics requires us to risk ourselves precisely at that moment of unknowingness, when what forms us diverges from what lies before us, when our willingness to become undone in relation to others constitutes our chance of becoming human.[67]

APPREHENSION AND VULNERABILITY

Critique, for Butler, involves a troubling of norms that is a challenge to our deepest sense of who we are. Butler urges us to *remain in the space of trouble* rather than to escape. Staying in this place of discomfort allows one to learn from the unease and unsettlement of such spaces. Fiona Jenkins[68] offers the notion of "apprehension" as a response to being troubled and that involves a mode of staying in the troubling space of always reworking *but never overcoming* the norms that do violence. "Apprehension" is an attitude in which one refuses the move to restore the norms that constitute us and a willingness to inhabit the space of anxiety.

Jenkins further maintains that such "apprehension" requires a sense of "unknowing" in which we suspend any definite answer to the question about "what we are" and, most significantly, encounter the other in "the open-endedness of the question *who are you*?"[69] Jenkins calls upon us to consider how we can respond to the troubling experience of difference non-violently and to "exist in a way that is exposed to dissonance and yet able to imagine surviving, *even flourishing* within its living potentiality."[70]

"Apprehension," it should also be noted, does not imply a position that stands outside of our field of meaning "as conscious intentional subjects capable of 'seeing through' social illusions to reach a better truth, and a changing and remaking of ourselves in its light."[71] We always remain "a part of that circuitry."[72] In his discussion of whiteness, John Warren makes a similar point when he acknowledges that "I cannot escape whiteness, nor can I discount the ways I am reproducing whiteness. . . . I cannot claim to be nonracist, to rest in the ideal of a positive racial identity." Yet this does not immobilize him but instead leads him to remain in the uncomfortable position of trying "to do whiteness differently."[73]

Trouble, or "being a problem," is not something that should be overcome because it is the space of the ethical and can lead to the transformation of a normative field of intelligibility. It is where new possibilities of the human can emerge. It is in this space that such questions as "What is real? Whose lives are real? How might we remake reality?" can be negotiated.[74]

Vulnerability is another concept that is central to Butler's ethics. Butler contends that we need to accept, rather than deny, our own vulnerability because disavowing vulnerability enflames fantasies of invulnerability that lead to continued violence and war. In *Precarious Life*, Butler maintains that vulnerability is a primary human condition. Not only are humans corporally dependent on others for survival as infants but also in the process of grieving and mourning our interdependence and vulnerability becomes apparent. In mourning, Butler claims, we are dispossessed in the sense that we lose something of ourselves that is part of our relation with the lost other. We are not the same person after such a loss as the questions "Who am I?" "Who might I now become?" bring to light that others are part of who we are. Grief and mourning makes possible the recognition that we are given over to others in our self-constitution. Recognition of this vulnerability can be "conducive to developing wider modes of commonality and co-operation"[75] and helps to reveal who is not considered grievable.

Butler notes how easy it was for her to mourn the loss of journalist Daniel Pearl, who was kidnapped and murdered, because she could imagine bonds of kinship with him. Both shared a religious faith, both had similar Hebrew names. It is not difficult to mourn the death of someone who is familiar, who could be me. Yet Butler insists that this effortlessness to mourn is what requires critical interrogation. Butler asks us to consider: Whose death is grievable and whose is not? Butler's point is that acknowledging vulnerability can become an opportunity to understand those for whom vulnerability is a constant condition of existence.

Expanding on the notion of vulnerability, Erinn Gilson[76] highlights that vulnerability has been traditionally understood as the state of being exposed to harm and injury and, thus, something to be avoided. Moreover, the common definition of vulnerability implies weakness, defenselessness, and dependency. Gilson refers to this as the *negative* definition of vulnerability understood as a characteristic of certain individuals that is not desirable. Butler, in contrast, references the term in ways that are not negative—as involving an openness to being affected and affecting. According to Gilson, Butler's work shifts the meaning of vulnerability from its negative connotation to "a more general term encompassing conceptions of passivity, affectivity, openness to change, dispassion, and exposure."[77]

For Butler, vulnerability is not exclusively limiting but also enabling—it is what makes it possible for us to be open to affect. Gilson explicitly argues that the *ideal of invulnerability* is a form of willful (in the sense that it is in one's interest) ignorance that is actively cultivated and that encourages a *closure* towards anything that might unsettle us. Gilson insists that this valuation of invulnerability invites *closure*.[78] In a powerfully insightful move, Gilson argues that invulnerability is a position that "enables us to ignore those aspects of existence that are inconvenient, disadvantageous, or uncomfortable for us, such as vulnerability's persistence. *As invulnerable, we cannot be affected by what might unsettle us.*"[79]

Denials of vulnerability, thus, are problematic because they invite ethical and epistemic closure.

CONCLUSION

What does it feel like to be a white problem? To be a problem for whites should not feel like guilt and blame which carry all the dangers of the sovereign subject discussed above. To think in terms of guilt and blame would still be to recenter and privilege white feelings. How then to answer Yancy's question?

In *Look, a White!*[80] Yancy offers a detailed analysis of the notion of "tarrying." For Yancy, tarrying is

> an important process whereby whites remain open to the experience of nonwhites and thereby allow for the *possibility of being touched.* Part of the function of tarrying is to create a space for whites to ask themselves the question: How does it feel to be a problem?[81]

Yancy cautions whites to tarry with what people of color are trying to tell them—to stay with the feeling that one is the problem—and not constantly attempt to evade responsibility for their privilege and complicity in racism. Moreover, acknowledging one's self-limits facilitates the ability to tarry. As Yancy explains,

This feeling of opaqueness is a manifestation of awareness that whiteness (as the transcendental norm) is the condition of their formation, is the condition of dispossession, is the condition that links them to heteronomous white networks and matrices of power and privilege. [82]

His aim is to get whites "not to rush past the question of accountability or responsibility."[83]

Like Butler, Yancy is calling for whites to live in the anxiety of critiquing white norms without closing such questioning down too hastily. Like Butler, Yancy is calling for whites to acknowledge their constitutive self-limits. This can help whites to understand that they will not be able to "ascertain their own racism through a sincere act of introspection."[84] The white racist subject is not "transparent, fully open to inspection"[85] because whiteness constantly ambushes[86] white subjects and implicates them in racism. For Yancy, dispossession takes the form of an acknowledgment of uncertainty requiring a shift from presumptions of mastery to a focus on incompleteness. Yancy urges whites to realize that "I *don't* know myself as I thought I had" or "I am other to myself despite my assumptions to the contrary."[87]

The notions of apprehension and vulnerability are dispositions that whites can develop that encourage whites to be sceptical of their desires for redemption. The point is not to transcend "bad feelings" but rather to fashion a new relationship to such feelings. As a result, the development of better possibilities for listening and speaking will become possible. Such an approach to being "a problem" that does not dwell on feeling bad may inspire whites to be receptive to the point that they will be changed by what they hear.

Shannon Sullivan notes that white feminists often ask, "Does being white make it impossible . . . to be a good person?" Sullivan explains that, while understandable, this is the wrong question to ask because "it is a loaded question: it contains a psychological privilege that white people need to give up, which is the privilege of always feeling that they are in the right."[88]

Ironically, trying to "be good" may be beside the point. Instead, whites must be vigilant about their desires to "be good" so that they can form alliances with people of color to challenge systemic racial injustice. Marilyn Frye's quote that introduced this chapter wonders how whites can be ethically responsible without something "sturdy and firm underfoot." She proposes that white feminists find new ways of being. I hope this chapter has offered some suggestions in that direction.

Yancy argues that the black counter-gaze from which the question "What does it feel like to be a white problem?" arises can function as a "gift."[89] It can function as a gift when whites take up this question in a way that assists us/them to understand whiteness more effectively. Understanding that one is a problem in this sense can lead to ways of being newly accountable and can encourage an acknowledgment that there is always so much more to learn.

And that feels like an incredible and genuine gift. Yet it is a gift that does not relieve one from doing work. Nor is it the type of gift that brings liberation, transcendence or consolation. And finally, it is clearly not a gift that releases one from being a problem. Rather it is a gift that encourages one not to rush to solutions and instead to negotiate complicity "not as injury" but "as a form of critique . . . that is the starting point and the condition of ethics itself."[90]

NOTES

1. Marilyn Frye, "White Woman Feminist," *Willful Virgin: Essays in Feminism* (Freedom, CA : Crossing Press 1992): 148.
2. Christine Clark and James O'Donnell, "Rearticulating a Racial Identity: Creating Oppositions Space to Fight for Equality and Social Justice," in C. Clark and J. O'Donnell (eds) *Becoming and Unbecoming White: Owning and Disowning a Racial Identity* (Westport, Connecticut: Bergin & Garvey, 1999): 5.
3. For an excellent illustration see Joy Simmons, "My White Self," *A PA Newsletter on Philosophy and the Black Experience*, Vol. 6, No. 2 (Spring 2007).
4. Sara Rushing, "Preparing for politics: Judith Butler's ethical dispositions," *Contemporary Political Theory*, 9/3, 284-303
5. Marilyn Frye, "White Woman Feminist," 286.
6. Ibid., 151.
7. Marilyn Frye, *The Politics of Reality: Essays in Feminist Theory* (Trumansburg, NY: Crossing Press, 1983): 113.
8. Alison Jones, "The Limits of Cross-Cultural Dialogue: Pedagogy, Desire, and Absolution in the Classroom," *Educational Theory* Vol. 49, No. 3 (1999): 299-316.
9. Damien Riggs,"Benevolence and the Management of Stake: On Being 'Good White People'," *Philament*4 (2004) http://www.arts.usyd.edu.au/publications/philament/issue4_Critique_Riggs.htm (accessed June 19, 2012).
10. Eduardo Bonila-Silva, *Racism Without Racists: Color-Blind Racism and the Persistence of Racial Inequality in the United States* (Lanham: Rowman& Littlefield, 2003).
11. Peggy McIntosh, "White Privilege and Male Privilege: A Personal Account of Coming to See Correspondences through Work in Women's Studies," in R. Delgado and J. Stefancic (eds.) *Critical White Studies: Looking Behind the Mirror* (Philadelphia: Temple University Press, 1997): 291-299.
12. Cynthia Levine-Rasky, "Framing Whiteness: Working through the Tensions of Introducing Whiteness to Educators," *Race, Ethnicity and Education* 3, no. 3 (2000): 271-292.
13. Ibid., 277.
14. Cynthia Kaufman, "A User's Guide to White Privilege," *Radical Philosophy Review* 4, no. 1-2 (2002): 30-38.
15. Ibid., 32.
16. Zeus Leonardo, "The Color of Supremacy: Beyond the Discourse of 'White Privilege'," *Educational Philosophy and Theory* 36, no. 2 (2004): 137-152.
17. Ibid., 144.
18. Ahmed, Sara. "Declarations of Whiteness: The Non-Performativity of Anti-Racism." *borderlands* e-journal 3, no. 2 (2004) http://www.borderlands.net.au/vol3no2_2004/ahmed_declarations.htm (accessed June, 19, 2012).
19. Probyn, Fiona. "Playing Chicken at the Intersection: The White Critic in/of Critical Whiteness Studies." *Borderlands* 13, no.2 (2004) http://www.borderlandsejournal.adelaide.edu.au/vol3no2_2004/probyn_playing.htm (accessed June 19, 2012).
20. Sara Ahmed, "Declarations of Whiteness."
21. Ibid.

22. Cynthia Willett, "Book Review: Black Bodies, White Gazes." In APA Newsletter, Fall 2009, vol. 9. no. 1, p. 26.

23. Audrey Thompson, "Not the Color Purple: Black Feminist Lessons for Educational Caring," *Harvard Educational Review* 68, no. 4 (1998): 524.

24. George Yancy. *Black Bodies, White Gazes: The Continuing Significance of Race* (Lanham, Maryland: Rowman & Littlefield, 2008).

25. Ibid., 4.

26. Ibid., 23.

27. Ibid., 19, emphases added.

28. bell hooks, "Representations of Whiteness in the Black Imagination," in her *Black Looks: Race and Representation* (Boston, MA: South End Press, 1992).

29. George Yancy, *Black Bodies, White Gazes,* 227.

30. Ibid., 228.

31. Ibid.

32. Ibid.

33. Deborah Britzman, *Lost Subjects, Contested Objects: Toward a Psychoanalytic Inquiry of Learning* (Albany: State University of New York Press, 1998).

34. George Yancy, *Black Bodies, White Gazes,* 160.

35. Charles Mills, *The Racial Contract* (Ithaca: Cornell University Press, 1999).

36. Nancy Tuana, "The Speculum of Ignorance: The Women's Health Movement and Epistemologies of Ignorance, *Hypatia* Vol. 21, no. 3 (2006): 1-19.

37. Ibid. 11.

38. Marilyn Frye, *The Politics of Reality*

39. Charles Mills, *The Racial Contract*, 120.

40. Eduardo Bonilla-Silva, *Racism without Racist: Color-Blind Racism and the Persistence of Racial Inequality in the United States* (New York: Rowman and Littlefield, 2003).

41. Stephen McNamee and Robert Miller Jr., *The Meritocracy Myth* (Lanham, MD: Rowman& Littlefield, 2004).

42. Estella Williams Chizhik and Alexander Williams Chizhik, "Are you Privileged or Oppressed? Students' Conceptions of Themselves and Others," *Urban Education* 40, no. 2 (2005): 116-143; Rudolfo Chavez Chavez and James O'Donnell, *Speaking the Unpleasant: The Politics of (non)Engagement in the Multicultural Education Terrain* (Albany: State University Press, 1998); Ann Berlak, "Teaching and Testimony: Witnessing and Bearing Witness to Racisms in Culturally Diverse Classrooms," *Curriculum Inquiry* 29, no. 1 (1999): 99-127; Audrey Thompson, "Entertaining Doubts: Enjoyment and Ambiguity in White, Antiracist Classrooms," in *Passion and Pedagogy: Relation, Creation, and Transformation in Teaching,* ed. Elijah Mirochick and Debora C. Sherman (New York: Peter Lang, 2002): 431-452; Kevin Kumashiro, Leslie G. Roman, "White is a Color! White Defensiveness, Postmodernism and Anti-racist Pedagogy," in *Race, Identity and Representation in Education,* ed. Cameron McCarthy and Warren Crinchlow (New York: Routledge, 1993): 71-88; Bonnie TuSmith, "Out on a Limb: Race and the Evaluation of Frontline Teaching," in *Race in the College Classroom,* ed. Bonnie TuSmith and Maureen T. Reddy (New Brunswick, New Jersey: Rutgers University Press, 2002): 112-125.

43. Kim Case and Annette Hemmings, "Distancing: White Women Preservice Teachers and Antiracist Curriculum," *Urban Education* 40, no. 6 (2005): 606-626.

44. Kathy Hytten and John Warren. "Engaging Whiteness: How Racial Power Gets Reified in Education." *Qualitative Studies in Education* 16, no. 1 (2003): 66.

45. Alice McIntyre, *Making Meaning of Whiteness: Exploring Racial Identity With White Teachers* (Albany, New York: State University of New York Press, 1997), 45.

46. Judith Butler, *Undoing Gender* (New York: Routledge, 2004): 35, emphasis added.

47. Judith Butler and William Connolly, "Interview," (2000) *Theory & Event* Vol. 4, No. 2 (2000) http://muse.jhu.edu/journals/theory_and_event/toc/archive.html,

48. George Yancy, "Whiteness as Ambush and The Transformative Power of Vigilance," in his *Black Bodies, White Gazes: The Continuing Significance of Race*, 231.

49. Ibid., 240.

50. Ibid., xxii

51. Ibid.
52. Ibid., 231.
53. Judith, Butler. *Giving an Account of Oneself* (New York: Fordham University Press, 2005).
54. Ibid., 19.
55. Ibid., 124.
56. Ibid., 77.
57. Ibid., 21.
58. Ibid., 36-37.
59. Ibid., 78.
60. Judith Butler, *Undoing Gender* (New York: Routledge, 2004) p. 21.
61. Judith Butler. "What is Critique? An Essay on Foucault's Virtue." In *The Political*, ed. David Ingram (Boston: Blackwell, 2002): 212.
62. Ibid.
63. Ibid., 214.
64. Judith, Butler. *Giving an Account of Oneself*, 23.
65. Judith Butler. "What is Critique?" 222.
66. Sara Rushing, "Preparing for politics," 296, emphasis added.
67. Judith, Butler. *Giving an Account of Oneself*, 136.
68. Fiona Jenkins, "Judith Butler: Disturbance, Provocation and the Ethics of Non-Violence," *Humanities Research,* Vol. XVI, No. 2 (October 2010) http://epress.anu.edu.au/apps/bookworm/view/Humanities+Research+Vol+XVI.+No.+2.+2010/1331/jenkins.xhtml (accessed June 18, 2012)
69. Fiona Jenkins, "Judith Butler," 9.
70. Fiona Jenkins, "Judith Butler," 12 (emphasis added).
71. Ibid. 3.
72. Ibid.
73. John Warren, *Performing Purity: Whiteness, Pedagogy, and the Reconstitution of Power (New York: Peter Lang, 2003)*, 465.
74. Judith Butler, Precarious Life: The Powers of Mourning and Violence (New York: Verso, 2004): 33.
75. Angela McRobbie, "Vulnerability, Violence and (Cosmopolitan) Ethics: Butler's *Precarious Life,*" *British Journal of Sociology* 57, no.1, 2006, 78.
76. Erinn Gilson, "Vulnerability, Ignorance, and Oppression," *Hypatia* 26, no. 2 (2011): 308-332.
77. Ibid., 310.
78. Ibid., 313.
79. Ibid., emphasis added.
80. George Yancy, *Look a White! Philosophical Essays on Whiteness* (Philadelphia, PA: Temple University Press, 2012).
81. Ibid., 16, emphasis added.
82. Ibid., 166.
83. Ibid., 167.
84. Ibid., 168.
85. Ibid.,
86. Ibid., 170.
87. Ibid.
88. Shannon Sullivan, *Revealing Whiteness: The Unconscious Habits of Racial Privilege* (Bloomington, Indiana: University of Indiana Press, 2006): 184.
89. George Yancy, *Look a White!* : 6, 10.
90. Fiona Probyn, "Playing Chicken at the Intersection: The White Critic in/of Critical Whiteness Studies." *Borderlands* 13, no.2 (2004) http://www.borderlandsejournal.adelaide.edu.au/vol3no2_2004/probyn_playing.htm (accessed July 8, 2012).

Chapter Two

Feeling White, Feeling Good

"Antiracist" White Sensibilities

Karen Teel

How might we learn to [act] if we gave up the need to feel like and to be seen as good whites?—Audrey Thompson[1]

When the great American thinker W. E. B. Du Bois prophetically identified the problem of the twentieth century as the color line, the problem was not black people but white supremacy.[2] Du Bois rightly named this as a global problem. Today, within the context of the United States, I understand white supremacy, or whiteness for short, to be the fact that people who are or are perceived to be of European descent consistently receive privileges and advantages over people who are or are perceived to be of color. These unearned benefits accrue to whites as a direct result not only of the personal prejudice often called "racism" but also of a system of white advantage that is largely invisible to white people. This is the ongoing legacy of historical events and processes in which we of European descent explicitly valued ourselves over Africans, Asians, and indigenous Americans. Unquestionably, substantial progress has been made, yet any person willing to consider the evidence— persistent racial inequalities in employment, housing, incarceration rates, health care, and so on—can see that this whiteness problem Du Bois articulated so elegantly did not magically resolve itself by the turn of the twenty-first century.

I am white, female, a practicing Catholic, an academic, relatively young (for an academic), and a parent of small children. All of these characteristics, and more, influence my social, political, and ecclesial experiences. As a U.S. citizen and resident, however, I experience my whiteness as my most salient feature, the one that most profoundly shapes my ordinary lived reality. Whatever the occasion, by virtue of my whiteness, I am complicit in, I participate in, I perpetuate the problem of white supremacy. I am a white problem.

When I say that my whiteness shapes my ordinary lived reality, I mean that there is to it both an *orderliness* and an *ordinariness* so all-encompassing, so finely tuned, that I can easily remember being completely oblivious to the fact that my whiteness rendered me part of a very serious problem. (As I recall, this felt pretty good.) How it feels to me to be a white problem has changed dramatically from year to year, and at times from week to week, as my understanding and awareness of racism have developed and my own raced ways of being in the world have shifted. Even now, after years of conscientization,[3] I often don't notice when I am functioning as a white problem. I doubt I will ever arrive at a complete or exhaustive understanding of whiteness, so I expect this process to continue indefinitely into the future. For me, then, there are many ways of feeling like a white problem, some of which I don't know about yet and some of which I may never know.

For these reasons, here I aspire neither to articulate a grand theory of this feeling nor to elucidate my entire personal history as a white problem. Instead, after outlining my initial ambivalence about discussing this question, I offer a snapshot of how it feels to me to be a white problem as of this writing, in the summer of 2012. To show how feeling white cuts across my everyday experiences, I build my analysis around three recent events related to particular aspects of my white identity: as a practicing Roman Catholic, as a parent choosing a kindergarten for her first child, and as a professor at a university. My whiteness, and increasingly my feeling of being a white problem, profoundly shapes my participation in each of these sites where I work, live, and worship. Critiquing some of the specific feelings I have experienced in such situations, I submit that feeling like a white problem is ultimately tangential to, yet deeply entangled with, the question of how white people can combat racism.

FEELING AMBIVALENT ABOUT WRITING THIS CHAPTER

To admit that I am a white problem is simply to state a fact. Yet asserting it makes me uncomfortable, in seemingly paradoxical ways: I am embarrassed to be a problem, yet admitting it feels like boasting (*Isn't it wonderful that I've recognized that I am a problem by virtue of being white?*). In beginning to write about how it feels to be a white problem, I have felt much as I often do in the face of my own and others' racism: paralyzed, uncertain how to begin.

Catholic theological ethicist Maureen O'Connell rightly reminds us that white people trying to deal with racism by talking about it is a catch-22.[4] On the one hand, if we want to understand what it means to be a white problem and learn to deal with it, we have to be able to talk about it. Yet, on the other hand, placing our hope in a "talking cure" for racism[5] involves the risk of exacerbating the problem, in several interrelated ways. First, to fetishize "talking about race" can give white people the impression that simply by being willing to engage in conversation about racism, by feeling bad about it, we can solve it. I do not want to encourage us to think white navel-gazing is worthwhile as an end in itself. As philosopher of education Audrey Thompson insists, the problem that needs to be solved is racism and its concrete effects, not white feelings of guilt or helplessness.[6] Second, to speak about myself in relation to white supremacy risks giving the mistaken impression to other whites that I, a white person, am an expert on racism, and that if they simply listen *to me*, all will be well. Third, I do not wish to ask people of color, from whom whites have always taken far too much, to help me feel better. In short, though it is necessary, to speak of how it feels to be a white problem can perpetuate the worst kind of white racial narcissism and self-congratulation.

Talking about *me* and *my* whiteness problem, then, risks reinforcing patterns I would rather interrupt. Yet, if I do not openly and consistently acknowledge that my whiteness is a problem, I collude with those who believe that it is ruder to speak of this than not to speak, or, conversely, that nothing needs to be said, because white people are not really a problem at all. Thus, in deciding whether to speak (or, more precisely in this case, to write), I had to choose, proverbially, between the lesser of two evils. Both are fraught. Both carry serious risks. Both have the potential to exacerbate the problem, rather than diminish it. Even narrating this initial dilemma makes me uncomfortable, because it sounds to me like so much white whining.

Yet the editor of this volume, George Yancy, a black philosopher who reflects critically upon race and racism and whiteness in particular, has requested that white thinkers theorize how it feels to be a white problem. Depressing, demoralizing, and downright ugly as white racist self-disclosure can be, it appears that he finds it illuminating when white people attempt to expose honestly the racist workings of our minds.[7] On reflection, this makes sense. People of color know the effects of racism much more intimately than most white people ever will, but they can't get inside our white heads.[8] They can and do develop brilliant theories about the preposterous mental gymnastics that must go on in there—Christian womanist ethicist Emilie M. Townes has dubbed this the "fantastic hegemonic imagination"[9] —and they're likely to be right, but no one (including white people) can know for sure unless those of us who are inside those white heads chime in to corroborate and clarify their hypotheses. Moreover, my own field of Catholic and (more broadly) Christian theology, like virtually all other "traditional" academic disciplines, is unfairly dominated by European scholars and sensibilities, and I have made it a rule to try to follow the lead of scholars of color who have long exhorted white theologians to face up to white supremacy.[10] So, here goes.

THREE VIGNETTES

For many years now, I have been consciously engaged in a process of becoming more and more aware of the pernicious and pervasive nature of whiteness and my complicity in it. My disgust and outrage at the injustice of this system has steadily deepened, and accordingly, my desire to perform antiracism rather than racism has increased. Still, in specific situations in which the workings of whiteness become evident to me, I often fail to intervene, feeling more or less paralyzed by *anonymity*, *helplessness*, and *embarrassment*. The intensity of these feelings varies according to the circumstances, especially including whether I succeed in making what I judge to be an adequately antiracist intervention. I think these feelings merit some scrutiny. To what extent, if any, do they reflect reality in any given situation? Relating personal experiences with whiteness at church, at an elementary school, and at work, I critically examine these feelings for what they might reveal about the inner workings of whiteness.

Attending Church: Feeling Anonymous

One Saturday, I attended Mass in a city I was visiting. The late-afternoon sun poured through the tall windows of the old cathedral as the white priest gave a sermon reflecting upon the suffering and death of Jesus. Appealing to African American history and experience, and referring to lynching and the blues in turn, the priest went on at length about "our brothers and sisters" who are suffering, and how "we" need to "help them." I thought as I listened that while I never hear this kind of rhetoric in the mostly black church I now usually attend, I often hear it in ethnically white churches. It always communicates the erroneous assumption that no one present is suffering, let alone a member of the group being discussed. In this case, I thought I recognized in the priest's voice (as, in other contexts, I have heard in my own) an undercurrent of pride in being open-minded enough to devote the theme of his homily to "them," "those" black people out there somewhere to whom "we" white people, should "we" happen to encounter "them," ought to express "our" sympathy.

Although I was certain the priest meant well, I experienced his homily as terribly violent and insensitive. I felt distressed and angry that people of color, and white people too, including myself, had to hear it. Feeling helpless to stop it, I could not wait for it to end. I felt acutely embarrassed to be white, both for myself and on behalf of the other whites present, especially the priest. Indeed, most (not all) churchgoers appeared to be white. As I sat there,

I felt invisible, sharply aware that my white skin blended in perfectly with that of my fellow white churchgoers. Some of them (I squirmed at the thought) were undoubtedly being confirmed in their belief that occasional feelings of sympathy comprise an adequate response to the overwhelming legacy of whiteness. This anonymity, being one in a sea of white faces, meant that I was helpless to communicate my feelings simply by assuming a look of disapproval; had the priest looked my way, surely he would never have noticed.

The discomfort I felt was exacerbated by the fact that I was sitting with a black friend whose body language indicated that she was also offended, or at least disgusted. I wanted to jump up and down and call out to the priest, "We're right here! Stop talking like we're not!" Respecting the solemnity of the Mass, however, I did not, nor, not expecting to see the priest again and not wanting to upset him, did I approach him after the Mass ended.

This feeling of anonymity has also arisen in similar situations in which my whiteness renders my antiracist aspirations utterly invisible. I feel my particular identity being effaced by whiteness itself. I want to be able to censure whiteness simply by *looking* a certain way, through the use of facial expressions and body language, but I can't. I feel trapped, rendered invisible behind a screen that makes all white people look identical.[11] Since I can't change the fact that I am white, I can't get out from behind the screen. Subtle gestures toward resistance or cross-racial solidarity, such as looking angry or irritated, rarely make any difference: they are easily ignored or misinterpreted by other screened-in whites, and they are usually indistinguishable to those on the other side. If I yell loud enough or jump high enough, the people out there may be able to hear me or see me, and a large enough disturbance stands a chance of being noticed by those on my side, too. But as soon as I cease to make this tremendous effort, I return instantly and by default to the anonymity guaranteed by the hegemonic screen of whiteness.

My protest against feeling "anonymous" may signal that I have realized the impossibility, in this racialized society, of being judged on my individual merits and not according to my race. Before noticing that whiteness is a problem, and a problem *for me*, I was able to enjoy the presumption (mine and other white people's, that is) of my own goodness and the assurance that my individual acts, good or bad, would never reflect on my race, but only on me personally.[12] This exposes my mistaken white belief that U.S. society had already become, as the Reverend Dr. Martin Luther King Jr. dreamed, a meritocracy where we are "not . . . judged by the color of [our] skin but by the content of [our] character."[13] I now realize that white people generally feel this way only about white people, and that people of color are justified in assuming white people, including me, to be racist (actively participating in whiteness) unless we demonstrate otherwise.[14] This realization is sobering, especially the latter. It feels unfair, though, of course, it is not, to have to prove myself, not to be considered "innocent until proven guilty."

Is this in any way analogous to what individual people of color experience when white people make assumptions about them based on their actual or perceived race? Does my sense of "anonymity" in a white crowd signal that what I am up against is nothing less than racial stereotyping? By asking this question, I do not intend to blame people of color for stereotyping white people or to cry "reverse discrimination." Insofar as white people can be "stereotyped" as part of the oppressor group, it is our own fault for having been and continuing to be oppressors; it is our own racism, coming home to roost. Neither do I intend to imply that all stereotyping has equally detrimental effects. In my experience, the white stereotype of a white person as good works to the psychic advantage of white people who are clueless about whiteness. It is extremely pleasant to be able to expect to be received warmly, or at least civilly, by virtually everyone I encounter in my daily life. I am chafing against this stereotype because working to diminish the power of whiteness and gaining the good opinion of antiracists, especially people of color, has become important to me. But unless I am carving out a path different from the masses of white people who don't do a whole lot to counteract whiteness, it is perfectly logical for everyone, whites and people of color alike, to assume that I am part of those masses. If I'm not taking such steps, I *am* just like them.

While stereotyping of any kind may be unjust, then, it is also true that in any given situation, I have the significant advantage of getting to choose whether or not to hide behind the screen of white anonymity. When I do, I personally don't notice any negative consequences, other than perhaps feeling disappointed in myself. I remain "good" in the eyes of other whites, and people of color, who cannot possibly be aware that I knew better, can usually be counted on not to express their dissatisfaction. If, resisting my white anonymity, I attempt an antiracist action that is recognizable as such, then I risk some white people thinking I'm bad or crazy, but I stand to gain the approval of people of color and white antiracists who may suddenly see me with new eyes. In such situations, I really can't lose.

This analysis makes clear that what I have called anonymity may be closer to laziness than I care to admit. I have often experienced this anonymity as helplessness, but clearly the two are not synonymous. At the church, I made various excuses when I could have chosen to act. My reasoning that I should not interrupt the service, and that to explain my concern to the priest afterward would require a different and less comfortable kind of conversation than the typical post-service greeting normally invites, upheld the typically white values of "niceness,"[15] "politeness,"[16] and "colorblindness."[17] Thinking it over, I probably would not have interrupted the service in this particular case, but there was no good reason not to approach the priest afterward.

By surrendering to the feeling of anonymity-cum-helplessness, by acting on white values rather than antiracist values, I colluded with the perpetuation of white supremacy. I felt like a white problem, and I was.

Choosing a School: Feeling Embarrassed

This past year my husband and I reached the parenting milestone of choosing a kindergarten for our elder child. Touring several schools, we heard various principals describe their schools' assorted merits. One white principal rhapsodized about his school's tremendous diversity, emphasizing how great this was because "everyone" will be out there in the real world, and it is so important for kids to learn to get along with "everyone." I was surprised to hear this because I had thought this school was majority white. When the time came for questions, therefore, I inquired about the statistics for racial/ethnic and socioeconomic diversity. The principal quickly stated that 25 percent of the schoolchildren qualified for the free or reduced-cost lunch program, indicating financial need, but he hemmed and hawed about race and ethnicity. He said hesitantly, "The biggest group is Hispanic . . ." At last he appealed to the school secretary, who quietly stated that the majority of the students are white, with a substantial minority of Hispanic students, and no more than 3 percent from any other group.

I was embarrassed for this principal and, by extension, for white people in general. He had set himself up as a champion of diversity only to reveal that he did not know the most basic statistics for his school, and he did not seem to realize this was a problem. I felt less embarrassed for myself personally than in church, because here I had at least attempted to overcome my anonymity by asking a question. I was sure, however, that others heard my question and the principal's answer as purely informational, not as exposing the foolishness of the notion that if you mix a few people of color into a sea of white folks, all your diversity problems—past, present, and future—will vanish. I could not assume that any of the other parents (most appeared to be white) had noticed my "test" of the principal's assumptions about diversity, or his "failure." As has happened elsewhere, I did not know whether it would be wise to intervene further or, if so, how best to do it.

An overwhelming concern to minimize further embarrassment also deterred me from pursuing a follow-up intervention. I felt helpless to expose this manifestation of whiteness while still adhering to the rules of civility (i.e., not embarrassing other white people) that feel all-important in such situations. So I fell silent. I allowed my (white) desire for politeness to trump my desire to call out the principal's whiteness (or at least, his sadly inadequate "antiracism").

Reflecting on this situation prompts the observation that perhaps an initial, relatively non-threatening strategy for the beginning white antiracist could be to cultivate the skill of asking incisive questions. I am thinking here of questions that would expose how the *situation* is racialized, rather than focusing attention on the *person* through whose choices, actions, or intentions whiteness is manifesting itself at the moment. For example, rather than leaving it up to my fellow parents to conclude that a 60 percent white school might not be diverse enough, I could have asked, "What programs or curriculum does the school have in place that actively promote positive engagement with diversity?" This question could have remained non-confrontational, non-judgmental, even informational, yet the principal's answer would have revealed whether the school had allocated any resources to the diversity issues it claimed (through him) to value.[18] One way to challenge whiteness, then, is to ask for the right kind of information, and in particular to question the distribution of resources, so the powers that be must acknowledge that their mouth is somewhere their money is not.[19]

To sum up, in this and other situations, I have felt terribly embarrassed to be associated with white people who don't notice the whiteness we're perpetuating and, when we do notice, don't do enough about it. I think this feeling is more than warranted. Whiteness is embarrassing! I also notice that although I cease to be embarrassed for myself personally when I am able to act decisively, as I will describe next, my fear of failing and of being embarrassed by that failure often prevents me from doing what needs to be done. Perhaps I need to get to a place where I am *more* embarrassed by allowing myself to remain associated with whiteness than I am by doing a less-than-perfect job of confronting it.

At Work: Feeling Capable

At the university where I work, I participated in a discussion about teaching "diverse students." During the conversation, a white colleague reported the following: Some of his white students feel surprised and betrayed when, toward the end of a course he teaches on race and ethnicity in the United States, he reveals his conviction that the "problem" of racial injustice has not entirely been "solved" but continues to the present day. I was surprised to hear that someone would teach such a course without contextualizing this from the outset as an area of ongoing concern, and my initial response was, as usual, to feel embarrassed on behalf of white people, including my anonymous self. Because I immediately knew how I would intervene, however, I felt neither helpless nor overly bothered by my (temporary) anonymity.

When the opportunity arose, I stated that this approach seemed odd to me. I asked my colleague whether he thought it responsible to allow his white students to remain comfortably ignorant of whiteness for so long, and whether he has considered using an honest appraisal of the current state of affairs to frame the course from the outset. There followed an earnest and thoughtful exchange about what my colleague's teaching strategy does and does not accomplish.

Both during and after this discussion, I felt pleased that, rather than hiding behind my white anonymity, I had found a direct, productive, and non-combative way to engage another white person on a whiteness issue. I felt good about taking responsibility for drawing attention to it, rather than leaving this task to the people of color who were present. This is one of the few times I have felt like a strong and effective advocate of antiracism. I was proud of myself.

Looking back on it, though, I wonder whether these positive feelings were entirely warranted. The exchange felt, and still feels, like a major break-through. Perhaps, for me, it was. Yet in the grand scheme of things, it was a small effort; it was undertaken in a relatively safe space, one that, in fact, had been designated for the discussion of just such concerns; my concern with politeness remained primary, as I posed my question in such a way as to convey that I was interested in thinking about this *with* my colleague, rather than trying to accuse him of anything nefarious; moreover, given his prior comments, I had every reason to expect that he would be receptive to my challenge. Perhaps most troubling, in framing my colleague's strategy as a missed opportunity to engage white students in a sustained confrontation with white racism, I failed to point out that it requires students of color—most of whom probably come in with a more sophisticated awareness of contemporary racial dynamics—to endure virtually an entire course on race and ethnicity with no acknowledgment of the crucial currency of these matters.

Besides signaling how far I have still to go in becoming anything like consistent in my antiracist activism, these reflections lead me to a question: When one intervenes to challenge a racialized or racially charged dynamic, must the encounter include a combative element in order for one's action to "count" as antiracist? While I currently have no answer to this question, in the next section I want to examine critically my concern with what "counts."

IF WHITENESS FEELS SO BAD, WHY DON'T I INTERVENE MORE OFTEN?

My analysis of these experiences leads me to the fairly obvious conclusion that no matter how disgusted and outraged I may feel about whiteness, unless these feelings translate into action, they do no one any good. I would argue that being a white problem means that I can't decrease the whiteness quotient of any situation simply by showing up. In fact, given my own whiteness, the reverse is true. To perform antiracism, I have to decisively act, drawing critical attention to myself, to other white people, and to whiteness.

It will take time to learn to do this well, and every situation is different; nevertheless, there is always something that I can do, even if I feel (as I often do) that it is imperative to remain studiously calm. Sometimes, though, polite intervention may not be enough. Townes insists that antiracism has to be loud, bossy, and insistent: "being polite (dispassionate) about it has not worked."[20] To intervene in what will be perceived as an impolite manner raises the possibility that other white people will become defensive or write me off as a nutcase. Yet here too, I suspect, whiteness will work to protect itself. Many white people will conclude that although I may have had a "moment," I am really still a trustworthy white person. Townes may be right: We have to jump and yell for all we're worth just to get people to notice we're trying to shake things up behind this screen.

It is one thing to realize that whiteness is a problem and that I am part of it. Given the considerable (for a white person!) sensitivity to whiteness that I have developed, however, I am also compelled to ask why I have not done more about it. By reflecting further on what goes on inside my white head whenever I notice that I am in the midst of a whiteness event, I want to suggest two possible explanations.

Feeling Fearful

First, when faced with an unfolding whiteness event, I do not always know what to do. I am still developing my awareness of whiteness, and I am often uncertain of whether my analyses are correct; I need to think through some situations more carefully than the moment allows. More importantly, when I do become aware of whiteness, I usually find myself uneasily doing what amounts to a cost-benefit analysis regarding whether and how to act. No matter what kind of intervention I imagine, the thought of forfeiting my white anonymity feels dangerous. To speak plainly risks isolating me from (white) friends, family, colleagues, and strangers. Some may take offense, be disappointed in me, think I am overreacting, accuse me of inventing racism where it does not exist, and generally decide that I am not, after all, a "good person."[21] Since I feel I have a lot to lose, I prefer to be reasonably confident that a given intervention is warranted and has a fair chance of success before I embark on it. In short, sometimes I do nothing about whiteness because the situation passes before I have decided whether or how to act.

Ultimately, this seems to come down to a concern with my own credibility, with whether my action will "count" as antiracist. I worry about how exactly to intervene because I want to do it "right." This concern, I think, is not unrelated to a genuine desire to be successful at decreasing the power of whiteness, rather than reinforcing it through my own clumsiness. But when I look closely, it also appears to be related to anxiety at the prospect of giving up certain benefits attached to my white privilege. To expose whiteness to white people successfully, to mark myself as anti-whiteness, risks being dismissed by whites, excluded from the white "club." If I am going to risk being ostracized behind the screen, entering into a kind of white "homelessness," then I want to be fairly certain people of color and their allies will perceive me as a credible and competent antiracist, someone who "gets it."

Engaging in this cost-benefit analysis always makes me feel unsettled. Even as I don't know how else to respond, I am haunted by the suspicion that such uncertainty represents a colossal moral failure (*If whiteness is bad, then surely I should challenge it!*). I now believe that this vaguely troubled feeling has stemmed largely from an inchoate awareness of the fact that while I dither, people of color suffer. [22] For even if none are present at the moment, every unchallenged whiteness event functions to reinforce and perpetuate the socio-political structure of white dominance that oppresses bodies of color. When people are suffering, what kind of a person indulges in the privilege of deliberating over whether to intervene? Yet it has felt necessary to do so. It appears I have become ensnared in the trap Thompson describes in which "the desire to be seen as a friend substitutes for the engagements and ways of knowing required to *be* a friend." [23] My fear of not being accepted by whites or people of color as a "good," relatable person has directly competed with, and often defeated, my desire to fight racism.

Feeling Proud

Second, I suspect I often fail to act when participating in whiteness events because underlying all the *uncomfortable* feelings I have described is already a *good* feeling. Namely, I am proud of myself for "getting it," for being able to identify racialized social dynamics. For a white person, I seem to myself to be extraordinarily aware of white supremacy as a problem that shapes so many institutions and communities to which I belong, and I find it impossible to avoid congratulating myself on this. It is strangely thrilling to analyze the racialized dynamics in a given situation, knowing that many of my fellow whites are unconscious of these implications. I feel like a clever spy, sneaking around behind the screen of whiteness and secretly passing judgment on us all. No matter how bad I feel about whiteness, I feel good even when I fail to intervene, just for having wanted to. Clearly, my strong feelings in the face of racism sometimes substitute for action in ways that feel like (but obviously are not) a satisfactory response.

On the one hand, I suppose pride is a natural response to acquiring and practicing a new skill. On the other hand, I suspect it signals that I do not truly understand the seriousness of my own situation. After all, I am *not* a spy who infiltrates whiteness from the outside and can observe without implicating herself. I am part and parcel of whiteness. Surely, then, far from making me better than other white people, knowing and still doing nothing actually

makes me worse. My feelings of anonymity, helplessness, and embarrassment implicate me in the sin I warned against earlier: thinking that feelings
of protest or sympathy in the face of whiteness constitute an adequate response. Considering my concern with wanting to appear "credible" to other
whites in order to convince them that antiracism is the way to go, as a
Christian I am reminded of Jesus's admonition to remove the plank from
one's own eye before bothering about the speck in another's (Mt 7:5). It
seems I have more work left to do than I thought.

What Needs to be Done?

I have come to believe, in theory at least, that remaining complicit in whiteness is objectively worse than all other outcomes. I want to heed Thompson's
call to "g[i]ve up the need to feel like and to be seen as [a] good white," by
myself and others.[24] But I haven't figured out how. My fear and pride, my
concern with safeguarding my own credibility, comfort, and self-respect—
advantages that stem (at least in part) from my white privilege—remain
centrally important to me.

What would it take to overcome this? Do I need, as I myself recently
suggested, to figure out how to feel worse than ever about whiteness, so that I
will be compelled to act?[25] As far as I can tell, my feelings of anonymity,
embarrassment, and helplessness seem to function at least sometimes to identify racist situations correctly. But, no matter how acute, these feelings of
personal discomfort are insufficient to produce antiracist action. Indeed,
when I successfully performed what I understood to be an antiracist action at
work, it was not because I felt so bad that I had to speak up. It was because I
felt confident that I understood what was happening and could intervene
effectively. I can't help but conclude that feeling bad about whiteness,
though wholly appropriate, is not the silver bullet to antiracism I hoped it
might be.[26]

Along these lines, Thompson suggests that feeling bad or guilty about
racism does not necessarily lead whites to act, and that in fact, it can lead us
to disclaim responsibility altogether. To illustrate, she relates a story about
two of her friends who went away on vacation, leaving her in charge of their
children but forgetting to leave the key to their car.[27] She and the children, at
considerable inconvenience, had to walk, ride bicycles, and take buses every-
where. She received many phone calls in which her friends assured her that
they felt tremendously guilty about forgetting to leave the key but declined to
solve the problem by actually sending it to her. They said that they already
felt bad enough about their mistake and that having to take responsibility to
redress it would only make them feel worse. They were unconcerned with the
fact that they had the power to resolve a material inconvenience that they
themselves had caused; they were satisfied that their feelings were an ade-

quate response. In my case too, focusing on my own anxieties has kept me at the center of my analysis and actions in situations that cry out for antiracist intervention. As Thompson implies, I need to stop worrying about how I feel and start doing what needs to be done.[28]

FEELING WHITE, FEELING GOOD[29]

By way of conclusion, I would like to return to the problem of discussing how it feels to be a white problem. Thompson warns white people that "the very acknowledgment of our racism and privilege can be turned to our advantage."[30] How right she is. I cannot avoid benefiting from racism and white privilege, no matter what I do. If I ignore whiteness, I experience no obvious ill effects; I get to feel good about myself, as is white people's *modus operandi*, and put all my energy to advancing the cause of me. If I fight whiteness, I get to feel good about myself, as well as sometimes receiving accolades and admiration from people of color and white people who (aspire to) "get it," which also advances the cause of me.

To illustrate, let me offer one last personal example. I hope soon to be awarded tenure and promotion at my university, based chiefly on my accomplishments in teaching and research. My research output that is likely to be judged adequate consists largely of publications on the problem of racism and whiteness, including this very chapter. Now, there is something repugnant about a white person, already the recipient of so many unearned advantages,[31] building a career on analyzing white supremacy, even when one intends to move oneself and other white people toward greater awareness and active rejection of whiteness. Given how dearly people of color have paid for white power and privilege, I shudder when I consider that I live a life of relative luxury while exercising what for me is truly an *option* to try to redress that privilege. It would seem reasonable for white people to have to suffer for our whiteness sins, yet my penance so far includes constructing theories from a quiet private office with a view of a lush San Diego canyon. (This view is framed by a palm tree waving in the breeze. I am not making this up.) Irony and injustice notwithstanding, here I am and here, for the time being, I remain.

All this is to say that, because I share Thompson's concern about "keep[ing] whiteness at the center of antiracism,"[32] I am still uneasy about offering these reflections to the world. Yet Thompson also suggests, connecting her car-key story to racism, that "people of color are not really interested in daily phone calls about how bad we feel. They just want us to send the key."[33] So if Yancy believes that, at this socio-historical moment, the disclosure of the inner workings of white minds might function as a "key" to unlock further aspects of our collective ability to combat whiteness, then the least I can do is to try to send it along. Since this "key" should never have been mine in the first place, I am only doing what I should, and I do not deserve to be congratulated for it. I also don't deserve to be congratulated for declaring that I don't deserve congratulations, although it is impossible to avoid feeling like I do. And any embarrassment that may arise at this exposure of my own white privilege and ignorance feels like something to celebrate as well, because it is the "right" response.

You get the picture. As a white person, even if I want to, I can't lose. Such, perhaps, is the nature of twenty-first-century whiteness.

NOTES

1. Audrey Thompson, "'Tiffany, friend of people of color': White investments in antiracism," *International Journal of Qualitative Studies in Education* 16, no. 1 (2003): 7–29, at 12.

2. W. E. B. Du Bois, *The Souls of Black Folk* (New York: Penguin, 1996), originally published in 1903 by A. C. McClurg & Company.

3. This term, *conscientização* in Portuguese, comes from Paulo Freire, *Pedagogy of the Oppressed, New Revised 20th-Anniversary Edition*, translated by Myra Bergman Ramos (New York: Continuum, 1996), 90. I understand it to mean becoming aware of an oppressive situation such that one begins to recognize one's role and agency in it.

4. Maureen H. O'Connell, "Confessing Complicity: Catholic Moral Theology and White Claims to Moral Goodness in Racial Injustice," paper presented at the meeting of the Catholic Theological Society of America, St. Louis, Missouri, 9 June 2012.

5. Alison Jones, "The Limits of Cross-Cultural Dialogue: Pedagogy, Desire, and Absolution in the Classroom," *Educational Theory* 49, no. 3 (September 1999): 299–316, quotation at 306; Thompson, "Tiffany," 17.

6. Thompson, "Tiffany," 24.

7. See, for example, George Yancy, "Introduction: framing the problem," in *Christology and Whiteness: What Would Jesus Do?* edited by George Yancy 1–18 (London and New York: Routledge, 2012), at 9–10.

8. See, for example, Charles Mills's call for close examination of white moral and political cognition in *The Racial Contract* (Ithaca and London: Cornell University Press, 1997), 95, 109.

9. Emilie M. Townes, *Womanist Ethics and the Cultural Production of Evil* (New York: Palgrave Macmillan, 2006). The term "womanist" was coined by Alice Walker and means, briefly, "a black feminist or feminist of color"; see Walker, *In Search of Our Mothers' Gardens: Womanist Prose* (Orlando: Harcourt, 1983), xi–xii.

10. For example, see James H. Cone, "Theology's Great Sin: Silence in the Face of White Supremacy," *Union Seminary Quarterly Review* 55, nos. 3–4 (2001): 1–14; M. Shawn Copeland, "Racism and the Vocation of the Christian Theologian," *Spiritus* 2 (2002): 15–29; Townes, *Womanist Ethics*.

11. Readers will note that this metaphor of a "screen" echoes Du Bois's idea of the "veil" in *The Souls of Black Folk*.

12. See, for example, Tim Wise's account of how he, a white man named Tim, was able to rent a truck with no hassle right after Timothy McVeigh bombed the Oklahoma City federal building. Wise, *White Like Me: Reflections on Race from a Privileged Son*, Revised and Updated (Brooklyn, NY: Soft Skull, 2008), 53.

13. Martin Luther King Jr., "I Have a Dream," Speech at the March on Washington, 28 August 1963, in *I Have a Dream: Letters and Speeches that Changed the World*, edited by James Melvin Washington with a foreword by Coretta Scott King 101–6 (New York: Harper-Collins, 1986), quotation at 104.

14. Prominent second-wave white feminist Sandra Lee Bartky recounts her surprise upon learning that her students of color had long assumed she was racist, despite her efforts to

include readings by people of color on her syllabi and lead discussions on race in her classes. In her analysis, she suggests that, to put it in the terms I have used here, she had not yelled quite loud enough or jumped quite high enough for these students to discern her intentions clearly. For me, her reflections also prompt the clarification that the onus must always be on the white person to perform antiracism effectively, not on people of color to notice and affirm it. See Bartky, "Race, Complicity, and Culpable Ignorance," in *"Sympathy and Solidarity" and Other Essays* 151–67 (Lanham, MD: Rowman & Littlefield, 2002), at 153–4.

15. See Wise, *White Like Me*, 84–87.

16. See Townes, *Womanist Ethics*, 60–63.

17. See Eduardo Bonilla-Silva, *Racism Without Racists: Color-Blind Racism and the Persistence of Racial Inequity in the United States, Second Edition* (Lanham, MD: Rowman and Littlefield, 2006), and Tim Wise, *Colorblind: The Rise of Post-Racial Politics and the Retreat from Racial Equity* (San Francisco: City Lights, 2010).

18. It seems to me a clear indication of my white cluelessness, and of the sustained and focused reflection required to overcome it, that this question did not occur to me until about six months later, while I was writing this chapter.

19. It might work the other way, too: if privileged people could be persuaded to share resources, perhaps no one would need to care about what we were thinking.

20. Townes, *Womanist Ethics*, 60–63, quotation at 63.

21. For an extended discussion and analysis of white people's need to feel like good people, see Barbara Applebaum, *Being White, Being Good: White Complicity, White Moral Responsibility, and Social Justice Pedagogy* (Lanham, MD: Lexington, 2011).

22. I am grateful to George Yancy for rendering explicit the fact that the cost-benefit analysis I describe here is conducted at the expense of suffering bodies of color.

23. Thompson, "Tiffany," 24.

24. Thompson, "Tiffany," 21.

25. See Karen Teel, "What Jesus wouldn't do: a white theologian engages whiteness," in *Christology and Whiteness: What Would Jesus Do?* edited by George Yancy, 19–35 (London and New York: Routledge, 2012), at 29–30.

26. The fact that my confidence in this as a possible strategy has already waned shows just how fast my understanding of whiteness can change, as I mentioned above.

27. Thompson, "Tiffany," 15–16.

28. Thompson, "Tiffany," 16.

29. This heading, and the chapter's title, are indebted to Applebaum's *Being White, Being Good*. I am also grateful to Sarah Azaransky for serving as a sounding board at key moments during the writing of this chapter, and to Matt Watkins for reading and critiquing a final draft.

30. Thompson, "Tiffany," 12.

31. See Peggy McIntosh, "White Privilege: Unpacking the Invisible Knapsack," in *White Privilege: Essential Readings on the Other Side of Racism*, ed. Paula S. Rothenberg, 97–101 (New York: Worth, 2002).

32. Thompson, "Tiffany," 8.

33. Thompson, "Tiffany," 16.

Chapter Three

"White Talk" as a Barrier to Understanding the Problem with Whiteness

Alison Bailey

I have often wondered, and it is not a pleasant wonder, just what white Americans talk about with one another. I wonder this because they do not, after all, seem to find very much to say to me, and I concluded long ago that they found the color of my skin inhibiting. This color seems to operate as a most disagreeable mirror, and a great deal of one's energy is expended in reassuring white Americans that they do not see what they see.

—James Baldwin [1]

I urge each one of us to reach down into that deep place of knowledge inside herself and touch that terror and loathing of any difference that lives there. See whose face it wears.—Audre Lorde [2]

Being a good white is part of the problem, rather than the solution to systematic racism.—Barbara Applebaum [3]

FLUTTERING AROUND THE WHITE PROBLEM

Quick: How does it feel to be a white problem? I want to hear what it's like for you. How do you think being white is a problem? Tell me in your own words. Tell me how you exist in your whiteness. What's so special about it? What's valuable about being white? Tell me, how does it feel to be a white problem?

What do you mean a white problem? You see this is really NOT my problem. I'm a good person. I'm not prejudiced. My ancestors never owned slaves. Anyway, that was a long, long time ago. I'm not responsible for the

Indian Removal Act, Japanese internment, or the Black Codes. I wasn't even born yet. Yes, I know America has a history of racism and genocide, but our nation has come a long way. And, you can't dwell on the tragedies of U.S. history—that was in the past. We can't teach that to our children if we want them to be proud of this country. Things are much better now. And, anyway, I'm not the problem—it's only racists that are the problem. I'm not like my bigoted father. I don't care if you're black, red, or yellow with polka dots, everyone should be treated equally. The problem is that some people don't treat others equally. It's really not a white problem; I didn't choose to be born white. Anyway, I have black friends. I regularly contribute to the Dolores Huerta Foundation. My church does charity work in the Chicago barrios. I'm from a poor white family. We suffered too, and you don't hear us complaining. The problem is that people of color make everything about race. I don't think of you as black. Right, I understand the problem; I've read James Baldwin and bell hooks. I'm a lesbian, so I know what it feels like to be oppressed. I feel so awful about my whiteness. I don't think of myself as white. I'm Irish, Dutch, and German. I've always felt as if I were an Indian in another life. It's not like I'm a member of the Aryan Nation or some Arizona militia group or something. . . . You can trust me! I'm on your side! I'm open-minded, fair, supportive, and empathetic. My heart is in the right place. I mean well. I'm innocent. I'm good! I'm a good white person! It's all good! There is no problem here.

It's no accident that these responses are often the first words out of white people's mouths when we talk about race, white privilege, and racism. They are not a random constellation of utterances. What Alice McIntyre calls "white talk" is a predictable set of discursive patterns that white folks habitually deploy when asked directly about the connections between white privilege and institutional racism.[4] I used to believe that white talk was a welcomed response to the request that I examine my whiteness. I routinely (and very sincerely) made many of the above declarations. Sometimes, in moments of defensiveness, I still do. I used to imagine that my remarks would be interpreted as expressions of solidarity, compassion, friendliness, and support. I thought that by pointing to my goodness that people of color would feel safe around me, and see me as a trustworthy ally, one of the good ones, an exception.[5] I was wrong. It's so much more complicated.

White talk has a long and annoying history. W. E. B. Du Bois alludes to it in the opening lines of *The Souls of Black Folk* (1903) where he reflects on his many conversations with white folks about what at the time was called "the Negro problem." He begins:

> Between me and the other world there is an ever-unasked question: unasked by some through feelings of delicacy; by others through the difficulty of rightly

framing it. All, nevertheless, flutter round it. They approach me in a half-hesitant sort of way, eye me curiously or compassionately, and then, instead of saying directly, How does it feel to be a problem? They say, I know an excellent colored man in my town; or, I fought at Mechanicsville; or, do not these Southern outrages make your blood boil. At these I smile, or am interested, or reduce the boiling to a simmer, as the occasion may require. To the real question, how does it feel to be a problem? I answer seldom a word. [6]

Du Bois's exchange not only marks the burdens of blackness but also points to white folks' discomfort with the possibility that the so-called Negro problem's origins are closer to home. It lies not in the character of some "problem people" but in white folks' general fears and anxieties. As Lerone Bennett Jr. later observed in his essay "The White Problem in America":

> When we say that the causes of the race problem are rooted in the white American and white community, we mean that the power is in white Americans and so is the responsibility. We mean that the white American created and invented the race problem and that his fears and frailties are responsible for the urgency of the problem.
> When we say that the fears of white Americans are at the root of the problem, we mean that the white American is a problem to himself, and that because he is a problem to himself he has made others problems to themselves.
> When we say that the white American is a problem to himself, we mean that racism is a reflection of personal and collective anxieties lodged deep in the hearts and minds of white Americans.
> By all this we must understand that Harlem is a white-made thing and that in order to understand Harlem we must go not to Harlem but to the conscience of white Americans and we must ask not what is Harlem, but why have you made Harlem? Why did you create it? And why do you need it? [7]

Du Bois's interlocutors' implicit queries can be traced back to these fears and anxieties. They flutter not only around the so-called Negro problem but also around their whiteness. A century later, white folks rehearse this familiar chorus: "my best friend is black"; or, "I marched in the Not in Our Town anti-racism rally"; or "doesn't the Trayvon Martin shooting in Sanford, Florida, make your blood boil?" We flutter.

My project in this chapter is to explain why the question "How does it feel to be a white problem?" cannot be answered in the fluttering grammar of white talk. The whiteness of white talk lies not only in its having emerged from white mouths but also in its evasiveness—in its attempt to suppress fear and anxiety and its consequential [if unintended] reinscription and legitimation of racist oppression. For this reason it is ontologically impossible for white talk to answer the question "How does it feel to be a white problem?" [8] White talk is designed, indeed scripted, for the purposes of evading, rejecting, and remaining ignorant about the injustices that flow from whiteness and its attendant privileges. I want to suggest a new point of entry—a way to flip the script, so to speak.

I begin with some observations about the basic advantages and disadvantages of using white talk as a route into the white problem. My account develops an expanded version of Alice MacIntyre's definition of white talk that is attentive to the racialized bodily scripts that accompany white talk. I argue that white talk persists because it has an enduring and powerful moral, ontological, and epistemic payoff for white folks. I explore each payoff with an eye toward clarifying how white talk functions to maintain the illusion that we are invulnerable beings. Next, I pause to reply to the popular objection that this particular critique of white talk silences white people in conversations on race. If we cannot address the question "how does it feel to be a white problem" in the fluttering grammar of white talk, then how shall we begin? In closing, I suggest that we might reduce fluttering by replacing white talk with a discourse of vulnerability, where vulnerability is defined not as weakness but as a condition for potential. I offer some brief guidelines for how we might start this conversation.

WHY START WITH WHITE TALK?

I regularly use white talk as an entry point into classroom discussions on race. There are good reasons for this. First, white talk is a manageable artifact of the white problem.[9] It offers an accessible and tangible illustration of white people's resistance to understanding our complicity in maintaining racial inequalities. White talk is also a convenient point of agreement: it undeniably exists. Well-meaning white folks can't explain away white talk with the same finesse as we explain away white privilege. No one says, "You're making this up. Maybe we used to talk this way, but things have changed. White people don't say these things anymore!" Instead, we blush. *Yes! I've said many of these things. I hear myself in these utterances.*

There are also very good reasons for not using white talk as an entry point. With rare exceptions, the burden of patiently listening, educating, correcting, and explaining racism regularly falls on people of color. As a friend of mine once said to me after a three-day antiracism workshop: *No offense, but I'm so tired of having the race conversation with white people. It's frustrating, and it always leaves me feeling tired, depressed, and vulnerable. I don't think white folks know how much courage it took for me to tell y'all what it's like to go through the day in a black woman's body. It's hard to trust white folks to begin with, but sometimes, in settings like this, I just take a chance. I share my stories in hopes that someone will believe me when I tell them that racism is still very real for us. I always hope that white folks will be empathetic, and some people are, but most don't listen. I know that when I'm talking, that you are up in your head all that time trying to explain my words away. Then, you find some reason to tell me that it's all in my head. You say I'm just seeing things, that I'm too sensitive, or too angry, or that I'm not trying hard enough. White people always politely say to me, maybe it's this, or maybe it's that. But, they rarely ask: Are you OK? Does this frequently happen to you? Do you think you were given the run around because you are black, and the white guy at the bank teller's window assumed that you were scamming him? I'm tired of white folks insisting that I must be mistaken about my own experience. I'm tired of them assuming that I'm the problem. You deal with them. I don't have the energy. Maybe they will get it if they hear it from a white person. You talk with them.*[10] I've heard folks of color say these things again and again. At some point in my journey I learned to hear what was being said. I stopped trying to explain away the harms by attributing them to individual character flaws and started looking for patterns and asking questions. I ask that white readers hold these voices in our heads and hearts.[11] I ask that we attend to these voices with the same love and care that use to listen to our best friend's voice. I ask that we center these voices, engage them, and feel their weight during our conversations.

WHAT IS WHITE TALK?

White talk is the *lingua franca* of race talk among white folks. It is a privilege-exercising discourse that usually springs from our lips without notice. White people habitually fall into white talk as a strategy for steering clear of entertaining the possibility that many of our actions, utterances, and thoughts contribute to the perpetuation of racial injustices and that we bear some responsibility for these. As Alice McIntyre argues, white talk "serves to insulate white people from examining our individual and collective role(s) in the perpetuation of racism. It is the result of whites talking uncritically with/to other whites, all the while resisting critique and massaging each others' racist attitudes, beliefs and actions."[12] White talk is a family of verbal strategies that whites regularly deploy to excuse us "from the difficult and almost paralyzing task of engaging [our] own whiteness."[13] We use white talk to derail conversations on race, to dismiss counterarguments, to retreat into silence, to interrupt speakers and topics, and to collude with other whites in creating a "culture of niceness" that makes it difficult to critique the white world.[14] White fear and anxiety drive these conversational detours, dismissals, and denials.

White talk mirrors Elizabeth Spelman's remarks on boomerang perception—"I look at you, and come right back to myself."[15] White talk is a "boomerang discourse": I talk to you but come right back to myself. This boomerang process points to another interesting aspect of white talk. In addition to its responsibility-evasive function, white talk also serves to construct the speaker as an imagined non-racist self. That is, it gives us a sense of ourselves as well-meaning white people to whom we can boomerang back when we feel that our perceived sense of ourselves as not racist is being challenged. When white talk is performed in front of others, especially among people of color, this public performance acts as a ritual of moral purification that seeks to evoke people of color's affirmation. Since we, as white folks, have become so adept at seeing only the self we want to see, we will either interpret our conversations as exchanges in which our goodness is affirmed—"*See, LaKeesha thinks I'm a good person.*" Or, we favorably re-interpret our exchanges in ways we imagine that our goodness simply can't be seen—"*Diego is too trapped by his own oppression and victimhood to recognize that I'm a good white ally.*"

McIntyre's analysis is clearly directed at extra-discursive social change, yet its single-pointed focus on "the spoken" offers readers a narrow and disembodied account of white talk: one that privileges the content of the utterances and ignores the bodily performances that accompany them. I think this is a mistake. Attending to the bodily comportment of all speakers, regardless of race, during these conversations offers us a deeper reading of what's going on during these exchanges. It's important to cultivate mindfulness not only of white talk, but also of our bodily comportment during these conversations for the simple reason that what our words say and what our bodies do are not always in concert. Over the years, I've cultivated the habit of watching bodies while I listen to what students have to say about race. For example, I regularly hear white folks declare their goodness and offer examples of why they haven't a racist bone in their bodies. Yet I watch their bodies tighten and withdraw, their hands tense up and their eyes dart about looking for a safe place to rest their gaze. What I've learned is that most white speakers attribute their goodness to the content of our utterances even when those utterances spring from bodies that are ill at ease, restless, fearful, or anxious. We must be mindful of this tension. Body language is a form of nonverbal communication: our posture, facial expressions, subtle gestures, and tone of voice provide additional cues about white talk's emotional content.[16] How do people of color react when a white student responds, deploying white talk, to a Muslim student's story about being harassed by airport police? How do our bodies interact with one another when the conversation takes an uncomfortable turn? What fears and anxieties trigger those reactions?[17]

White talk—its utterances and accompanying gestures—mark our fluttering. The verb "to flutter" is etymologically linked to "float," which connotes the sense of remaining on the surface, failing to go deep. Hence, "white talk" might be construed as that which remains on the surface of things. We flutter when we resist lighting upon or dwelling in spaces where we feel unsafe and vulnerable. We flutter when we look for detours, distract ourselves, and pull into our bodies. We flutter when we blame others, become defensive, or treat people of color as our confessors. We flutter to avoid hearing people of color's histories, experiences, and testimonies. We do everything imaginable to avoid confronting and owning our anxieties and fears. Cherríe Moraga's description of white women's fluttering clearly illustrates the embodied, affective, and relational nature of white talk that I have in mind.

> I watch white women shirk before my eyes, losing their fluidity of argument, of confidence, pause awkwardly at the word, "race," the word, "color." The pauses keeping the voices breathless, the bodies taut, erect—unable to breathe deeply, to laugh, to moan in despair, to cry in regret. I cannot continue to use my body to be walked over to make a connection. Feeling every joint in my body tense this morning, used. [18]

What I like about this passage is how Moraga observes white women's fluttering while attending to its impact on *her* body. Learning to be mindful of these dynamics has taught me to tune into my own words and bodily responses and to think carefully about white talk's psychological costs for people of color. What must it feel like to hear the word "black"—a word that describes your core identity—stick in the white people's throats? What must it feel like to watch white bodies tighten up in your presence? How painful must it be to politely listen to white folks constantly try to convince you that you must be wrong about your feelings? Returning mindfully to the problem of whiteness requires white folks to ask ourselves: What must it feel like to recognize, however dimly, our contributions to this pain, anxiety, and anger? Or, how can I recognize my contributions in ways that focus on the space in between us, on our interactions, and that don't boomerang back to finding ways to restore my goodness?

THE PROBLEM WITH WHITE TALK: MORAL, ONTOLOGICAL, AND EPISTEMIC PAYOFFS

What's the matter with white talk? Here's the short answer. White talk distracts us from rather than engages us with the heart of the white problem: fear. The long answer is more complicated: white talk has a deep moral, ontological, and epistemological payoff for white folks. It permits us to feel as if we are thoughtfully engaging race and racism but allows us to do so from a place of imagined invulnerability, comfort, and safety. To understand this, I need to spell out more carefully how white talk bolster's white folks sense of moral goodness, well-meaning white identity, and epistemic authority.

White talk has a strong moral dimension.[19] As Barbara Applebaum clearly and convincingly argues: Its central aim is to convince listeners that the
speaker is an innocent, well-meaning, and good-intentioned person who
bears little or no responsibility for the continuing harms of racism. We do
this by dividing the world into two kinds of white folks—[bad] racist white
people, and [good] well-meaning white people—and repeatedly offering evidence for our membership in the "good white people" group. Goodness is the
magnetic north of white talk. It bolsters our sense of moral goodness by
steering conversations away from discursive spaces that reveal our fears,
anxieties, and vulnerabilities and into discursive spaces where our goodness
is reified. When I say: "*My ancestors never owned slaves; I have black
friends; I grew up in a mixed neighborhood; my father's the bigot in the
family; or, it's not like I'm a member of the Aryan Nation or something,*" I
am not making random claims about myself or family members. Words are
never just words. Words are always doing things.[20] To understand this point,
it's helpful to make the distinction between the literal and the functional
meaning of white talk. The utterance "I'm not a member of the Aryan Nation" is not meant to be taken literally in this context; that is, its function is
not to alert listeners to an interesting factual aside about my political alliances or about who I don't hang out with after work. The actual content of
the sentences uttered in white talk may be true, but that's not the point. When
asserted in response to the white problem question, these remarks do something else: they are offered as evidence of one's innocence. One might also
note that the extreme nature of these examples allows for a form of contrast
that sets a very low threshold for goodness. Being good requires only that we
not be moral monsters. When white folks make these claims we grant ourselves permission to flee the messy and unfinished business of racism by
placing ourselves in the company of "good white folks," who, because of our
goodness, imagine that we have nothing further to think about on the subject.[21] White talk redirects our conversations onto discursive terrain where
white folks are innocent bystanders rather than part of the problem. Focusing
exclusively on white moral goodness, as Barbara Applebaum argues, makes
it extremely difficult to entertain the possibility that our words, actions, body
language, thoughts, and beliefs make us complicit in systemic injustices.[22]
After all, if you think you're good, then you assume that you are invulnerable
to criticism. There is nothing more to learn.

Next, the moral work that is done by white talk also performs a specific
ontological function: it repeatedly directs us back to an imagined pure, un-
complicated, unproblematic understanding of what it means to be a well-
meaning white person. In short, white talk reflects the ontology of whiteness.[23] To get at this, I need to say something about how the presence or
absence of problems is tied to the social construction of racial identities. This
becomes clearer if we return to Du Bois's original question: What does it

mean to be a problem? The question, as George Yancy argues, is "directed at the ontological core of one's being as in—how does it feel *to be* a problem?[24] To *be* a problem is different than to *have* a problem. Having a problem means an obstacle has been placed in your path. I *have* a problem when I can't find the keys to my car or when I forget to bring my driver's license to the airport. To *be* a problem means that your entire racial group is imagined to be an obstacle by their very nature. "Within the white imaginary, to be black means to be born an obstacle at the very core of one's being."[25] The process by which some groups move from defining themselves to being defined by outsiders as "problem peoples" is part of the machinery of colonization and nation building. For example, there is a predictable script that runs through U.S. history that positions and repositions so-called non-white peoples as problems in this sense. Consider how the Middle Passage transformed African identities [plural] from Ashanti, Yoruba, Imbangala, and Nyamwezi into an artificially homogenized class known as "Negroes" [singular]. Consider how European colonization of the Americas turned the Quechua, Maya, Anazasi, and Cherokee into "Indians." These classifications were tied further to the mission of colonization. If African labor was needed for agriculture, then Africans were understood as identical to beasts of burden. If colonial expansion required land and resources, then Native peoples and their land management practices were recast as wasteful and uncivilized. Consider further, how the new categories "Negro" and "Indian" rapidly morph into "Negro Problem" and the "Indian Problem." Peoples are problematized when their very being is imagined to be defective, deviant, childlike, irresponsible, criminal, immoral, dirty, animalistic, culturally and intellectually inferior, savage, primitive, barbaric, lazy, hypersexual, predatory, violent, slothful, addicted, deceiving, or untrustworthy. And it is their being that is understood to be fixed, permanent, eternal, and inescapable.

The problem of whiteness can't be engaged critically by extending this "the core-defines-the-identity logic to white folks." Recasting the script does not mean re-imagining white people as racist-at-core in the same way people of color have been historically represented as lazy, childlike, or violent at core. Flipping the script is not the scholarly equivalent of an adolescent backseat quarrel on a long road trip. It's not…*"You're the problem! . . . No, You're the problem! . . . No! YOU'RE the Problem! It's a black problem! No, it's a WHITE problem."* The construction of African and Native peoples as problems is part and parcel of the construction of Europeans as responsible, civilized, human, chaste, clean, trustworthy, citizens, hardworking, moral, pure, and good.[26] They are two sides of the same ontological coin. Positioning some groups as problems invariably places other so-called civilized groups in the position to "solve these problems." So, I'm not suggesting that we answer the white problem by flipping the ontological coin: that is, by making the problem-solvers the ontological problem, as if by "nature." The white problem is ontologically different from what has been historically called the Negro problem, the Indian problem, the yellow peril, the Mexican problem, the Arab problem, the Muslim problem, or the immigrant problem. When the script is flipped, the referent of "problem" is recast: the shift is from looking at the so-called ontological problem of blackness, to "the performative power of whiteness."[27]

White talk is one example of this performative power of whiteness. The conversational detours that characterize it reinforce the essential core of well-meaning white identity by repeatedly redirecting our gaze to goodness. The French root (*détour*) means literally to turn away. To paraphrase James Baldwin, white talk helps to manage white identity by allowing white folks to turn away from those "disagreeable mirrors" that reflect our whiteness back to us in its plurality. When we turn away, we convince ourselves that "we do not see what we see."[28] Disagreeable mirrors show white folks as no other mirror can. María Lugones uses mirror imagery to highlight how white folks' single-pointed focus on our goodness makes it difficult to see plurality of selves that disagreeable mirrors reflect back to us. For example, think about how white folks regularly appeal to our charity work in either poor countries or low-income neighborhoods as evidence of our goodness. Often in our rush to bolster our good works, we fail to consider how the residents of those communities sometimes resent outsider's help. When outsiders impose their reform agenda on communities based on what they *believe* a community needs and not what residents *know* they need they act ignorantly and arrogantly. In these contexts, well-meaning whites are not simply "good." They are "good-arrogant-innocent-imperious-well meaning, perhaps misguided" white folks. Considering the community perspective helps to reveal our plurality. When we are open to seeing ourselves as others see us, we become what María Lugones calls "plural selves." We block plurality because learning to see ourselves as others see us is frightening and inconsistent with the view we have of ourselves as wholly good. White folks block identification with our arrogant or imperious selves because, as Lugones reminds us: "'remembering that self fractures you into more than one person. You know a self that is decent and good, and knowing yourself in [that] mirror frightens you with losing your center, your integrity, your oneness.' And, 'you block identification with that self because you are afraid of plurality.'"[29] When we respond to the white problem question in white talk we block the possibility of seeing our plurality. Our whitely utterances reinscribe the contours of goodness, rather than reveal our goodness-arrogance-ignorance. Recasting the script means that white folks have before us the burden of identifying and problematizing whiteness in its plurality by learning to see what is not seen, and understanding how whiteness poses a problem for humanity.[30]

Finally, white talk is an expression of epistemic resistance driven by fear and anxiety. I'll have more to say about the epistemic consequences of white talk in my final section. At this point, I will mark the epistemic dimensions of white talk, and pause to consider a common objection.

OK, SO JUST TELL ME WHAT TO SAY!

OK I get it. I can't engage whiteness critically using the fluttering grammar of white talk because these utterances bolster white privilege on moral, onto-logical, and epistemological grounds. So, what should I say? How should I have this conversation? Tell me what to say, I don't want to offend anyone! I feel silenced! I feel trapped! I feel as if everything I say is going to be wrong, and that I'll be called a racist, so why bother?

I want to make three observations. First, as some readers may have guessed, this objection follows the discursive contours of white talk by steer-ing the conversation back toward white people's goodness and comfort. *I don't want to be seen as a racist, I don't want to offend anyone, so tell me what to say! I want to avoid discomfort at all costs!* Responding to critical accounts of white talk with "what do *you* want *me* to say?" is boomerang discourse—it repositions white subjects as fixers, missionaries, rescuers, and thus as outside of the critique of whiteness. Further, it suggests that white folks rely exclusively on members of oppressed groups for answers rather than trying to figure it out for ourselves. *White folks can fix this nasty racism business if we just learn to say the right things!* As Barbara Applebaum so nicely puts it, these objections "center the question on 'what can *I* do?, rather than 'what can be done?' and this encourages moral solipsism, heroism, and white narcissism."[31]

Next, there is a strong connection between white privilege, goodness, and rule following. Marilyn Frye once observed that white morality was rule governed: "by believing in rules, by being arbitrators of rules, by understand-ing agency in terms of the applications of principles to particular situations, whitely people think they preserve their detachment from prejudice, bias, meanness, and so on. White people tend to believe that one preserves one's goodness by being principled, by acting according to rules instead of accord-ing to feeling."[32] We may take comfort in following rules because rules often minimize risk and bolster illusions of invulnerability. *If I follow the rules of the road, then I'll minimize my risk of accidents; and, I'll be a good driver. If I follow the rules for interacting with people of color, then I'll minimize the risk of being called a racist; and, I'll be a good white person. So, what are the rules? Don't call black folks "articulate." OK. Don't touch black peo-ple's hair. Check. Never say I don't think of you as black, Indian, Chinese, and so on. Check.* Rules act as insurance against slipping from goodness. *What do you mean I'm prejudiced? I followed the rules. I said all of the things you told me to say!* Rules are a quick path to comfort. It's easier to memorize a rule such as "Don't touch black people's hair" than it is to work toward a deep understanding of the history and the politics of uninvited touching.[33] Rules can be used in place of genuine interactions and conversations. Following rules need not require a profound change of heart, deep self-examination, or risk taking. It's easier to follow a set of guidelines than it is to interrogate whiteness deeply, to listen to people of color, or to read alternative histories that call into question everything we've been taught to believe about what it means to be white in the United States of America.

Finally, I find it interesting that this objection almost always gets framed as a choice between white talk and silence. White talk is so deeply rooted in the sense whites have of ourselves as essentially well-meaning that we assume it's our only voice. It is not. It is the voice of insecure goodness, imagined invulnerability, ontological wholeness, and epistemic closure. Ironically these are expressions of invulnerability that are driven by a fundamental vulnerability at their very core. There are other voices—vulnerable voices—that shake the boundaries of the white self and that reorient our attention away from restoring goodness and comfort and toward listening to people of color's voices and questioning our own responses. What if we ditched white talk and retreated to what Pema Chödrön calls "the places that scare us" rather than to the places that comfort us?[34] What if we made a sincere effort to engage our fluttering? What if we touched down and spent some time in uncomfortable spaces.[35] How might we start thinking about this? How might we have these conversations in ways that recognize our plurality?

WHITENESS WITH MINIMAL FLUTTERING: "VULNERABILITY-AS-POTENTIAL" AS A NEW POINT OF ENTRY

Quick! Stop fluttering just for a moment! Touch down, even briefly. Be still. Breathe. Observe. Let's talk about how it feels to be a white problem. Can you talk through this without falling back into white talk? Can you understand how white talk skirts the issue and silences those voices we've been asked to hold in our heads and hearts? Can you grasp how white talk privileges white folks' comfort over people of color's lived experiences? Can you acknowledge how white talk erases your plurality? Can you understand how retreating to white talk closes off opportunities for knowledge?

I want to return to the epistemic dimensions of white talk. The question "how does it feel to be a white problem?" can never be answered in the fluttering grammar of white talk. The detours and distractions of white talk promote epistemic closure by confining our discussions to discursive comfort zones where evidence of white innocence has greater epistemic weight than people of color's own testimony. As such, it will not take us into Chödrön's "places that scare us," that is, the places where we can take risks and be epistemically open to seeing ourselves as plural and often contradictory.

White talk closes off alternative ways of knowing. The epistemic closure I have in mind here is a form of willful ignorance. Ignorance [literally, "to ignore"] is a central feature of racism, and white talk is a means of willfully managing our ignorance in ways that keep white folks from feeling vulnerable. Nancy Tuana defines willful ignorance as the condition of "not knowing, and not wanting to know."[36] People with race privilege, she argues, commonly exhibit a "determined ignorance" of the lives, histories, and cultures of those whom we believe to be either inferior or unimportant.[37] Willful ignorance is not a *passive* form of ignorance. It is a complex result of endless acts of negligence and omission. It cannot be explained as a simple gap in our knowledge.[38] That is, it's not the product just missing information. As in, *"Hey, it's not my fault, I was never taught about the Tulsa Race Riots, the Indian Removal Act, or the Chinese Exclusion Act.* White willful ignorance requires repetitive and diligent effort to resist knowing what is before you. Willful ignorance is *actively* produced: It is an achievement that must be managed.[39] Managing ignorance requires keeping the habitual detours, dismissals, and denials that characterize white talk in good working order. When we say: *"Why do we need to know about the Sand Creek Massacre? That was all in the past, and things are so much better today,"* we opt for epistemic closure. We refuse to consider how current injustices are tied to the history of European colonization of the Americas. White talk is an expression of willful ignorance, not because the speaker has a gap in her knowledge. Remember: Words *do* things. When we fall back on white talk we *actively* give ourselves permission to put racism and genocide in the past, dismiss historic atrocities as insignificant, dismiss people of color's very real day-to-day grievances, or to privilege our own desire not to talk about it. We opt to dwell in an imagined state of invulnerability, where past atrocities are conveniently severed from present realities.

The epistemic effects of white talk remain powerful because willful ignorance, in a twisted way, has a huge payoff for white folks. Following James Baldwin, Elizabeth Spelman describes how white folks actively remain ignorant about people of color's contemporary grievances because we fear that they might be true. It's not simply that we *suspect* that they might be true and choose not to believe them. Her point is more subtle and unsettling: "[We] want the claim 'black America's grievances are real' to be false, but we know that if we treat [this claim] as something that could be false, then we would also have to regard it as something that could also be true. Better to ignore [the claim] altogether, given the fearful consequences of its being true. Better not to have thought at all than to have thought and lost."[40] Spelman's argument points to a powerful and astonishing conclusion: Not only is the whitely desire to parade oneself as good, pure, and innocent driven by willful ignorance but also the costs of this ignorance to black, brown, Native, and Asian bodies is so astonishingly pervasive and enduring that it "drains off the moral capital" we imagine ourselves having accumulated![41] When bolstered by willful ignorance, white folks' sense of our own goodness collapses into a form of solipsism and narcissism that negates any genuine form of respect and recognition for the "Other" that might reveal the plurality of white selves. Almost all of the evidence of our goodness offered by white talk collapses under the weight of our refusal to engage alternative explanations.

We need a new entry point into the white problem question: one that resists turning the conversation into either a forum about white goodness or into an ignorance-management project. Remember fear is at the root of the white problem. But what drives the conversation is not fear itself but how vulnerable we feel in the face of this fear. We can either plaster over our fears with white talk, or we can humbly acknowledge that they make us feel vulnerable and learn to treat this vulnerability as a source of knowledge. What if we made a conscious choice to embrace that vulnerability and used that realization as an entry point into the question of what it means to be a white problem? What if we replaced white talk with a discourse of vulnerability?

Conventional understandings equate vulnerability with being weak, helpless, defenseless, dependent, or susceptible to harm or injury. This sense of vulnerability-as-weakness is not the one I want to use to ground the new entry point. The definition of vulnerability I have in mind is closer to Erinn Gilson's account of vulnerability-as-potential. On this view vulnerability is not just what happens to some humans in particular circumstances. It is the basic character of human existence. [42] In Gilson's words:

> Taken . . . as a fundamental state, vulnerability is a condition of potential that makes possible other conditions. Being vulnerable makes it possible for us to suffer, to fall prey to violence and be harmed, but also to fall in love, to learn, to take pleasure and to find comfort in the presence of others, and to experience the simultaneity of these feelings. Vulner*ability* is not just a condition that limits us, but also one that can *enable* us. As potential, vulnerability is a condition of openness, openness to being affected and affecting in turn. [43]

The enabling features of vulnerability-as-potential surface when we stop fluttering.[44] Lee Mun Wah once said, "If you accept and acknowledge your mistakes, what I see is your goodness. If you cover up your mistakes with excuses, claiming your goodness, all I see are your faults."[45] Naming our ignorance requires releasing our attachments to goodness and comfort and recognizing fear and discomfort as sources of knowledge and connection rather than as sources of closure and flight. What if we treated fear, anger, shame, and guilt not as feelings to be squashed, escaped, ignored, or reconfigured favorably but as genuine sources of knowledge? What if we followed people of color's lead into discursive spaces where we felt fragile, rather than into spaces where we felt comfortable? What if we attended to our feelings through our interactions with one another?

I don't want to define the exact nature of a discourse of vulnerability. I'm not interested in offering a new set of rules. Following Frye, I want us to "act according to feeling."[46] However, I do think that a discourse of vulnerability demands that speakers cultivate an attitude of epistemic openness as we enter these conversations. If we carry that attitude into our discussions then alternatives to white talk may emerge. Discourses of vulnerability will no doubt take on the shape and the character of their epistemic communities. I want to offer the following guidelines as a way to begin:

Begin where you are and not where you think you should be.
If you keep falling back into white talk then mark these moments and cultivate a healthy curiosity about why these patterns persist. Ask yourself: What buttons were pushed for me to respond with white talk? Name the barriers, detours, and diversions you habitually use. Write them down. Keep talking. Don't beat yourself up. If you don't see the white problem right away, then remind yourself that white talk is an expression of privilege, so there is a reason that many of us retreat to this discourse when challenged.

Actively listen to one another, and hear what is being said.
This requires being present when others are speaking and not trying to map out a reply to their words while they speak. Talk *with* each another, not *at* each another. Notice what is and is not being said and how it is expressed. Be mindful of key words and themes that repeat themselves. Ask yourself what emotional work these words and themes do, and why they continue to surface. Be curious about others' stories and observations, and use active language to engage their words. If you are unsure about someone's meaning then ask for clarification. Cultivate a reflective discourse of engagement: What I heard you say was . . . Why did you find that frustrating? What angers or frightens you? What makes you feel unsafe? Tell us more about that? How did that experience affect you? What do you need?[47] Don't forget to listen non-verbally to the messages that are being physically communicated.

Be mindful of what makes you shut down.
Be attentive to what your words and body tell you and those around you about race, racism, and whiteness. Observe the paths each conversation takes. Have you unconsciously changed the topic or shifted the focus? Are speakers being interrupted? How does your body react to what is being said? Where do you direct your gaze when the conversation takes an uncomfortable turn? Do you fidget or look at your phone? Cultivate an awareness of what makes you feel comfortable or uncomfortable during these conversa-

tions. You might try to write down the words and gestures that trigger strong feelings. Be honest, authentic, and forgiving. Trust yourself, but at the same time recognize that self-trust is slippery and can very easily collapse into white talk that re-centers white epistemic authority.

Take responsibility for your mistakes and learn from them.
Vulnerability requires letting go of the fear that you will make mistakes, offend people, and say foolish things. Most of us don't want to talk about race because we are afraid that we might say something offensive. As Lee Mun Wah once said: "Good luck. This country has five hundred years of a 'don't ask, don't tell policy' when it comes to diversity issues." More than likely you will say something that will hurt or be painful to someone. The important thing is to take responsibility for your mistakes and to be open to talking about them. Understand that taking responsibility does not mean beating yourself up. Be kind to yourself and others. This is difficult work. Period! There is no easy or correct way through these conversations. Take comfort in your courage and ability to take risks, rather than your ability to 'get it right.'

Treat discomfort as a source of knowledge.
Treat anger, fear, and anxiety as natural reactions to moving closer to knowledge. Crafting a discourse of vulnerability requires settling into our discomfort rather than continuing to flutter. You might practice moving toward the places that scare you by making a conscious choice to engage your fears and discomforts in ways that are not aimed at managing your ignorance or merely at protecting yourself from feelings of vulnerability.

Focus on being open and curious.
If white talk maintains the illusion of invulnerability through "not knowing, and not wanting to know," then a discourse of vulnerability-as-potential requires cultivating an attitude that is open to knowing. So . . .

Quick: What does it mean to be a white problem?
That is a really complex and difficult question. I wonder why it makes me uncomfortable? Why do I resist? Why do I become so defensive? I've never thought of whiteness as a problem. I wonder if this omission is significant? Perhaps having white privilege means not having to consider the possibility. What do you think? There must be something very big at stake for white folks to hang on to white talk so tightly. This is telling. What can we learn from this? It's so awkward. I'll admit that this question makes me feel fragile, angry, guilty, and defensive. Do you feel the same way? I am open to exploring what's behind these reactions. Can you say that again? I want to be sure I understood you clearly. It must be frustrating for people of color to have to

listen to white folks continually dodge this topic. What's that like? I'm scared that there is a lot more riding on the white problem than I can see right now. What if it's really deep? What if collective white fears and anxieties have been the source of real life injustices and harm from the start! What if racism really is a white problem! This is immense. What if we took time to dwell together in our anger, fear, and discomforts together? What if we listened patiently and carefully to one another's stories and to the connections between these narratives? Would a more complete picture emerge? Would the problem at least come into focus?

NOTES

Many thanks to Kristie Dotson, Kyle Powys Whyte, Michael Monahan, and Lawrence Solum, and George Yancy for helping me puzzle through these issues with clarity and honesty.

1. James Baldwin, "White Man's Guilt," in *The Price of the Ticket: Collected Nonfiction 1948–1985* (New York: St. Martin's Press, 1985), 409.

2. Audre Lorde, *Sister Outsider: Essays and Speeches by Audre Lorde* (Berkeley, CA: The Crossing Press, 1984), 113.

3. Barbara Applebaum, *Being White, Being Good: White Complicity, White Moral Responsibility, and Social Justice Pedagogy* (Lanham, MD: Rowman and Littlefield, 2010), 20.

4. Alice McIntyre, *Making Meaning of Whiteness: Exploring Racial Identities with White Teachers* (Albany, NY: SUNY Press, 1997).

5. The fact that I understood white talk as an expression of solidarity rather than a conversational slight of hand is a perfect example of an epistemology of ignorance. As Charles Mills once asked: "How are white people able to consistently do the wrong thing while thinking that they are doing the right thing?" Charles W. Mills, *The Racial Contract* (Ithaca, NY: Cornell University Press, 2007), 94.

6. W. E. B. Du Bois, *The Souls of Black Folk* (New York: Dover Publications, Inc., 1994), 1.

7. Lerone Bennett Jr. "The White Problem in America," *Ebony* (August 1965), 29–30.

8. Many thanks to Michael Monihan for his clarification of this point.

9. I'm grabbing onto one corner of the white problem. A complete understanding requires more time. As Charles Mills's once quipped about white ignorance: "It's a big subject. How much time do you have? It's not enough." Charles W. Mills, *The Racial Contract*, 13.

10. I've tried to capture the basic message of the conversation.

11. Like many white writers, I struggle with the question of voice when writing on race. Sometimes I use third person plural to refer to white people. This keeps the question of audience open. Other times I place my whiteness front and center to mark my location. I realize that both strategies run the risk of misinterpretation. My understanding is that this collection is directed primarily, but certainly not exclusively, at white readers, who resist seeing themselves as a problem. For this reason I've decided to use first person singular.

12. McIntyre, *Making Meaning of Whiteness: Exploring Racial Identities with White Teachers*, 46.

13. McIntyre, 46.

14. McIntyre, 46.

15. Elizabeth V. Spelman, *Inessential Woman: Problems of Exclusion in Feminist Thought* (Boston: Beacon Press, 1988), 12.

16. Chinese American filmmaker and community educator Lee Mun Wah's teaches bodily observation as a central means of understanding conversational dynamics. I'm drawing on his use of this practice. See http://www.stirfryseminars.com/resources/. For a phenomenological account of the impact of fear on bodies see Sarah Ahmed's The Affective Politics of Fear, in her *The Cultural Politics of Emotion* (New York, NY: Routledge, 2004).

17. I confine white talk to verbal communication and its accompanying gestures. This does not mean that white folks sometimes communicate our anxieties corporeally without uttering a word. We may clutch our bags when a person of color sits next to us on the Metro, lock our car doors when we drive through black or Latino neighborhoods, or flinch when young black men reach into their pockets. I recognize these as forms of communication. For the present purposes, however, I follow Lee Muh Wah's practice of focusing on bodily comportment *during* conversations on race, because they offer important affective information about these utterances.

18. Cherríe Moraga, "Introduction," *This Bridge Called My Back: Writings By Radical Women of Color*, 3rd edition (San Antonio, TX: Third Woman Press, 2002), xlvi.

19. My comments here are deeply inspired by Barbara Applebaum's careful discussion on the connections between whiteness and moral goodness in her *Being White, Being Good* (2010). I'm working with her basic argument and observations.

20. I have in mind here John Austin's *How to Do Things with Words*, 2nd ed. (Cambridge, MA: Harvard University Press, 1975).

21. As Barbara Applebaum notes, standard accounts of responsibility that tie culpability to actions and chains of causality define responsibility in narrow terms. This makes it difficult to understand how white folks perform and sustain whiteness and racism in our everyday ordinary actions. Applebaum does a remarkable job of clarifying the distinction between complicit as a matter of being, and complicity as a matter of doing, and argues for a new conception of responsibility that does not rely so heavily on blame and causal links between individual actions and institutional systems. See Applebaum, *Being White Being Good*, and Sandra Bartky,"Race, Complicity and Culpable Ignorance," in *Sympathy and Solidarity: And Other Essays* (Lanham, MD: Rowman and Littlefield), 2002.

22. Applebaum, *Being White, Being Good.*

23. George Yancy, "Fragments of a Social Ontology of Whiteness," in *What White Looks Like: African American Philosophers on the Whiteness Question* (New York: Routledge, 2004), 1–25.

24. George Yancy, *Black Bodies, White Gazes: The Continuing Significance of Race* (Lanham, MD: Rowman and Littlefield Publishers, 2008), 86–87.

25. When we have historically imagined people of African descent to be brutish, Mexicans to be lazy, Jews to be stingy, Indians to be uncivilized, or Asians to be cunning we are not making remarks about particular individuals in these groups, we are making claims about the essential nature of that group. George Yancy, *Black Bodies, White Gazes,* 87.

26. James Baldwin offers one of the clearest accounts of the white practice of dumping our anxieties and fears into dark bodies for the purpose of shoring up our own identities. He says: "I know this, and everyone who's ever tried to live knows this. What I say about you, about someone else, about everybody else, reveals you . . . what I think of you as being, indicated by my own necessities, and my own psychology, my own fears and desires. I'm not describing you when I talk about you, I'm describing me." The historical invention, in his words, of 'the nigger' as a placeholder for white anxieties is central to the maintenance of white identity. He remarks, "But you [white folks] still think that the 'nigger' is necessary. But he's unnecessary to me." See Baldwin's 1963 KQED interview available: http://www.youtube.com/watch?v=L0L5fciA6AU. See also George Yancy's discussion in *Look, A White!: Philosophical Essays on Whiteness* (Philadelphia: Temple University Press, 2012), 1–16.

27. Yancy, *Look, A White!,* 3.

28. James Baldwin, "White Man's Guilt," 409.

29. Now, people of color also see themselves reflected in white mirrors. The difference here is that survival under white supremacy requires a complex understanding and constant awareness of the plurality of one's selves; that is, a people of color regularly move between understandings of how whites seen them, and how they see themselves. White survival does not require a working understanding of our plurality in this sense, and so we focus on those selves that comfort rather than disturb us. María C. Lugones, "On The Logic of Pluralist Feminism," in *Feminist Ethics*, ed., Claudia Card (Lawrence, KS: University of Kansas Press, 2003), 73.

30. For a detailed account of 'flipping the script' see Yancy, *Look, A White!,* 1–17.

31. Applebaum, *Being White, Being Good,* 5.

32. Marilyn Frye, "White Woman Feminist," in *Willful Virgin: Essays in Feminism* (Freedom, CA: The Crossing Press, 1992), 155.

33. Unwanted touching smacks of ownership and entitlement to another person's humanity. It turns people of color into exotic objects of curiosity. Unwanted touching also *references* the psychological torment that Africans experienced during slavery—the invasive poking, prodding of auction block inspections. For example, in *The History of Mary Prince: A West Indian Slave Related by Herself*, Mary Prince recalls, "I was soon surrounded by strange men, who examined and handled me in the same manner that a butcher would a calf or lamb he was about to purchase, and who talk about my shape and size in like words—as if I could no more understand their meaning than a dumb beast." Cited in Yancy, *Black Bodies, White Gazes* 141. Amoja Three Rivers gives examples of these rules in a contemporary context. See her *Cultural Etiquette: A Guide for the Well Intentioned* (Indian Valley, VA: Market Wimmin Press, 1991).

34. Pema Chödrön, *The Places That Scare You: A Guide to Fearlessness in Difficult Times* (Boston: Shambala Press, 2001).

35. Yancy describes this as tarrying. In his words, "[t]he unfinished present is where I want whites to tarry (though not permanently remain), to listen, to recognize the complexity and weight of the current existence of white racism, to attempt to understand the ways in which they perpetuate racism, and to begin to think about the incredible difficulty involved in undoing it." Yancy, *Look a White*, 158.

36. Nancy Tuana, "The Speculum of Ignorance: the Women's Health Movement and Epistemologies of Ignorance," in *Hypatia* 21, no. 3 (2006), 1–19. Tuana's account of willful ignorance borrows from insights in Marilyn Frye (1992), Charles Mills (1997), James Baldwin (1963), and Elizabeth Spelman (2007). I am following the thread she has woven as I think it applies to white talk.

37. Tuana, "The Speculum of Ignorance," 10.

38. Frye, "On Being White," 118.

39. See Mills, *The Racial Contract*, and Tuana, "The Speculum of Ignorance."

40. Spelman, "Managing Ignorance," 121.

41. Spelman draws on the work of Carolyn Betensky here. I've revised this citation to emphasize how ignorance undercuts white folks efforts to be seen as good. See Spelman, "Managing Ignorance," 212.

42. Recently scholars have explored this sense of vulnerability as both an alternative to the autonomous, independent subject of liberal philosophy and as a means of exploring the connections between the illusion of invulnerability and violence and oppression. See Applebaum's *Being White, Being Good*. See also Debora Bergoffen, "February 22, 2001: Toward a Politics of the Vulnerable Body," in *Hypatia* 18, no. 1 (2003), 116–34; Judith Butler, *Precarious Life: The Power of Mourning and Violence* (New York: Verso, 2004); Martha A. Fineman, "The Vulnerable Subject: Anchoring Equality in the Human Condition," in *Yale Journal of Law and Feminism* 20, no. 1 (2008), 1–23; and, Erinn Gilson, "Vulnerability, Ignorance, and Oppression," in *Hypatia* 26, no 2. (2011), 308–32.

43. Gilson, "Vulnerability, Ignorance, and Oppression," 3.

44. The pivotal moment in Lee Muh Wah's documentary *The Color of Fear* (1994) illustrates this perfectly. The film documents a three-day conversation between eight men on race in America. About half way through the film Victor (an African American man) and David (a well-meaning white man) have a powerful exchange. Throughout the film David has repeatedly resisted, dismissed, and rejected all the evidence the men of color in the room have shared with him about the daily obstacles they face as black, brown, and Asian American men in the United States. David habitually refuted all of the men's stories by insisting that the harms and fears each speaker described could be more accurately attributed to their actions, choices or attitudes, but not to racism. At some point the conversation between the two breaks down. Victor asks David point blank why he refuses to hear what they have been telling him. For some reason, instead of retreating to white talk, David replies, "Because I don't want to believe that America is like this." To which Victor responds, "From here on in, I can work with you." The conversation becomes productive, honest, and informative only when David stops fluttering and becomes vulnerable to the possibility that others don't share his lived experience.

45. Lee Mun Wah, *Stir Fry Seminars and Counseling Newsletter*, April 2012. Available: http://www.stirfryseminars.com/pdfs/newsletter.pdf. Accessed April 2012.

46. Frye, "White Woman Feminist,"155.

47. I'm drawing partially from Lee Mun Wah's list of "Nine Healthy Ways to Communicate." A complete list is available through Stir Fry Seminars: http://www.stirfryseminars.com/pages/offer.php

Chapter Four

Unforgetting as a Collective Tactic

Alexis Shotwell

How can people currently racialized as white come to understand the ongoing production of whiteness as a problem? How do we understand ourselves as a white problem? Historian of indigenous struggles and revolutionary Roxanne Dunbar-Ortiz formulates the beautiful concept of *unforgetting*. In this chapter, I want to dwell with conceptions of critical memory practices as a way to think about how white people can work with anticolonialism and decolonizing as praxis. For me, the aspiration to this kind of practice has intimately to do with memory and with the process of understanding the work of memory in two national contexts: Canada and the United States. I'll focus here on the question of indigenous sovereignty and critical whiteness as a challenge to forgetting. Dunbar-Ortiz says:

> The definition of lying is what white South African anti-apartheid writer Andre Brink plays with in his book *An Act of Terror*. What's the opposite of truth? We think immediately "the lie." But in Greek, the opposite of truth is forgetting. This is a very subtle thing. What is the action you take to tell the truth? It is un-forgetting. That is really meaningful to me. It's not that the origin myth is a lie; it's the process of forgetting that's the real problem. . . . Alliances without un-forgetting at their core aren't going to go anywhere in the long run. So, it is a dilemma, but we have to find a way. We have to find ways to go through a mountain. We have to find that pass to get through it. [1]

Unforgetting, on this view, is an activity, just as forgetting is an activity. Political forgetting names an epistemology—a way of knowing—and an ontology—a way of being. Epistemically, forgetting is a core piece in colonial practice. Charles Mills and others call this an *epistemology of ignorance*: just as what we know arises from political situations and choices, what we do not know is actively shaped and carries politics. [2] Ignorance is not just an absence of knowledge; it is a way to (not) know things. In our being, ontologically, we become who we are in part through what we know and what we are made (or made able) to forget.

It is my contention that a central feature of white settler colonial subjectivity is forgetting; we live whiteness in part as active ignorance and forgetting. In situations where facts of the matter are routinely brought to our attention, forgetting must be an active and ongoing thing. In general, I believe that systemic oppression is in fact present enough in our world that the kinds of ignorance and lack of knowledge running alongside oppression deserve explanation. Consider that some people think that they "just don't see race," or that poverty doesn't exist in their community, or that indigenous people aren't part of their national consciousness. One way to understand what's at play here is through imagining a kind of benign ignorance—people just haven't been taught the facts of the situation, and so they can't be held responsible for not understanding how race, poverty, indigeneity, and more are present in their lives. If this were the problem, just giving people more and better information would correct their knowledge problem. But we don't just have a knowledge problem—we have a habit-of-being problem; the problem of whiteness is a problem of what we expect, our ways of being, bodily-ness, and how we understand ourselves as "placed" in time. Whiteness is a problem of being shaped to think that other people are the problem. Another way to understand this dynamic is via a conception of forgetting following Dunbar-Ortiz: forgetting as the active process of not telling, seeing, or understanding the truth of the matter.

This can be very subtle and it can be very blatant—sometimes at the same time. In my experience, it can take quite drastic shifts in context to bring to white consciousness the work of forgetting. I've experienced such shifts primarily through moving across the Canada-U.S. border several times in my life, and these shifts have been the main site for having some critical conception of whiteness as a problem. When I was fourteen, my family moved from Boulder, Colorado, to Halifax, Nova Scotia. It was 1989. In 1990, something happened near the city we know as Montreal. It's difficult to tell what happened, because how I tell it matters to what it was, what it is. I think of this as the difference between a no problem/problem narration and memory, or we could say a forgetting/unforgetting difference.

In the no problem/forgetting narration, here is what happened: My family decided to move to Canada, applied to immigrate through the normal channels, achieved landed immigrant status because we were assessed as good, prosperous prospective citizens, and moved. We left behind Boulder—a small, pretty idyllic town on the edge of the Rocky Mountains that happened to be full of mostly white mostly hippies. The summer after we arrived in Halifax, there was an armed conflict near a small town called Oka—Aboriginal Canadians had suddenly blockaded a road going into town to prevent a golf course being built on land that they claimed. A nearby reserve blockaded an important bridge in solidarity, and the Canadian government called in the army to calm things down before they got violent. We watched the events on television.

The problem/unforgetting narrative is much longer and more complex, and in a minute I'll unpack it more. But I want to remember here the point at which I started to notice that there was something not quite right about the narrative even as I tell it above, which was indeed for the most part how I experienced it. I had, as many U.S. Americans have, a conception of Canada as an affable, somewhat vague, helpful neighbor—the kind of person who would try to de-escalate a fight and encourage everyone to get along. I had some sense of the international Canadian presence as a peace-keeping force of good, mostly because I had a clear critique of U.S. foreign policy and militarism shaped through my early-teen opposition to Reagan and to a nuclear reactor close to Boulder. But I would say also that I had virtually no specifically racial content for any of these feelings and senses. Moving to Canada felt—aside from generalized teenage angst—like being invited to move into someone's slightly nicer than normal house on a quieter block than I was used to.

This feeling of there being no specific racial content to the act of moving from one country to another is actually an extremely racialized feeling. My family ran a used bookstore and café in Colorado; my parents both had university degrees; we all speak English, and my father is fluent in French. These facts about us look neutral, and as though they are not about race—we have to turn the story slightly, like shifting a translucent stone in sunlight, to notice the codes the Canadian government used and uses to prioritize white immigrants to the country through their "points" system. Education, country of origin, class status, occupation, language competency—all these characteristics of prospective immigrants also have racial dispositions, and how you weight what feature of an applicant "counts" shifts the racial composition of your immigrant pool. So although it's slippery to name, my feeling of "neutrality" and no-big-dealness is something, in retrospect, that shows up as very white.

In that summer, watching native women, men, and kids blockade roads and bridges, watching the army bring in tanks, I began to have a different or supplemental feeling. I began to feel as though, indeed, someone had invited me to move into a house—but without mentioning that it wasn't actually their house they were inviting me to live in with them. And that while they lived there they'd been flushing their toilet directly into the basement, sewage saturating the walls, sowing salt in what used to be the garden, shutting the children of the genuine owners into a shed out back, starting campfires in the living room. That kind of thing. I began to feel profoundly uneasy about the country I'd moved to in a way that has deepened and continued through the cross-border moves that have followed. I began to feel a sense of whiteness as a site of shame, and of Canadian whiteness as built on past and ongoing violence.

A start on a problem/unforgetting narration makes whiteness show up differently in this story. Boulder turns out not to be a neutral, idyllic place full of innocent actual and neo-hippies who just happen to be mostly white but something much more difficult. Historically, Boulder was the territory of the Ute, with significant presence from Cheyenne and Arapahoe peoples. (Most Boulderites don't "know" this, although one of the main roads through town is called "Arapahoe.") Mostly white settlers moved in as part of the westward genocidal push to quell permanently indigenous resistance to the formation of the United States, a push fueled in Colorado as elsewhere by a prospecting gold rush.[3] In the Boulder area, the 1864 Sand Creek Massacre is notable—a group of more than one hundred Arapahoe and Cheyenne flying the American flag and a white flag were butchered, and their scalps paraded through Denver. If this is not a race thing, what is it? And what does it mean not to remember this context?

In the wake of World War Two, the area just outside of Boulder participated in the origin and waging of Cold War politics, paying host to Rocky Flats, one of hundreds of nuclear power plants on U.S. soil that along the way naturalized a US narrative of world domination through nuclear capacity.[4] Nuclear weapons and energy may seem not to be about whiteness, in part via complex ways that the Soviet Union was framed as a white-ish Second World threat to the United States (the presumed whiteness of the communist was one of their dangers—they could be anywhere!). When we look at how the plutonium triggers manufactured in Rocky Flats were to be used, or where depleted uranium gets weaponized and used, it is mostly against what used to be called the Third World. The military industrial complex that produced Rocky Flats, and other nuclear facilities in the United States, relies on a racializing logic of defending a particular (American) form of life. If this is not a race thing, what is it? And what does it mean not to remember this context?

Colorado was not a slave state (it was a territory, not a state, before the U.S. Civil War), but it enacted and supported some of the central contradictions of a white-black binary; in the fifties, for example, Denver was a major site of struggle around the practice of real-estate "redlining," which aimed to create racially delineated, de facto segregated, housing, and schooling. Someone once told me that in 1994 the Klu Klux Klan held a rally in Boulder; one of the speakers congratulated Boulder on achieving a more than 90 percent white population, saying it was a perfect example of how to create a white-only city through economic means. This may be a myth (an online search finds various blogs repeating this claim), but I believed the story immediately. There are a lot of African dance and yoga classes in Boulder, and it is home to a substantial convert Tibetan Buddhist community, members of Shambhala International (the community I grew up in and still practice as part of), along with a number of other meditation groups. If this is not a race thing, what is it? And what does it mean not to remember this context?

So when my family moved from Boulder to Halifax, we left a city that is, like most of the United States, soaked in blood spilled in genocidal wars, structured by ongoing systemic oppression, and complexly implicated in a form of ongoing cultural and economic colonialism sustained through consumerist orientalism—there are very few people of color in town, but you can participate in lots of cultural and health activities that come from the lifeworlds of brown and black people from around the globe. I didn't know any of this when we left, and I didn't know it on a very deep level. How is it possible to live in Boulder and think that it is simply and primarily a really nice place to live—beautiful, with an interesting climate, full of nice people who want to live healthy and get in touch with their spiritual side? How can people think that it is an innocent accident that makes living healthy and getting in touch with one's spiritual side actually about taking yoga, hanging a dreamcatcher from their car mirror, listening to Bob Marley, as though these were not practices densely rooted in non-white communities, anti-colonial struggles, and contexts? I want us all to see how this is a white problem; I want us to feel how this is about history and another concept: the "social organization of forgetting."

This is a concept we can place next to Dunbar-Ortiz's articulation of unforgetting. We unforget, actively and resistantly, because forgetting is shaped by forces bigger than us. In their book about Canadian regulation of sexuality through state surveillance, Gary Kinsman and Patricia Gentile say: "In part, capitalism and oppression rule through what we call 'the social organization of forgetting,' which is based on the annihilation of our social and historical memories. . . . We have been forced to forget where we have come from; our histories have never been recorded and passed down; and we are denied the social and historical literacy that allows us to remember and relive our past, and, therefore, to grasp our present."[5] We white people might, on some level, *like* living with annihilated social and historical memories—we might like to think that the present is innocent of the past that produced it. We might like to think, though we're ashamed to admit it, that we don't need to tell or hear the painful stories of the actions that created the world we live in. That feeling, of wanting to be people unmoored from history, of endorsing the pretense that we have nothing to do with the past that constitutes our material conditions and our most intimate subjectivities, is a feeling that defines us. The social organization of forgetting means that our actual histories are lost, and it means that we have a feeling of acceptance and normalness about living with a lie instead of an unforgetting.

My family moved to a place that has different histories and different
present practices of racialization than Colorado, and the United States. But I
would say now that these differences didn't, don't, make the situation better.
And, indeed, the differences are not so different. My sense of Canada as an
affable, well-meaning neighbor turns out to be a truly masterful lie, a story
rather than history that would be impressive if it weren't so vile and harmful.
Start with the sentence I used to tell the story of what happened in 1990, just
above. I said: "there was an armed conflict near a small town called Oka—
Aboriginal Canadians had suddenly blockaded a road going into town to
prevent a golf course being built on land that they claimed." Now, I am not
going to be able to tell you the full complexity of what it would be to retell
that sentence in a mode of unforgetting, challenging the social organization
of forgetting that defines Canada. But I can do a little. Let me start with the
town. Oka is indeed a small town in the province of Quebec; they make what
people say is a pretty good soft cheese. But Oka could be understood as
actually Kahnehsatake, a winter stopping place of the Kanien'kehá:ka, one of
the five Nations that founded the Haudenosaunee Confederacy. When the
Kanien'kehá:ka were forced out of the area that is now Montreal, they were
"given" land by the then King of France across the Ottawa River (this was in
1716). The Society of St. Sulpice, a Catholic order, was "given" land next to
them; the order changed the terms of the grant in 1717, stealing the land.
They established what became Oka. After Confederation, in 1868, Chief
Joseph Onasakenrat, himself a seminarian, learned about the stolen land
grant and undertook various legal, political, and (probably) direct actions
against the Sulpicians. These efforts didn't succeed in winning back the land
title.[6]

So when in 1961 the city of Oka built a private golf course on land the
Sulpicians had stolen hundreds of years before and then sold, and the Kani-
en'kehá:ka protested and filed a failed legal suit, there was some long history
already behind them. And when in 1990 the city decided to expand the golf
course by another nine holes and to put up some luxury condominiums on
top of the Mohawk graveyard, there was a longer history there. It's hard to
see how I and other white settler Canadians could believe that the road
blockade the Kanien'kehá:ka put up was a sudden thing. And yet, that was
definitely the sense you would have gotten from the media. One simple
version of the story we got and get about indigenous resistance comes from
the racist colonial view: unreasonable and violent natives, ungrateful for the
many gifts the Canadian state had/has bestowed upon them, get uppity. It
sounds as though I'm just being sarcastic when I say it like that, and I wish
that this story was not still so widespread, but actually this continues to be a
very widespread view, expressed by a lot of people who would not self-
identify as racist.

Another simple story, which is less of a lie, in Dunbar-Ortiz's terms, is a reversal: Aboriginal peoples are the first peoples of this continent; this land is their land, stolen from them by military force, systemic duplicity, traitorous betrayal, legal double-standards, and outright genocidal policies. The Canadian state and all of the people who live here are profoundly indebted to indigenous peoples. Any wealth "we" have rests on the foundations of a primary and ongoing land theft, and returning the nine square-mile piece of land stolen by the Suplicians (and later Oka) to the Kanien'kehá:ka would be a step so tiny as to be a drop in the ocean of restitution needed to approach anything like justice. This account would say that the Kanien'kehá:ka own the land the golf course expansion and luxury condos were to be built on and that no one should trample on their rights to it. As I say, this is a truer story, a more accurate way to understand the situation. But part of the trouble in retelling this story is that because of the layers of colonial violence it is actually complicated to resist the simple racist colonialist story with a simple reversal. So I think the unforgetting approach would need to go deeper: How do we tell a resistant, anti-colonial story without using colonial frameworks? What would it mean to understand this history without foregrounding a conception of property and land ownership that may be completely unintelligible within indigenous social and legal systems? How can we tell this history without replicating another colonial trope, that of the innocent, pure, all-good natives? That is, how can we see the Kanien'kehá:ka as victims of profound injustice, and also people who fought with other tribes in the area, sometimes because of the pressures of colonists but sometimes for other dominative reasons? How can we understand them as having a right to the land but also as people who were forced to live in the area now called Oka because of decisions made in France but who did not primarily use that place in their lives? In other words: How can we tell the full complexity of this narrative in a way that foregrounds the needs and interests of people most affected by vectors of oppression and vulnerability—in this case, the Kanien'kehá:ka? And what would inhabiting the full complexity of that narrative do to white settlers? When I, as a white settler woman living on stolen land, narrate these questions or take up and amplify other people's engagement with questions like these, can I simultaneously take responsibility for whiteness and undo it?

These are not meant to be rhetorical questions, but they are difficult to answer, and they become even more difficult when the questions apply not just to one place and one golf course/condo development but to an entire area now constituted as a country, Canada, and the entire network of relations threading through it. And it is this entire network and this complex and dense history that we would stand in relation to in doing the work of unforgetting. Paulette Regan is the research director with the Truth and Reconciliation Commission of Canada, a body tasked with reckoning with another piece of Canada's specifically genocidal colonial project: Indian Residential Schools.

The schools were organized toward, in the infamous words of one of the early commissioners, "killing the Indian in the child"—to this end, children were taken away from their parents, not allowed to speak their language or practice their cultures, and, in too many cases to count, actually killed. The schools were in operation in Canada from the 1890s; the last school closed in the mid-nineties. The TRC's mission statement states: "The Truth and Reconciliation Commission will reveal the complete story of Canada's residential school system, and lead the way to respect through reconciliation ... for the child taken, for the parent left behind."[7] Telling the complete story of Indian Residential Schools involves substantial struggle against a social organization of forgetting; in Canada, unlike in places in more profound transitional contexts such as South Africa in the wake of apartheid, there has not been widespread attention to the TRC process from white people and settlers most generally. Also, the process itself has been delimited; it does not involve a reckoning with the entire history of colonialism and its violence—it addresses itself to the more historically and socially bounded wrong of residential schools.[8]

Still, the TRC process is a major struggle against the social organization of forgetting. In reflecting on the responsibilities settlers hold to undertake an engagement with this process, Regan quotes theorist Roger Simon. She says:

> Such an undertaking would enable us, as Simon states, not only to "correct memory" by "engag[ing] in an active re/membering of the actualities of the violence of past injustices" but also to "initiate rememberance of the discursive practices that underwrote the European domination, subjection, and exploitation of indigenous peoples." Engaging in these acts of "insurgent rememberance" makes visible to non-indigenous people the colonial roots of historical patterns and structures that shape our contemporary thinking, attitudes, and actions towards indigenous people: . . . my own act of insurgent remembering involves deconstructing the peacemaker myth, linking the discursive practices of nineteenth-century treaty making and Indian policy to a flawed contemporary discourse of reconciliation, and thus tracing the continuity of the violent structures and patterns of indigenous-settler relations over time.[9]

Insurgent remembrance, unforgetting, reveals salient lines of history, dwelling with how the past shapes the present. Above I said about this period shortly after my family moved to Canada that "the Canadian government called in the army to calm things down before they got violent." The presumption that the Canadian state keeps peace rather than practicing violence, or that things were not already profoundly violent, is part of a dense process of forgetting. The Canadian military has been deployed relatively rarely on Canadian soil, but for the most part against indigenous peoples and often in relation to land claims. From a different view, then, we can say that the military brings the violence, rather than quelling it. But let me nuance this stance more. It would be truer, less of a forgetting mode of thinking, to understand the historical context of the founding and grounding violence of the Canadian state—violences directed toward many immigrant and enslaved peoples, as well as toward indigenous peoples.

Regan says: "[O]ur willingness to negotiate outstanding historical claims with indigenous people is mediated by our willful ignorance and our selective denial of those aspects of our relationship that threaten our privilege and power—the colonial status quo."[10] Unforgetting, in these terms, can be understood as requiring not only the acknowledgment—the coming into knowledge—of things that threaten the colonial status quo. Unforgetting, following Regan, will also require a will, a willingness. This, again, involves a shift from *knowing about* particular things to *taking action* in particular ways informed by that understanding. This is because more is at stake than the truth; the colonial status quo involves truly vast apparatuses and histories. The point of reckoning with the social organization of forgetting is, if it is anything, to craft a future different than the horrific past we have inherited and live in the present. Such crafting would change the material conditions of our lives, though in ways that we cannot completely predict or determine. When I've taught university classes about Canadian colonial histories, my mostly white settler students worry that if we reckoned for real with the histories they're learning about, often for the first time in their lives, they and their families would be kicked out of Canada. They worry about the effects of Canada ceasing to exist. Some of them know where their families came from, and many of them don't. But they consistently say "where would we go, and what country would take us in?"

The assumptions my students make in these worries tell me something about how they see themselves. They assume that if indigenous people were in charge of the geographical place now called Canada that they would expel and expunge all the white people and all the settlers of color. They assume that the social relations of oppression, violation, and dispossession would be merely reversed and not transformed. They assume that there is no way to reckon with the past that does not reiterate the founding and ongoing violences they've learned about for the first time. This tells us something useful about how people, even when they have not reflected on the problem very deeply, view whiteness—these students see one part of the historical role of white people with accuracy, and it is a shameful role, one that terrifies them to imagine being reversed. I am profoundly sad about these conversations, and in this way working with well-intentioned mostly white settler young people has shown me something about my own experience of seeing whiteness as a problem. When we learn even small parts of the shared histories that constitute racialization, most of the time we encounter those histories as something above and outside us—as reified, settled, and unchangeable. This more often produces despair than actuates possibility.

Unforgetting, then, if it can have the potential Dunbar-Ortiz claims for it, to sustain alliances, has to be collective. And, as she notes, it cannot be elitist or only happening in academic or guilty liberal contexts. She argues that:

> It means organizing working-class whites. There's just no question about it. We've just got to do it. We've been trying to avoid it for so long. They're the carriers of the origin stories and the people who have the most invested in them, especially the descendants of the original settlers. But I think the commitment to getting history straight has to come first. If you're trying to change a society and you don't know its history, you will never get anywhere. [11]

Gentile and Kinsman's reflections on the importance of resisting the social organization of forgetting are useful in thinking about how memory might be involved in this kind of organizing. They say: "Remembering and memory are produced socially and reflexively. The liberal individualist notion that memory is some sort of asocial and ahistorical essence is not consistent with how memory works as a social practice. Memory always has a social and a historical character. Our experiences are remembered through social language and through how we make sense of them to ourselves and others." [12] I think that unforgetting produces a will and an energy to act and not simply an enhanced knowledge or understanding, because of the social and historical character of memory and remembering. This is why thinking about history is useable in organizing.

If the will to take action is generated in collective contexts, if we can't self-generate it, it makes sense that my students feel frozen to the extent that they don't see what they might be able to do to *individually and personally* change the world. They can't be white all alone, because our whiteness exists as a problem only in the context of complex social relations. So unforgetting in relation to understanding and acting in response to the overwhelming complexity of everything, refusing the lie, only makes sense as a collective venture. Anything else is a kind of conceit.

In trying to think about the situations in which whiteness has shown up as a problem for me, I've tried to think about the kind of problem I am for others. It's more interesting though more difficult to think of "me" as a collective situation experienced individually than it is to think about "me" individually. Of course, I have a hundred mortifying and cringeful stories about times my whiteness has individually hurt someone else—times I recognized as they were happening, times I was told about later, and some I can only suspect. And all of those happenings are legible only in the context of systemic and structural racism that traumatizes and harms people of color, often through the clumsy, self-entitled "ignorance" arising from my whiteness and the whiteness of people much like me. I am not telling a lot of other stories I could tell here—about times when I messed up, gaffed, slipped, didn't get the point, or did other things as a direct result of my whiteness—

which is also to say that these things were some of the ways that my white-ness is constituted. I've focused here on some of the points of friction where big systems and institutions have shown up in my personal experience. The social organization of forgetting is, in my view, one of the core ways that whiteness as a system is perpetuated. How we resist that organization will produce maybe more incidents of personal messing up, but these things can and maybe should be seen as valuable indications that we have put ourselves at risk for failure—and this is a better place to be than never trying anything.

NOTES

1. Roxanne Dunbar-Ortiz 2008, "The Opposite of Truth Is Forgetting: An Interview with Roxanne Dunbar-Ortiz by Chris Dixon." *Upping the Anti* 6 (May): 47–58, quote on p. 57.
2. See Charles Mills "White Ignorance," in Shannon Sullivan and Nancy Tuana *Race and Epistemologies of Ignorance*. State Univ of New York Press, 2007.
3. In 2012, a community awareness arts project began in Boulder, called "One Action—One Boulder County/Niwot's Arrow." This project aims to bring into public consciousness, dialogue, and action the history of racial and economic injustice in the Boulder area. They say: "We cannot change history. We can only remember it, but that very remembrance is a powerful choice. OAOB/Niwot's Arrow, a community conversation project, aims for a vision of dig-nified choices in the understanding and acceptance of history, no matter the reality: To stand both within the parts worth celebrating and within the more painful moments; to resist defen-siveness and guilt, replacing them with strength and courage as we make inequities visible for reflection, engagement and education; to ask profound questions of ourselves, our communities and our nation, examining our worst moments so we might avoid repeating them." (http://www.one-action.org/learn-together/choices-of-dignity/)
4. Rocky Flats was shut down after a 1989 raid on the facility, run by the Department of Energy, by the FBI.
5. Gary Kinsman and Patrizia Gentile, *The Canadian War on Queers: National Security as Sexual Regulation.* UBC Press, 2010, 21.
6. For some of the history of this area, see Leanne Simpson and Kiera L. Ladner eds., *This Is an Honour Song: Twenty Years Since the Blockades* (Arbeiter Ring Publications, Winnipeg, Manitoba).
7. Truth and Reconciliation Commission. "Truth and Reconciliantion Commission of Can-ada: Interim Report," 2012, 2.
8. Residential schools have been a widespread colonial technology; in addition to Indian Residential Schools in the Canadian context, there were Indian Boarding Schools in the United States and forced removal of Australian Aboriginal children, though they were held in more dispersed institutional housing and schooling situations. For more on these contexts see: Ward Churchill, *Kill the Indian, Save the Man: The Genocidal Impact of American Indian Residential Schools* (City Lights Publishers, 2004); A. D. Moses, ed., *Genocide And Settler Society: Fron-tier Violence and Stolen Indigenous Children in Australian History* (Berghahn Books, 2005); Andrea Smith, *Conquest: Sexual Violence and American Indian Genocide* (South End Press, 2005); Margaret D. Jacobs, *White Mother to a Dark Race: Settler Colonialism, Maternalism, and the Removal of Indigenous Children in the American West and Australia, 1880-1940* (Univ of Nebraska Pr, 2009).
9. Paulette Regan, 2010, *Unsettling the Settler Within: Indian Residential Schools, Truth Telling, and Reconciliation in Canada.* UBC Press, 49–50.
10. Regan 35.
11. Dunbar-Ortiz, 58.
12. Gentile and Kinsman 37.

Chapter Five

On Not Making a Labor of It

Relationality and the Problem of Whiteness

Crista Lebens

As a white lesbian and anti-racist feminist, much of what I have learned about racism can be found in a poem by the late Pat Parker, black lesbian poet, feminist, and activist, titled, "For the White Person Who Wants to Know How to Be My Friend."[1] In the more than two decades since I first read the poem, I have found that I return to it frequently as a touchstone for racial awareness.[2] The first two lines present a seeming contradiction: she advises the reader to *forget* that she is black and *do not forget* that she is black. The last lines caution the reader, finally, to *not make a labor of it.* Learning what that means and how to put that in action is, in Parker's words, the way to be a good friend, and, philosophically, the path to developing a relationality in which whiteness as a problem is minimized for all. Hence, I use the injunction to "not make a labor of it," (especially for people of color, but also for myself) to analyze my experience of whiteness as a problem and suggest a remedy, though not a cure for it.

A CONVERSATION

I am staying with friends, Rita and Pam, in another city. While sitting in their living room, another friend, Sonia, comes over to visit, and an important conversation took place.[3]

Sonia had been having ongoing difficulties at work. Having completed an advanced degree earlier that year, this was the first full-time job she'd gotten after graduation, and it had gone bad. Some background is necessary: she is an African American social worker working with clients dealing with severe poverty. The clients are largely African American; the social workers are almost exclusively white. At first, her supervisors were impressed by her successes: clients that others had worked with for months with no change were able to make significant progress in a very short time working with Sonia. The supervisors were pleased and said so, but that began to change. Her successes continued, but her supervisors began to be critical of her methods. Suddenly, they began suggesting that she should act more "professional" with clients. They were referring to the way she would speak to clients directly and bluntly, rather than couch her statements in more "polite" phrasing. The picture that emerged was of a black social worker communicating effectively with black clients in language and manners that made the white social workers uncomfortable. Sonia said that "It's weird" how the other social workers responded to her. What she didn't come out and say was, "It's racist; they were intimidated by a bunch of black folks talking to each other." Rita and Pam did say so. They speak the plain truth, too. The visiting friend needed a reality check to assure herself that she wasn't crazy, and she got it from us.

Sitting there in the living room, I agreed with my friends' take on the situation. My support was there without question, but something else was going on that I could not participate in fully. As the only one in the room who was not a person of color, I didn't want to interfere with the important work that was happening, that was a kind of meaning-making. I wanted my presence there to not be a problem. Frankly, I don't think it was, much, anyway, and I was appreciative of the gift of honesty and trust all of my friends had given me.

I was invited to write an essay for this anthology shortly after this conversation took place. When I heard that the topic would be "How does it feel to be a white problem?" I thought immediately of this conversation.

Now, I have no problem naming actions like those of Sonia's supervisors, actions that are racist and messed up. That kind of racism was not the way my whiteness was a problem. Rather, my whiteness is a problem, both for people of color and for me, because it affects my relationality in the sense that it shapes the kind and depth of my response to others. In a sense, I understand this as a lack of ability. This lack can be understood structurally within the framework of the epistemology and ethics of ignorance, as developed by Charles Mills[4] and expanded by Sarah Hoagland,[5] and as an intersubjective phenomenon as delineated by the related concepts of "whiteliness," developed by Marilyn Frye[6] and "knowing, loving ignorance" as developed by Mariana Ortega,[7] and at the level of the psyche, the "opaque white self," as outlined by George Yancy.[8] Structurally maintained white ignorance about racial dynamics diminishes the intelligibility of narratives describing racism. The lack of intelligibility diminishes white people's ability to recognize and respond appropriately to racism. Whiteliness and opacity present additional barriers to comprehensibility. All of these dynamics influence the way in which white people understand ourselves in relation to people of color. This is whiteness as a problem.

Back to the story. A few days before the conversation took place, Sonia had finally decided to quit the job—a drastic response in a terrible economic climate, but one that was finally a question of preserving her health and well-being. Sonia and Pam left the house after a while, leaving Rita and me to continue talking about the situation. Among my responses was to consider my position as a white teacher who encounters white students in the classroom, many of whom will go on to be social workers. This was a clear example of how institutional racism works. How could I begin to convey that knowledge to my students, and how could I be sure that I do not, myself, participate in maintaining such racist institutional dynamics? First and foremost, I wanted to support my friend. *". . . don't make a labor of it. . . . Remember."*

Sometimes I can feel myself being the white, middle-class, educated professional, and I feel the barriers to communication that presents. That recognition is not an expression of self-hatred or self-blame; rather, it is a recognition of the reality that I am implicated, by being white, in white supremacy. That is whiteness as a problem.

A PROBLEM FOR WHOM? WHITENESS AS A PROBLEM FOR PEOPLE OF COLOR

Certainly, whiteness causes problems for people of color. It's a double-whammy: the construction and maintenance of systems of white supremacy and all of the consequences of endemic racism, then, denial, mystification, and a refusal to take responsibility for it. That seems clear. This is what the white supervisors did with regard to my friend. They couched their discomfort in the language of professionalism. If they had criticisms of my friend's performance, then that was not made clear and seems strange if she was continuing to be successful in her case management. Sometimes, other white people can fail to recognize the racism in such situations and want to explain it away as a matter of personal differences, and so on. I did not do that. I recognized and affirmed that it was racism, and I responded as well as any white person could, which means my response was complicated, in part, for structural reasons.

EPISTEMOLOGIES OF IGNORANCE

To understand whiteness as a problem on a structural level, I turn to the work of Charles Mills and the concept of "epistemologies of ignorance." While whiteness as a problem encompasses more than this concept covers, the concept is still quite useful for understanding the nature of the problem. Mills distinguishes different kinds of white ignorance—that perpetuated by whites, which serves to maintain white supremacy (intentionally or not) and that maintained by people of color, which may work, to their detriment, to maintain white supremacy but also serves the function of protection and survival. I am concerned here with ignorance maintained by whites about people of color. Mills:

> racialized causality can give rise to what I am calling white ignorance, straightforwardly for a racist cognizer, but also indirectly for a nonracist cognizer who may form mistaken beliefs (e.g., that after the abolition of slavery in the United States, blacks generally had opportunities equal to whites) because of the social suppression of the pertinent knowledge, though without prejudice himself. So white ignorance need not always be based on bad faith. Obviously from the point of view of a social epistemology, especially after the transition from de jure to de facto white supremacy, it is precisely this kind of white ignorance that is most important. [9]

I am thinking specifically of the white ignorance of a "nonracist" cognizer, to use Mills's term, who does form mistaken beliefs because of the social suppression of pertinent knowledge, and this is done without prejudice on the part of the cognizer.

I am repeatedly made aware of my ignorance of history and how that prevents me from evaluating accurately contemporary race relations. Personally and professionally, I have been working to fill these knowledge gaps since becoming aware of them and so have at least a sense, as Socrates counsels, of knowing what it is I do not know. Professionally, I work to convey this complex message to my students and find that the ignorance of historical events makes it truly difficult for them (and can be for me) to grasp the significance of contemporary racial dynamics.

For example, I discussed with my students an example that I had read in Tim Wise's book, *White Like Me*. [10] Wise recounts a story from his hometown newspaper, where a white man brings his white wife to the emergency room. The physician on call is an African American man. The white man protests to another white male doctor that he does not want a black man to examine his wife. His protests are so vehement that the white doctor capitulates, though later the doctor admits he was wrong to do so. The point Tim Wise makes in retelling this story is to demonstrate the power of white supremacy to make the white man's request intelligible. To prove that white supremacy is "at work," he contends that the reverse situation, a black man refusing to let a white male doctor provide care to his African American wife (I'll not discuss whether the women in question are able to consent to treatment), would not only be unlikely, but Wise argues it would not be *compre-*

hensible.[11] Ignorance is more complex than a simple lack of knowledge. Within a system of structural ignorance, one cannot even learn (come to know) what is rendered unthinkable.[12]

When considering Wise's claim, a number of students voiced concern about the right of the patient (or the patient's husband, in this case) to have a say in who provides treatment. The situation could possibly be framed as one of patient autonomy in conflict with the principles of professional integrity (that of the white doctor, to whom this request was made). I redirected the discussion to reiterate Wise's point, that, regardless of whether or not a patient had such a right, the point Wise makes is that white supremacy makes the original demand intelligible and also renders unintelligible a situation where the roles would be reversed. Many of the students, almost exclusively white, did not recognize the racism because they focused on individual autonomy. They missed the racial harm.[13] An alternative explanation is that they recognized the racial harm but thought it justified in the interest of patient autonomy. Either way, many did not grasp, or did not want to grasp, Wise's point about the structural nature of white supremacy. And this is in a class where we have studied the nature of oppression as a structural phenomenon. When I briefly outlined the history of racialized gender relations between white men and women of color and the myth of black men preying on white women, it seemed they were unfamiliar with that history, as was I until after I began doing serious anti-racist work. That example of systematic white ignorance contributed, I think, to their failure to understand the point Tim Wise made. Thus, their lack of understanding was supported by several dynamics: (1) mere lack of historical information/knowledge; (2) the contribution that the lack of historical knowledge makes to a degree of incomprehensibility/unintelligibility; and (3) some degree of a will not-to-know/understand.[14] Another dimension of structural white ignorance that Mills highlights is relevant here:

> I want a concept of white ignorance broad enough to include moral ignorance—not merely ignorance of facts with moral implications but moral non-knowings, incorrect judgments about the rights and wrongs of moral situations themselves.[15]

The lack of knowledge is not just a lack of factual knowledge but a lack of ability to reason morally with regard to white supremacy and race relations. I recognize this sometimes in myself, and this is what I think I recognized in my students. Mills claims white ignorance is defeasible:

> So the idea is that there are typical ways of going wrong that need to be adverted to in light of the social structure and specific group characteristics, and one has a better chance of getting things right through a self-conscious recognition of their existence, and corresponding self-distancing from them.[16]

I agree that such self-conscious recognition can help to identify and circumvent some typical problems that result from white ignorance. And yet, white ignorance is a multilayered barrier to knowledge. Recognition comes about at different levels and is an ongoing (perhaps never-ending) process.

Mills brings into his analysis the recognition that concepts are not located in a neutral framework but rather in one oriented to certain understandings about how things work.[17] For example: Thomas Jefferson, in the *Declaration of Independence*, denouncing "savage Indians" in the same document where he asserts, "all men are created equal." For Jefferson (and the other "Founding Fathers") Indians (and other marginalized groups) are less than fully human, so there is no contradiction. As Mills points out:

> To speak of the "equality" of the savage would then be oxymoronic, since one's very location in these categories is an indication of one's inequality. Even a cognizer with no antipathy or prejudice toward Native Americans will be cognitively disabled trying to establish truths about them insofar as such a category and its associated presuppositions will tend to force his conclusions in a certain direction, will constrain what he can objectively see. One will experience a strain, a cognitive tension between possible egalitarian findings and overarching category, insofar as "savage" already has embedded in it a narrative, a set of assumptions about innate inferiority, which will preclude certain possibilities. "Savages" tend to do certain things and to be unable to do others; these go with the conceptual territory. Thus the term itself encourages if not quite logically determines particular conclusions. Concepts orient us to the world, and it is a rare individual who can resist this inherited orientation. Once established in the social mind-set, its influence is difficult to escape, since it is not a matter of seeing the phenomenon with the concept discretely attached but rather of seeing things through the concept itself.[18]

Racism creates an internal logic that perpetuates beliefs that maintain white supremacy. Those who seek to dismantle white supremacy face not just discrete incorrect beliefs but an entire framework within which the incorrect beliefs make sense. To give up the incorrect beliefs (or fill in the gap of simple ignorance with correct beliefs) necessitates a paradigm shift rather than individual correctives. The paradigm within which one apprehends statements about race determines the comprehensibility of those statements.

The effects of collective memory and collective amnesia are such that many whites now think colorblindness is the way to address racism—as if we can erase the inequities of the past and act as if now everyone is equal. In a striking reversal,[19] those people of color who point out racial differences are now the racists.[20] Beyond amnesia is the forgetting as an active deed, for example, in the Belgian Congo. In Brussels, they burned documents about the genocide. It took eight days.[21]

To sum up the effects of white ignorance, intentional and not, Mills turns to political theorists Kinder and Sanders:

Race is the primary social division in the United States, these two political scientists conclude, and whites generally see black interests as opposed to their own. Inevitably, then, this will affect white social cognition—the concepts favored (e.g., today's "color blindness"), the refusal to perceive systemic discrimination, the convenient amnesia about the past and its legacy in the present, and the hostility to black testimony on continuing white privilege and the need to eliminate it to achieve racial justice. As emphasized at the start, then, these analytically distinguishable cognitive components are in reality all interlocked with and reciprocally determining one another, jointly contributing to the blindness of the white eye. [22]

This is the kind of ignorance that I find myself still fighting in myself and that I encounter, for example, in my students. It is a simple not "getting it" because whites within the white ignorance bubble do not share the same framework as those who are cognizant of this history and the ways it has been erased. In my case, the experience of the white ignorance bubble is that of a blank, a sense that "I know there's something wrong, but I can't quite get it." And I experienced, to a slight degree, that "blank," a moral ignorance, with the friend who needed her friends to make sense of her experience, that is, to affirm the reality of the racism in that situation. I understood it, I affirmed it as racism, but I still felt a lack of something in my response because my understanding was based more on intellectual knowing than on one shaped also by having "felt the iron." At times I second-guess my ability to correctly interpret the racial dynamics of a situation.

A PROBLEM FOR WHOM? WHITENESS AS A PROBLEM FOR WHITE PEOPLE

Whiteliness

Whiteness is also a problem for white people. This barrier to clear communication and understanding is a barrier to human connection as well.

One way to understand this barrier is through the concept of "whiteliness." Marilyn Frye develops the concept of whiteliness as an analogy to masculinity. Men cannot cease to be male but can challenge male supremacy by rejecting values predicated on masculinity. Similarly, white people cannot cease to be white but can reject the values associated with being white, that is, whiteliness. Some elements of whiteliness are: denial of culpability, overwhelming belief in one's own goodness or good intentions, authorizing one's self or other white people to be the moral arbiters of the universe. (Frye, 152–57)[23] In constructing the concept of "whiteliness," Frye draws extensively on personal narratives collected in *Drylongso,* an ethnography of African American people, ordinary folks, or the "drylongso."[24] When reading their observations of white people, what I find most striking is their observation of the depth of white self-deception. Reading those observations, I wonder how any person of color could have a genuine relationship with a white person that deep in self-deception, and alongside that question, I hold the realization that no whitely person thinks of herself as whitely. Part of whiteliness is the failure to recognize it in one's self. This leads me to wonder about relationships between white people who act whitely. Is a genuine relationship possible between people in such deep denial? Perhaps it is in other regards but likely not with respect to race. White supremacy has held us all, but especially white people, in a diminished range of possibility for honesty in human relationships.

I considered whether my presence as a white person posed a problem for my friends, in that it might inhibit full disclosure, either of the reprehensible things done by the employers or the righteous rage in the face of such acts. That is another way whiteness poses a problem, that is, it is a barrier to simple truth telling. That was the problem with my friend's supervisors: Their whiteness (meaning their commitment to white supremacy—would that be whiteliness?) prevented them from being able to deal with my friend being direct and truthful with clients and also blocked her supervisors from facing the truth about their actions.

How was my whiteness a problem for me? I recognized that the way I participated in the meaning-making, the affirmation that, yes, indeed, this was racism in action, was different than for my friends. I was outraged as they were at the harm done to my friend and the harm done by white people to people of color all the time, every day. My outrage was not wholly and completely the righteous anger of one who has also been wronged. My outrage lacked that moral status, since I was aware that I was capable of perpetrating the harm done, just as those white professionals had. In fact, because of how whiteliness and denial work, I cannot know for sure that I have not done something similar. The possibility of culpability keeps me humble and tempers my righteous anger. I realize that makes me less able to support my friend in sorting out what this means, because my reaction is a bit mismatched to the harm done. That mismatch may be a kind of obfuscation that is another layer of the problem of whiteness. It is a barrier to simply naming a wrong.

I have encountered two objections to this interpretation. The first is that, given the anti-racist work I have done, I am unlikely to perpetrate this kind of racism in my professional capacity. I would be too aware of the dynamics of whiteliness to make this particular mistake.[25] To this I respond that whiteliness knows no bounds, and the mistake would be inadvertent. Part of the point of this essay is to recognize that white anti-racists can be whitely exactly when and because we do not recognize our whiteliness.

George Yancy explores this problem further. Using Judith Butler's analysis of subjectivity to reveal the unconscious dimensions of the self, he distinguishes the *subject* of structural racism from the *self* of racism at the level of the psyche, introducing the concept of the opaque white self. This is the whiteness or racism I, as a white person, cannot recognize. The message is that I am not a Cartesian self, completely transparent to myself. [26] He calls on white people to confront the existence of the opaque self and the evidence of one's racism at the level of the unconscious, despite conscious denials or a lot of anti-racist work.

A second objection to this interpretation of my response is that it was not mismatched to the situation and was not less than supportive. [27] To this I respond that I agree, to an extent. I think that my response was fine insofar as any white person could respond. But I do think that my recognition of possible similar culpability tempered my outrage, lest I become a hypocrite implying that I had never done something like that, that only *bad* white people do that. Such reflection is not a *mea culpa*; rather, it is a potential learning experience. So I do not really fault myself for my response; rather, I recognize that it may not be all that was needed in that situation. And that's OK, too, since others were there, and collectively we did give our friend the needed affirmation. Finally, it could be the case that I had something to offer as one who might be in the supervisor's position. In some instances, that could be, but in this case, that was not information that was called for.

Another way that my whiteness is a problem to me, and possibly to my friends, is that, as Patricia Hill Collins says, I don't "feel the iron" [28] of the pain of racism directly. The pain I feel is that of knowing the suffering it causes but not of being a target of systematic racism, at least not in that respect, though I do understand the pain of oppression, I have felt the iron, in other respects and I can empathize. So, again, my response is tempered by my lack of a standpoint. Sometimes the best I can do is recognize this limitation and not make it more of a problem than it already is, that is, "don't make a labor of it."

Relationality

Whiteness as a problem characteristically involves a kind of moral ignorance. Sarah Hoagland articulates this ignorance as a lack of relationality:

> We who are trained in responsibility in imperialist U.S. are trained to take charge (Pratt, Frye, Lugones, Hoagland). We are positioned to act for the other, to represent the other, but never to recognize ourselves as dependent on her. Particularly for white, middle-class women, those moral instincts are part of our socialization into whiteness. Thus we focus on our character and intentions rather than on our relations, and our sense of existence, our subjectivity, thereby appears to be in no way a product of the engagement. [29]

Hoagland asserts that the dependence she names is an ontological dependence not a moral dependence, though there is that too. [30] What it means to be white, to be the moral arbiters of the universe, is dependent upon the denial of relationality between white people and people of color. This concept of whiteness exists because white people had the power to define the subjectivity of non-white peoples. The denial of relationality makes possible an individualist focus on character and intentions.

It is this lack of relationality that allows my white students to characterize Tim Wise's example as a question of patient autonomy and miss the point Wise wants to make about the asymmetry of the situation—that not only could a black man not make the analogous request that a *white* physician not treat his wife but that such a request *would not make sense*, that the culture of white supremacy would render such a request incomprehensible. Then, when the example is discussed as a form of racism, the culture of white supremacy makes it possible to frame Wise's claim as a question of patient autonomy. This is a nice redirect, very effective for maintaining white ignorance and white supremacy.

Hoagland's concept of relationality is also at work in the living room conversation. While I feel the pull toward an individualist focus (did I do the "right thing," as if that is the crucial issue in that moment), I have done sufficient anti-racist work to allow me to recognize that question as a white-guilt trap. It's not about me, it's about my friend. Where I think a lack of relationality does come into play is, again, in my inability to fully affirm Sonia's interpretation of the work situation. I can recognize and affirm that her supervisors were racist but not with the same kind of moral authority. The moral position I hold is that of witness. I can be present as a white person who does get it, even as I recognize the possibility of my own culpability in a similar situation. I can work through the tendency of the white opaque self to mask my culpability without also getting caught up in my own guilt. Finally, I can improve my moral reasoning skills by doing one of the most important things a white person can do in such situations, which is to (mostly) keep quiet, listen, and learn something. [31]

In "learning something," I must also develop moral reasoning skills regarding how I use such knowledge. The trust my friends showed me included both the recognition that I would be supportive of Sonia, but also implicitly, that I would be careful with this knowledge. The other side of white ignorance, as Mills points out, is the protection that people of color have by keeping whitely people ignorant about their survival strategies. I return to Sarah Hoagland's work on relationality.

Hoagland takes the term "competent practitioners" of one's culture, or of the dominant logic, namely, whitely people skilled at maintaining white ignorance and white supremacy, from the work of María Lugones:

To avoid remaining fools, competent practitioners of the dominant logic can work to become critical practitioners. However, those working to enter an ethics of resistance can nevertheless become dangerous, particularly having been ignorant. In Sherley Anne Williams's story of the slave, Dessa Rose, a white woman named Ruth, in coming to know and then befriend Dessa Rose, became dangerous to her as they all plotted and executed an escape. As Ruth came to consider slaves human, she wanted to tell "everyone" (that is, whites) the "truth." Dessa Rose remarks: "Miz Lady . . . thought that if white folks knew slaves as she knew us, wouldn't be no slavery. . . . But it was funny, cause that was the thing I had come to fear most from her by the end of that journey, that she would speak out against the way we seen some of the peoples was treated and draw tention to us. And what she was talking now would sho enough make peoples note us" (1986, 231, 239). Ruth became dangerous because her understanding and empathy involved what Elizabeth Spelman calls, boomerang perception (1988)—Ruth looked at Dessa Rose and came right back to herself. Ruth's ignorance, even when coming to acknowledge Dessa Rose as human, was the failure to recognize how she herself was constructed in relation to Dessa Rose. As a result, she was not yet particularly competent to enter another world, changing her own relationality, not competent at "playful world travel" (Lugones 2003, ch. 4), and initially not particularly competent to maintain the ignorance of those in power and to keep the secrets of the con. Having been socialized in an ethics of ignorance, she lacked the skills, the virtue, of an ethics of resistance, skills that include promoting the ignorance of those who are in charge.[32]

At some point in resisting one's whiteliness, a white person changes from a *competent* practitioner of dominant culture to a *critical* practitioner, though presumably without losing one's "competence."[33] In Mariana Ortega's terms, one disabuses one's self of ignorance, including the "knowing, loving ignorance" (Ortega 2006) that can make one a fool and harm one's friends. One begins to "world travel" to the world one's friends occupy that is not one's own world and realize who one is in that world, as Lugones calls us to do. In Hoagland's example, Ruth overcomes the ignorance that allowed her to see Dessa Rose and the others as less than human. That might be the first "layer" of whiteliness. Ruth is still in the grip of white ignorance and is still whitely, in that she does not recognize herself in her friends' world—that she now has knowledge that, if revealed to those in power, would harm her friends. Ortega calls this "knowing, loving ignorance." In Hoagland's terms, Ruth is not able to "change her relationality" from an individualist perspective where she is a moral agent out to do good and end slavery to that of a relational being who has joined this moral community.

I recently watched the movie *Good Hair*.[34] The movie stars Chris Rock who investigates African American cultural values around black women's hair. He began by showing a picture of his two young daughters and observes that, even though he tells them how beautiful they are *every day*, his youngest daughter still told him, in tears, that she does not have "good hair." In answering the question as to where that message came from, he investigates hair straightening and hair weaves and explores just how ubiquitous these styles are.

I considered showing excerpts of the film in my feminist philosophy class (the same class referred to above). I was doing a section on beauty norms and had a text that challenged the myth that black women are not subject to norms the way white women are, and I thought this might be a good illustration of the point. I decided against showing excerpts in class, because I thought it would do more damage, by othering black women, than the good that might come from exposing and criticizing beauty norms that damage the self-esteem of little girls. I think this is an example of the kind of knowledge the character Ruth needed in order to not use the knowledge of subjugated communities in ways that harm them. This position—that of being a critical practitioner of dominant culture—requires one to drop the individualist "moral arbiter of the universe position" and take up recognition of one's relationality. One must judge carefully what one does with knowledge from the "worlds" of one's friends. As Hoagland observes, this world-traveling business is not so easy to do:

> My brief suggestions about becoming critical practitioners of dominant culture, playful world travel, border crossing, and traveling to non-dominant worlds of sense do not take on the extraordinary complexities involved in thinking concretely with others, in the communicative difficulties when going for coalition against oppression not through sameness but through difference.[35]

It is this complexity that I am trying to articulate in this essay, the multilayered nature of white ignorance, from whiteliness "unmodified," to a whiteliness characterized by knowing, loving ignorance, to an increasing awareness of relationality. As much as one's awareness increases, however, it is a lifelong process of both unlearning and learning.

Let us return to the focus of this essay, namely, the living room conversation, where my friend checked *her* interpretation of her white supervisors' actions to verify that yes, this was racism. I wonder whether I am still enmeshed in an individualist framework, analyzing my actions and trying to do the "right thing" rather than working out an analysis of whiteness as a structural problem.

At the individualist level, I might have either not recognized the racism of the supervisors (much like many of my students did not recognize the racism in Tim Wise's example), or I might have focused on my response or my past and present collusion with white supremacy. That could be both a result of and a contribution to the maintenance of white ignorance. That reaction could result from white ignorance of the way racism works and it would maintain that ignorance—a missed learning opportunity. Understanding the situation and my response at the structural level gets me out of whiteliness—white denial or white guilt and the temptation to "fix" the problem. My ability to move to the structural level is a direct result of my knowledge of racism and having adopted a paradigm in which structural oppression exists and makes individual acts of racism recognizable and comprehensible.

The third level of racism, the intrapersonal or psychic level, still remains. Because I am aware of my own racism at this level, I am suspicious of my ability to interpret the racial dynamics of an interaction. Sarah Hoagland writes about relationality and epistemic ability:

> whites and others in dominant relationalities lack epistemic privilege (conversation with María Lugones). This is not to say that from marginalized positions anyone holds knowledge which no one else has access to; nor is this about standpoint. It is to say that those lacking epistemic privilege lack critical abilities. It is to say that as we are materially privileged in particular ways, our epistemic abilities are suspect. It is to say that our abilities of understanding and analysis have been undermined or compromised in key ways as a result of our material privileging.
> For example, in working collectively with the *Escuela Popular Norteña*, a popular education school focused in Latino communities, I have come to realize that part of how many white feminists' abilities have been compromised is through our reaction to violence—turning to the state and organized police, legal, and medical forces . . . . We went from grassroots collective action to promoting state intervention. This is an epistemology and ethics of ignorance accomplished through a denial of relationality [The turn toward state intervention as a response to violence would be morally acceptable only through a denial of relationality with those targeted by the state] . . . . For men of color on the other hand, I suspect the compromising of abilities is something quite different.[36]

Hoagland's example demonstrates a group moving from a structuralist focus to an individualist one. An entire group, committed to radical, collective work, shifted to a dramatically conservative position as a result of epistemic and moral ignorance. The failure to recognize this shift could be attributed to whiteliness or the opaque white self, that is, an inability to recognize one's own racist actions or beliefs.

CONCLUSION

Whiteness as a problem can be encapsulated as a barrier to understanding, communication, and expression between people of color and white people. Within the context of personal relationships, at best, this barrier diminishes the well-intentioned white person's ability to be a good friend and, at worst, makes being her friend a labor for persons of color. Within the larger context of structural racism, whiteness is a problem in that it inhibits white people's ability to judge or interpret the racial dynamics of a situation; it inhibits white people's ability to recognize racism. This barrier/inhibition results from various types of ignorance on the structural and individual level, as well as dynamics that maintain these types of ignorance such as whiteliness and opacity.

The remedy, but not the cure, for this problem is twofold: First, recognition and acceptance of this diminished ability combined with an active awareness of and resistance to whitely tendencies. The concept of the white opaque self, as Yancy suggests, stands as a reminder that this process never ends. Second, continue working to dispel one's ignorance about past and present racism. While this will not end racism, for no other reason than many white people are not interested in such work, those white people who do may notice some changes over time. Eventually, these individuals may build skills that enhance their recognition of and ability to support relationality with people of color and to negotiate the seeming contradiction put forth by Pat Parker in the beginning of her poem. Perhaps this will diminish the extent to which white people constitute a problem.

NOTES

1. Pat Parker, "For the white person who wants to know how to be my friend" in *An Expanded Edition of Movement in Black* (Ithaca: Firebrand Books, 1999, 99). The full text of the poem can be accessed online via various websites, such as the following: http://condor.depaul.edu/mwilson/multicult/patparker.htm

2. The basis of my education in recognizing and dismantling white supremacy comes from radical lesbian feminists, both women of color feminists and white women. In this community (specifically, Lansing, Michigan) there was and is an expectation that one work on awareness and dismantling of multiple oppressions, including racism, and classism. In this essay I focus on whiteness, but my understanding of whiteness, and specifically my *gendered* whiteness, has been informed by this political community.

3. I am relating this conversation with "Sonia's" permission. I am not using my friends' real names.

4. Charles Mills, "White Ignorance," in *Race and Epistemologies of Ignorance*, ed. Shannon Sullivan and Nancy Tuana (Albany: State University of New York Press, 2007).

5. Sarah Lucia Hoagland, "Denying Relationality: Epistemology and Ethics and Ignorance." In *Race and Epistemologies of Ignorance*, ed. Shannon Sullivan and Nancy Tuana (Albany: State University of New York Press, 2007).

6. Marilyn Frye, "White woman feminist," in *Willful Virgin: Essays in Feminism, 1976–1992.* (Freedom, CA: Crossing Press, 1992).

7. Mariana Ortega, "Being Lovingly, Knowingly Ignorant: White Feminism and Women of Color," *Hypatia* vol. 21, no. 3 (Summer 2006), pp. 56–74.

8. George Yancy, *Look, a White!: Philosophical Essays on Whiteness* (Philadelphia: Temple University Press, 2012).

9. Charles Mills, "White Ignorance," in *Race and Epistemologies of Ignorance*, 21.

10. Tim J. Wise, *White Like Me: Reflections on Race from a Privileged Son.* (Brooklyn, NY: Soft Skull Press 2008).

11. Tim J. Wise, *White Like Me*, 76–77.

12. Marilyn Frye, comment, June 2013.

13. The very concept of individual autonomy might very well play a role in eliding their understanding. My point here is that I know many white students who deploy individual

autonomy as a way of avoiding being implicated in a historical and structural process called white supremacy. So, perhaps individual autonomy, at least in this case, is a site of whiteness itself. (George Yancy, comment, November 2013).

14. Marilyn Frye helped clarify this distinction.

15. Charles Mills, "White Ignorance," in *Race and Epistemologies of Ignorance*, 22.

16. Charles Mills, "White Ignorance," in *Race and Epistemologies of Ignorance*, 23.

17. Charles Mills, "White Ignorance," in *Race and Epistemologies of Ignorance*, 24.

18. Charles Mills, "White Ignorance," in *Race and Epistemologies of Ignorance*, 27.

19. Mary Daly introduces the concept of reversals as they function within a context of oppression. Mary Daly, *Gyn/ecology: The Metaethics of Radical Feminism* (Boston: Beacon Press, 1990) 46–48.

20. Charles Mills, "White Ignorance," in *Race and Epistemologies of Ignorance*, 27-28.

21. Adam Hochschild, 1998, ch. 19, cited in Mills, 29.

22. Quoted in Charles Mills, "White Ignorance," in *Race and Epistemologies of Ignorance*, 39.

23. Marilyn Frye, "White woman feminist," in *Willful Virgin*, 152–57.

24. J. Gwaltney, J., *Drylongso: A Self Portrait of Black America.* (New York: Random House, 1980).

25. Anne Courtney, conversation, Spring 2013.

26. George Yancy, *Look, a White!: Philosophical Essays on Whiteness* (Philadelphia: Temple University Press, 2012), 170.

27. Marilyn Frye, June 2013.

28. Patricia Hill Collins, *Black Feminist Thought: Knowledge, Consciousness, and the Politics of Empowerment.* (New York: Routledge, 2000), 35.

29. Sarah Lucia Hoagland, "Denying Relationality: Epistemology and Ethics and Ignorance." In *Race and Epistemologies of Ignorance*, 103.

30. Sarah Lucia Hoagland, "Denying Relationality: Epistemology and Ethics and Ignorance." In *Race and Epistemologies of Ignorance*, 99.

31. The suggestion to "just listen" came most recently from "Sonia" herself when I asked her about using this story in my paper, but it is a message I have gotten frequently from people of color, both friends and theorists I've read.

32. Sarah Lucia Hoagland, "Denying Relationality: Epistemology and Ethics and Ignorance." In *Race and Epistemologies of Ignorance*, 107.

33. George Yancy, comment, November 2013.

34. Jeff Stilson, *Good Hair* (Roadside Attractions, 2009).

35. Sarah Lucia Hoagland, "Denying Relationality: Epistemology and Ethics and Ignorance." In *Race and Epistemologies of Ignorance*, 111.

36. Sarah Lucia Hoagland, "Denying Relationality: Epistemology and Ethics and Ignorance." In *Race and Epistemologies of Ignorance*, 112–13.

Chapter Six

"You're the Nigger, Baby, It Isn't Me"

The Willed Ignorance and Wishful Innocence of White America

Robert Jensen

Two of the defining features of white America are its embrace of not knowing and the insistence on not being accountable. The essence of white pathology is contained in that willed ignorance and wishful innocence. By avoiding knowledge of what was done, and what is still being done, we can maintain our illusions about our own righteousness. And then we can sleep through the night, though fitfully. We can lie down and rest, comfortably but with a nagging feeling that something is wrong.

In this chapter, explore our white-supremacist system, and the white privilege that is the result of that system, by examining how white America constructs heroes, black and white. Such an examination, if honest, will lead to the only place that honesty in a white-supremacist system can lead white people—to an unsettling sense of ourselves, to an uncomfortable look in the mirror. Borrowing from James Baldwin, this is what we must see in that mirror: We white people are the nigger.

BLACK HEROES

In a class on democracy and mass media that I taught for several years, I assigned readings by Martin Luther King Jr., Malcolm X, and James Baldwin.[1] I asked the students to take note of what they knew about those three people before they did the reading. How do the men live in their imagination, in the public imagination? The answers, from overwhelmingly white classes in the early 2000s, were consistent: MLK was a great leader who, inspired by

85

his Christian faith, used non-violence to advance the cause of civil rights; Malcolm X was a dangerous radical who advocated violence against white people, whom he hated; and James Baldwin—never heard of him.

After the students read the essays and speeches, I asked them to discuss how their understanding of the three writers had changed. Again, the answers were consistent year after year: They had no idea that King had advanced such a radical critique, not only of white supremacy but of the U.S. war machine and the materialism in capitalism[2]; and they had not been aware of the sophistication of Malcolm X's critique and the depth of his humanity. [3]

Those reactions were predictable. Ever since white America allowed King to serve as the iconic figure for the "polite" civil-rights movement, white America has frozen him at an early point in his life, cast as the purveyor of the all-American dream. If black America demands a hero, white America will let them have King but an ideologically muted version. In the eyes of white America, Malcolm X—who once said, "I don't see any American dream; I see an American nightmare"[4] —plays the counter-iconic role, the dangerous black man. Neither caricature captures the man or the movement he led, of course, and one goal of the assignment was to spur students to ponder why white America needs the caricatures. Is the construction of the King and Malcolm X legends simply more evidence of the enduring white-supremacist reality in the United States?

About Baldwin, the students asked a simple question after reading: Why have I not read this man's work before? Typically, the only students who knew of Baldwin had encountered him in a black literature class, and the others were amazed that such a powerful writer was largely forgotten today. After screening *James Baldwin: The Price of the Ticket,*[5] a documentary about Baldwin that captures his energy and spirit, the students were even more stunned that Baldwin could be forgotten.

This lack of exposure to Baldwin can't be dismissed as merely generational. Baldwin died of cancer in 1987, when those students were babies, but MLK and Malcolm X died two decades before Baldwin, albeit by assassination in more dramatic and memorable form. The question remains: Why has white America (and much of non-white America, as well) pushed out of public view one of its most prophetic voices of the last half of the twentieth century?

I have no pithy theory about why Baldwin disappeared from the canon, why white America ignores him. It may simply be that in a culture that loves self-aggrandizing history and prefers glib experts, Baldwin was a formidable intellectual who refused to whitewash the past. He was relentless in his demand that white America abandon its willed ignorance and wishful innocence about that history:

This is the place in which it seems to me, most white Americans find them-selves. Impaled. They are dimly, or vividly, aware that the history they have fed themselves is mainly a lie, but they do not know how to release themselves from it, and they suffer enormously from the resulting personal incoherence.[6]

WHITE HEROES?

One of the reasons for my evangelical fervor about Baldwin's writings is that there is no other writer about race who sparks the range of intellectual and emotional responses in me. When I read Baldwin I learn and I feel, together. That capacity—to not simply intellectualize away a problem, nor to turn complex social problems into purely personal emotion—is crucial for white people who want to understand our own incoherence. For me, Baldwin's work has been a path down that frightening road.

I return to Baldwin and that path every few years or so. Like all great writers, Baldwin should not just be read, but re-read. After my most recent time spent with Baldwin to prepare this chapter, which included watching lots of video interviews, I realized that in recent years I have grown compla-cent, even a bit lazy in moral terms. For whatever reason, I had come to feel safe in the world, too self-satisfied; I was turning into the smug white person that it is so easy to be in this world.

In short: I realized I was losing the capacity for self-hatred. Baldwin helped me get that back, by reminding me that I am *the* nigger.

I am not *a* nigger, but *the* nigger. The difference in the article—*the* instead of *a*—is important. Here is Baldwin on the subject, taken from a 1964 public television documentary on racism in "liberal" San Francisco, in which he was featured:

> Well I know this, and anyone who has ever tried to live knows this. What you say about somebody else, anybody else, reveals you. What I think of you as being is dictated by my own necessities, my own psychology, my own fears and desires. I'm not describing you when I talk about you, I'm describing me. Now here in this country we've got something called a nigger. It doesn't, in such terms, I beg you to remark, exist in any other country in the world. We have invented the nigger. I didn't invent him. White people invented him. I've always known—I had to know by the time I was 17 years old—that what you were describing was not me, and what you were afraid of was not me. It had to be something else. You had invented it so it had to be something you were afraid of, and you invested me with it. Now, if that's so, no matter what you've done to me, I can say to you this, and I mean it: I know you can't do any more and I've got nothing to lose. And I know and have always known—and really always, that is part of the agony—I've always known that I'm not a nigger. But if I am not the nigger, and if it's true that your invention reveals you, then who is the nigger? I am not the victim here. I know one thing from another. I know I was born, I'm going to suffer, and I'm going to die. The only way you

get through life is to know the worst things about it. I know that a person is more important than anything else, anything else. I learned this because I've had to learn it. But you still think, I gather, that the nigger is necessary. Well, he's unnecessary to me, so he must be necessary to you. I'm going to give you your problem back. You're the nigger, baby, it isn't me.[7]

I am the nigger.

Let me be clear: I am not using this term in the way it is thrown around in pop culture today. I am not a nigger/nigga, in the sense that white people use the term to try to create the illusion of being hip, being part of their imagined version of black culture. I am not weighing in on the discussion within the black community about the pros and cons of using the term. I am not claiming to be a nigger to shock or offend.

I'm using the term as white people commonly use it, to express that ugly mix of fear and contempt. I recognize for all the changes in the culture since Baldwin used it in 1964, the term retains its power. Following Baldwin, I want to use it not as a weapon against others but as a tool for self-examination. I want to point the word inward rather than outward. To be a nigger is to be degraded, deficient, diseased, maybe even essentially deranged. In the racial game, we white people truly are the niggers.

I am the nigger, and so is every white person in the United States. Baldwin is right—white people are, as a class, less than fully human. We have created a world in which violence and coercion are routinely used to advance the narrow self-interest of the few at the expense of the many. That is inhuman. I am not *a* nigger, but as a white person I am *the* nigger. As long as the United States remains a white-supremacist society (more on that below), we can't escape this.

If the white projection of that status onto blacks was really about white fears of being those things, then I am those things. How could I not hate myself if I am a degraded person, not quite fully a person? If I am white in a white-supremacist society, and I want to claim any humanity, I have no choice but to hate the fact that we white people created the nigger, which means hating white people, which means hating myself.

There is a way out of this trap: Rather than pretend not to hate, we can acknowledge the hate so that it is possible not just to transcend it personally but to eliminate the need for it. I have to learn a loving self-hatred that can lead us out of this desperate place. If I am going to be honest, I can't evade the category; I have to help eliminate the category. We white people are the nigger until we get rid of the category we created. As long as the white-supremacist system continues, whether or not any white people ever aims the racial slur at a black person, then the idea of the nigger exists. And as long as that idea exists, any white person who wants to claim to be fully human has to accept that we are the nigger.

NOT ALL WHITE PEOPLE ARE ALIKE

The first reaction I typically get from white people to such a statement is: "That isn't fair. You are assuming all white people are alike. We aren't all bad."

Let's pause for a moment on that kind of comment: White people don't like being lumped together, treated as if their race defines them, being held responsible for the actions of their racial cohort. White people want to be viewed as unique individuals, not as less-than by virtue of their color. That doesn't feel good. So let's sit with that feeling for a moment. Before we talk about the varieties of white people, let's spend just a minute or two or three trying to understand the experience of being reduced to a category, the experience that white America has imposed on others for a century or two or three.

Of course not all white people are the same, on the issue of race or anything else. To assert that white Americans are "the nigger" is not to pretend there is a single white experience or political position. This isn't about describing the characteristics of individual white people; it's about asking white people collectively to be responsible. To say all white people are responsible is not to suggest all white people are the same on anything, including our opinions about race. It's not to pretend we all have the same political or economic power or all are equally responsible for the racialized inequality in the United States. All I am saying is no white person gets to opt out.

From that recognition of a collective identity and responsibility, it is important to think about the different ideological shades of white people. Just as with any ideology, there are many ways to organize the understandings white people have of whiteness. I'll divide that spectrum into reactionary, conservative, liberal, and radical white people.

Reactionary white people have never stopped believing in their inherent place on top of a racial hierarchy. They are proudly white supremacist; they still believe that black people—and usually also indigenous people, Latinos, and various other non-white groups—are biologically inferior. In recent decades this overt white supremacy has been pushed to the margins, but the racist backlash to the election of Barack Obama demonstrates how quickly that open expression of white supremacy can find its way back into the mainstream.

Conservative white people, who decry the ignorant bigotry of reactionaries, have abandoned genetic claims about racial inferiority and instead ponder how the pathologies of black and brown cultures might have developed. These conservatives—call them the "soft" white supremacists—are careful about how they speak in public, recognizing that in a multicultural society it is a more effective self-promotion strategy to prop up the mythology of white

America (the hardest-working chosen people in the world) rather than attack non-white America.

Liberal white people, who are quick to scold reactionaries and the conservatives, are more likely to ask how white America can "help" non-white people than ask how white America can transform itself. Rather than challenge the fundamental structures of the nation-state and economy to eliminate racialized disparities, liberals look for ways to smooth off the rough edges. Tepid affirmative action programs are a big hit with liberals.

And then there are radical white people (the category in which I put myself), who are bold enough to critique it all. We are the ones with the courage to tell the truth. We don't hesitate to describe the contemporary United States as a white-supremacist society. We are the heroes. And we are so humble that we deny our own heroism.

THE PROBLEM WITH WHITE HEROES

That last paragraph was meant to poke at white radicals. It was meant to poke at myself. It was meant to say: Don't forget, you are not the hero. You are the nigger.

Back to heroes: In general, I am skeptical of them. I think having heroes is almost always a bad idea because people are people, which means people are flawed, which means heroes are flawed, which means heroes betray us because we set them up to betray us. Why not just forgo heroes and avoid the whole messy business? Though everyone recognizes that no hero can withstand scrutiny—in other words, we all know that every hero is a person—we keep creating heroes, which means we eventually have to tear them down or lie about them, neither of which are attractive options.

Specifically, it's a very bad idea for white people to look for black heroes. When we hold onto black heroes, we focus on the admirable qualities of black individuals rather than the collective responsibility of white society.

The only thing worse that white people celebrating black heroes is white people creating white heroes. So, first, we need to kill all the white heroes.

For radicals, it's easy to reject the white heroes put forward by the dominant culture, such as the "founding fathers." Whatever their political achievements, they were also moral monsters. They were rich guys with slaves.

Is it unfair to judge people of another era by the standards of our time, to impose our moral judgments on people from centuries past? Perhaps it would be, but to recognize that someone like Thomas Jefferson—who not only owned slaves but wrote a famous racist tract (*Notes on the State of Virginia*[8]) and raped at least one of those slaves (Sally Hemings)—was a moral monster does not require us to transport our values back in time. We can evaluate him on the standards of the best of the white community of his own time. Among them was Thomas Paine, another founding father, but one rarely discussed today, perhaps because he wasn't wealthy, had radical politics, and critiqued organized religion. Paine, a major figure in the establishment of the United States who is best known for his 1776 pamphlet "Common Sense," was a vocal opponent of slavery; the first article he published in colonial America was an anti-slavery essay,[9] and a few weeks later an anti-slavery society was formed in Philadelphia with Paine as a founding member. Certainly Jefferson was familiar with Paine and the arguments against slavery. Certainly Jefferson was aware of the existence of the idea that all humans had an equal claim to liberty and the argument that Africans should be considered human in these matters. Jefferson lacked either the intellectual capacity or moral clarity, or both, to do the right thing. Not exactly the stuff of heroism.

Conquering heroes—the heroes who populate the history books of the United States—are not really heroes at all, unless we abandon basic moral principles, of their time and ours. But just as dangerous as treating conquerors as heroes are the stories of people with privilege who reject the system that produces the privilege—the resistance hero. The man who allies himself with feminists. The white person who takes up the anti-white supremacy cause. The American who fights for the revolution abroad. These people are cast as a kind of anti-hero, but anti-hero is just a variation on hero, and I still contend: Heroes are dangerous, no matter what category.

WHAT'S A WELL-MEANING WHITE PERSON TO DO?

If white people want to contribute to radical political movements, we should speak out against white supremacy. We have to do more than denounce the reactionaries, critique the conservatives, and challenge the liberals. We have to name white supremacy as the problem and offer a compelling analysis of that system.

First, the irony: Compelling critiques of white supremacy have been made, of course, by non-white people for centuries. When white people make the same critique, we are often taken more seriously precisely because we are white and presumed to speak more authoritatively. Black people who critique white supremacy are often labeled as angry or whiny, while white people who make the same critique are brave. We're not only presumed to be "objective" and therefore intellectually superior, but because we are arguing against a system that benefits us, we are morally superior.

Second, the double bind: When people suggest that it is heroic to speak about white supremacy and to contribute to organizing efforts to challenge the system, most white radicals point out that we should not be lauded simply for doing the right thing. And in rejecting heroic status, by offering humility in response to the praise, we add to our anti-heroic heroism.

We white people need to tell our stories, especially to other white people. How do we do that without casting ourselves as heroes? Is there a way to tell the story of white privilege without writing ourselves into that story as the hero, as the white person who "gets it?" The more we white radicals emphasize that white people will never get it in the same way as non-white people, the more we make the point that we really do get it. The more we deny heroic status, the more we can't help but imply we really are heroes.

Here's an example: I was recently at a "courageous conversations" discussion at a local church, one of about forty people, men and women, a variety of racial/ethnic identities. Three black women presented information about health disparities. About fifteen minutes into the presentation, at a point when it wasn't appropriate to interrupt with questions, a white man did just that, saying he was concerned that "we all will leave here feeling good about ourselves" but with no clear action plan. One of the black women answered politely and returned to her presentation.

I muttered to myself that the white guy should shut up and listen before he diagnoses the problem with a session that was providing valuable information, most of it new to me. But the presenters got things back on track, and I kept that thought to myself.

About five minutes later, another white man raised his hand and, making no connection to the material that the speaker was discussing, expressed his desire to talk about actions. "We know the statistics," he said. "We need to do something." Again, one of the women presenting tried to acknowledge his concern and return to the subject, but this guy ignored her and repeated his call to action.

At that point, I spoke up, saying, "I think your interrupting the speaker is disrespectful, and I would like to hear the rest of the presentation." My point was clear: You are exerting your privilege to define the purpose of the event, overriding a black woman who is in authority at that moment. Such behavior was at odds with his stated desire to contribute to an anti-racist project.

The white man got angry, kept talking, and finally blurted out, "Well, I don't like you either," though I had not attacked him personally and didn't know him. Apparently satisfied, he shut up and the program resumed.

I believe it was appropriate for me, as a white person, to challenge another white person who was unaware of how domineering his behavior was, especially in the context of the racial and gender dynamics. It seemed unfair to leave it to the presenter to sanction him, which would have left her open to accusations of not being willing to listen to feedback. I think I did the right thing. As we mingled after the event, several people thanked me.

But even if I did the right thing, I didn't feel good about it. By intervening, I was casting myself in the role of hero. I got to be the self-reflective white guy, compared with the clueless white guy. I got to be the white guy who "got it."

DRIVING WHILE WHITE

Here's one more example: Most discussions of "driving while black/brown" focus on the experiences of non-white people facing the threat of discriminatory treatment from law enforcement officers. But focusing on the flip side, how most white people don't worry about being stopped by police, helps us understand what it means to have privilege in a white-supremacist society. I often use a personal experience to explain that:

Late one summer night I was heading home after a long day at work. I was wearing an old t-shirt and shorts, driving a decaying 1970s-era Volkswagen Beetle, looking pretty raggedy. At an intersection I went through a yellow light (OK, maybe it had turned red) and saw the flashing lights in my rearview mirror. I pulled off the busy street onto a deserted side street and waited for the police officer. I was hot, sweaty, and tired, and I was in a bad mood. I complied with the instructions of the cop but with attitude.

When I opened the glove box to get my registration and insurance card, a small folding knife that I keep for emergencies popped out. The officer, who was white, asked me politely, "Do you mind if I hold that knife while we talk?" I gave it to him, and he ran my plates, wrote me a ticket, and returned the knife. I drove home.

When telling that story in an audience with non-white people, I routinely ask: What might have happened to me if I were black or brown? Most of the people laugh, recognizing that the officer would have been more likely to have treated the knife as a threat. One young black man asked: "Do you mean what would have happened after I'm on the ground with a gun to my head?" He wasn't suggesting that every police officer, white or not, is going to harass every non-white citizen in every traffic stop, but simply was recognizing the patterns in the targeting of black and brown people and the disproportionate use of force against non-white people. [10]

In telling that story, in acknowledging my privilege, I can't help but cast myself as the hero. I'm the kind of enlightened white person who can reflect on privilege in a white-supremacist society and see the truth.

Well, I can see most of the truth. During one talk when I told that story, I saw a middle-aged black man in the back of the room shaking his head, as if he disapproved of my account. That made me nervous, and I kept my eye on him through the discussion. Finally I asked him if he would like to comment, and he said that I didn't recognize all the ways my privilege had influenced my actions that night. "You pulled off onto a side street," he said. "I would never do that."

Robert Jensen

His challenge increased my nervousness. I explained that I had been pulled over on a main city street with a lot of traffic, and that I didn't want to block a lane so had turned off. "I understand why you did it," he said. "I'm telling you I wouldn't have." He said he would have stayed on the busy street, in view of as many people as possible.

I finally saw his point. My privilege dictated my choices long before the knife jumped out of the glove box. I could pull onto the deserted street because I didn't have to think about the potential consequences of being out of view, because I couldn't imagine a cop harassing or hurting me. I fumbled a bit more, trying to sound smart, and then realized there was nothing I could do but recognize that his analysis was correct. In telling a story designed to demonstrate that I'm one of the white people who gets it, all I did was make clear that I didn't get it all the way. Everyone ended up laughing, both at me and with me.

I still use that anecdote in lectures, updated to include that man's analysis. The story is designed in part to remind us white people that we aren't the experts with the definitive account and that it's important to listen. But in offering that story, of the heroic white person who is so humble that he doesn't mind using a story about his own shortcoming to illustrate the political point, I am simply reinforcing my own anti-hero heroic status.

And now, in writing down this account of the false heroism of white people, I am doing the same thing. By recognizing how there are times I don't get it, I am demonstrating how I really do get it. There's no way for me to speak without casting myself as the heroic anti-hero. The only way to avoid this trap is to not speak, but to not tell the story of white privilege is to abandon our responsibility to use white privilege to undermine it. To not speak because I feel immobilized by this trap would be cowardly.

But even making that point is problematic, since it highlights the struggle for me, a white guy. See how difficult this is for me? See how heroic I am to keep going, even when it's so difficult? Thinking about this too much can drive a person just a bit crazy.

THE RIGHT KIND OF CRAZY

This may sound like the self-indulgence of a white male professor (three identity categories especially prone to self-indulgence). Even if it is self-indulgent, I don't think I'm idiosyncratic. A question for the white people reading this: How many of you secretly write a story in your head in which you are a heroic anti-hero? How many of you have ever felt a sense of being special because a non-white person described you as "the white person who gets it?" How many of you feel a little creepy about this?

Most of the white people I know in political organizing are aware of this trap. We know that our value as public speakers and writers is rooted in this irony that being white gives our critique of white supremacy greater weight. As a middle-aged white man with a tenured academic position, my status not only gives me credibility but also a platform from which to speak and job protection if I choose to speak critically.

Since I have that position, I think my job is to be as radical as possible, to be the craziest person in the room, in a political sense. Much of the allegedly progressive work around race today has been reduced to watered-down diversity talk and celebrations of multiculturalism. There's nothing wrong with diversity and multiculturalism, unless those frameworks eclipse the much-needed critiques of white supremacy, as they routinely do. We need to keep the focus on the political, social, and economic effects of the enduring racism that is woven into the fabric of the United States. People with privilege can provide a service by pushing at the edges, working to create more space for non-white people to speak as bluntly as they want.

The best way I've found to do this is to identify the United States as a white-supremacist society. Even at a time when we have a black president, it's crucial to understand that we are still a white-supremacist society. The racial justice movements forced civil rights legislation and created a more civilized culture on many fronts, but we are still a white-supremacist society. In as many places and as many ways as I can, I repeat: The United States is a white-supremacist society. To most white people that sounds crazy.

In the United States today, everyone except an overt racist acknowledges our white-supremacist past and condemns the inherent injustice of that system, though often qualifying their positions with a demand that we see those historical crimes "in context." That leads to routine denial of the extent of the genocidal campaigns against indigenous people, the degree to which economic development was the product of African slave labor, the depth of the exploitation of Asian workers, and the brutal consequences of the U.S. aggression that took over Mexican territory.

But even with that hedging, white supremacy is widely understood to be a moral evil. That's why in the dominant culture, the term "white supremacist" is applied only to those overt racists, such as members of neo-Nazi groups or the Klan, and is not used to describe U.S. society. The United States was once a white-supremacist society, but how could that term be accurate today? We can answer the question by assessing the ideological and material realities—the way people think and the way people live.

First, the ideological: Studies consistently show that white-supremacist attitudes endure, even in people who are not overtly racist. Equivalent resumes sent to employers produce higher callback rates for a job interview when the applicant has a white-sounding name than a black-sounding name.[11] White people watching a video of a neighborhood evaluate the quality of the place as lower if there are non-white people walking the streets compared with white people in the frame.[12] Whatever the stated beliefs of white America, racist attitudes are deeply woven into the fabric of the culture. That's how we think, feel, and react.

Second, the material: There is a racialized gap on measures of wealth and well-being in the United States. On average, white people are doing better than non-white people, and the gap between white and black America is particularly pronounced. Even more dramatic is the fact that on some of those measures the gap between white and black has grown in the decades since the legislative achievements of the civil-rights movement, while on other measures the pace of the march to equality is so slow that it will be decades or centuries before we reach parity.[13]

The United States is the most affluent society in history. It is also a nation with a "can-do" spirit that believes that anything we want to achieve can be achieved. If the wealthiest nation in history claims to be committed to the end of racial injustice but remains white supremacist, both in ideological and material terms, what is the appropriate term to describe the racial system of the contemporary United States?

Only a crazy person would suggest that the United States in the twenty-first century is a white-supremacist society? That's the job of white people committed to a radical analysis: To be crazy, the right way.

GROWING UP

White people are the nigger until the category disappears. That means that self-respecting white people should focus not simply on helping non-white people deal with the worst of white racism (whether that help comes individually or through government) but on radically transforming society to eliminate white-supremacist ideas and conditions. If we white people don't want to be the nigger, that's the only way out.

I believe that transformation cannot happen unless we actively link the struggle against white supremacy to the struggles against patriarchy and capitalism as well.[14] A radical approach to race requires an equally radical approach to gender and class. We must recognize that whatever short-term material benefits we accrue in these systems, they lock us into what are essentially death cults: White supremacy, patriarchy, and capitalism are systems based on the naturalness and inevitability of hierarchy, of domination and subordination. To accept that is to surrender our humanity and join those death cults. The most important thinking in the movements for racial, gender, and economic justice has always pointed not to reform of systems but to the end of the systems.

Baldwin retained that radical spirit throughout his life. A year before his death he spoke at the National Press Club and gave several sharply worded answers to questions that amounted essentially to, "why don't black people get over it?" Just as he did in those powerful essays in the early 1960s, he threw the question right back to the mainly white audience and asked them why the white community won't be responsible for itself:

> White people don't know who they are or where they come from, and that's why you think I'm a problem. But I am not the problem, your history is. And as long as you pretend you don't know your history you are going to be the prisoner of it. And there's no question of your liberating me because you can't liberate yourselves. We're in this together. And finally, when white people— quote unquote white people—talk about progress in relationship to black people all they are saying and all they can possibly mean by the word progress is how quickly and how thoroughly I become white. I don't want to become white. I want to grow up. And so should you. [15]

That plea for us all to "grow up" struck me. That's exactly what I want to do, to grow up and out of my own compulsion to play the hero, to grow into a recognition that I must face the way in which I am the nigger.

I am in my mid-fifties, closer to the end of my life than the beginning. I've accepted that the fallen world into which I was born will fall further before redemption is likely. I have found ways to stay part of social justice movements even though I see little possibility of much progressive change in my remaining years. I am happy to keep working, even with no likelihood of progress in my lifetime and no guarantee of success in the longer term.

In taking the long view, I am rooting myself in religious traditions. By that I don't mean a particular set of supernatural claims, but rather an approach to the tragic nature of human existence, to the profound failures of the modern human. Earlier I used the term "prophetic" to describe Baldwin, who was—both during his life and after his death—often called a prophet. Baldwin seemed to prefer the term "witness." When asked in an interview what he believed he was witnessing, Baldwin said:

> Witness to whence I came, where I am. Witness to what I've seen and the possibilities that I think I see. . . . In the church in which I was raised you were supposed to bear witness to the truth. Now, later on, you wonder what in the world the truth is, but you do know what a lie is. [16]

Baldwin, who was raised in a strict Christian home,[17] uses these terms ecumenically, recognizing the power of the narrative from which the terms come without needing to embrace all the claims of the tradition. For me, that is part of why his writing and speaking have such power. He could invoke God without imposing a sectarian notion of God:

> To be with God is really to be involved with some enormous, overwhelming desire, and joy, and power which you cannot control, which controls you. I conceive of my own life as a journey toward something I do not understand, which in the going toward makes me better. I conceive of God, in fact, as a means of liberation and not a means to control others. Love does not begin and end the way we seem to think it does. Love is a battle, love is a war; love is a growing up. [18]

I don't like heroes, and I don't call Baldwin a hero. But I pay attention to those who have had the courage to bear witness. The goal is not to glorify the witness but to strive to live up to the challenge. The goal is to grow up, to be responsible adults. That requires a commitment to knowing, refusing to be willfully ignorant. And it means renouncing the wishful innocence that has been the hallmark of white America's mythology. It is our task to know and to name, honestly. We are not an innocent people. As Baldwin emphasizes, to claim innocence is morally unacceptable:

> [A]nd this is the crime of which I accuse my country and my countrymen, and for which neither I nor time nor history will ever forgive them, that they have destroyed and are destroying hundreds of thousands of lives and do not know it and do not want to know it. One can be, indeed one must strive to become, tough and philosophical concerning destruction and death, for this is what most of mankind has been best at since we have heard of man. (But remember, *most* of mankind is not *all* of mankind.) But it is not permissible that the authors of devastation should also be innocent. It is the innocence which constitutes the crime. [19]

THE END OF HATE

I believe that white people are afraid to face the truth because they are afraid that the truth can only lead to self-loathing, to hating ourselves and other white people. That is precisely what happens, but there is a path out. Baldwin, speaking about a conversation with a friend who had accused him of hating white people because they were white, explains it:

> [T]he moment she said it I realized it was true. It was as though I was looking at some pit at my feet, and the moment I realized it was true, if you see what I mean, it ceased to be true. Once I realized, and could accept in myself, in fact, it was true I hated white people, then I didn't hate them anymore. [20]

We transcend hate not by pretending to love but by acknowledging the reasons we hate. For white people, that starts not by looking at people of color to try to understand them, but by looking at ourselves and trying to fathom how we got to this place. As Baldwin said, "The only way you get through life is to know the worst things about it."

For people with unearned privilege in an unjust system, this is the worst, to look in the mirror honestly, both to acknowledge the damage we have done to others and to see what we have done to ourselves.

NOTES

1. The assigned readings were: Martin Luther King Jr., *A Testament of Hope: The Essential Writings and Speeches of Martin Luther King, Jr.*, James M. Washington, ed. (New York: HarperCollins, 1991), "Letter from Birmingham City Jail," pp. 289–302; and "A Time to Break Silence," pp. 231–44; Malcolm X, *Malcolm X Speaks: Selected Speeches and Statements*, George Breitman, ed. (London: Secker and Warburg, 1965), Chapter 3, "The Ballot or the Bullet," pp. 23–44; and Chapter 5, "Letters from Abroad," pp. 58–63; and James Baldwin, *Collected Essays* (New York: Library of America, 1998), "Color," pp. 673–77, and "The White Man's Guilt," pp. 722–27.

2. See Michael Eric Dyson, *I May Not Get There with You: The True Martin Luther King, Jr.* (New York: Free Press, 2000).

3. See Marable Manning, *Malcolm X: A Life of Reinvention* (New York: Viking, 2011).

4. Malcolm X, *Malcolm X Speaks: Selected Speeches and Statements*, George Breitman, ed. (New York: Grove, 1965), Chapter 3, "The Ballot or the Bullet," p. 26.

5. Karen Thorsen, dir., *James Baldwin: The Price of the Ticket* (San Francisco: California Newsreel, 1990).

6. James Baldwin, "White Man's Guilt," in *The Price of the Ticket: Collected Nonfiction 1948–1985* (New York: St. Martin's, 1985), pp. 410–11. Originally published in *Ebony*, August 1965.

7. James Baldwin, quoted in "Take this Hammer," produced by KQED-TV for National Educational Television, 1964. Online at 41:15, https://diva.sfsu.edu/collections/sfbatv/bundles/187041. Also online at http://www.youtube.com/watch?v=L0L5fciA6AU.

8. http://etext.lib.virginia.edu/toc/modeng/public/JefVirg.html.

9. http://www.thomaspaine.org/Archives/afri.html.

10. For information on how this plays out in New York City, see Center for Constitutional Rights, "Racial Disparity in NYPD Stops-and-Frisks," http://ccrjustice.org/stopandfrisk.

11. Marianne Bertrand and Sendhil Mullainathan, "Are Emily and Greg More Employable than Lakisha and Jamal? A Field Experiment on Labor Market Discrimination," *American Economic Review*, 94:4 (2004): 991–1013; Devah Pager, *Marked: Race, Crime, and Finding Work in an Era of Mass Incarceration* (Chicago: University of Chicago Press, 2007).

12. Maria Krysan, Reynolds Farley, and Mick P. Couper, "In the Eye of the Beholder: Racial Beliefs and Residential Segregation," *Du Bois Review*, 5:1 (2008): 5–26.

13. I summarize this data in my book *The Heart of Whiteness: Confronting Race, Racism and White Privilege* (San Francisco: City Lights Books, 2005), pp. 4–6. See also United for a Fair Economy, "State of the Dream 2012: The Emerging Majority," http://faireconomy.org/sites/default/files/State_of_the_Dream_2012.pdf.

14. See Robert Jensen, "Beyond Race, Gender, and Class: Reclaiming the Radical Roots of Social Justice Movements," *Global Dialogue*, 12:2 (Summer/Autumn 2010), http://www.worlddialogue.org/content.php?id=487.

15. James Baldwin, speaking at National Press Club, December 10, 1986. Online at 40:03, http://www.youtube.com/watch?v=SYka_Tq_mTI&feature=related.

16. Julius Lester, "James Baldwin—Reflections of a Maverick," New York Times, May 27, 1984. http://www.nytimes.com/books/98/03/29/specials/baldwin-reflections.html

17. For an account, see his first novel *Go Tell It on the Mountain* (New York: Dell, 1985/ 1953), which is typically described as semi-autobiographical.

18. James Baldwin, "In Search of a Majority," in *The Price of the Ticket: Collected Nonfiction 1948-1985* (New York: St. Martin's, 1985), p. 234.

19. James Baldwin, "My Dungeon Shook: Letter to My Nephew on the One Hundredth Anniversary of the Emancipation," in *Collected Essays* (New York: Library of America, 1998), p. 292. This essay was originally published in *The Progressive* magazine in 1962 and was subsequently published along with another essay ("Down at the Cross—Letter from a Region of My Mind," first published in *The New Yorker*) in book form as *The Fire Next Time* in 1963 by Dial Press.

20. "Race, Hate, Sex, and Color: A Conversation with James Baldwin and Colin MacInnes, James Mossman/1965," in Fred L. Stanley and Louis H. Pratt, eds., *Conversations with James Baldwin* (Jackson: University Press of Mississippi, 1989), p. 46–47.

Chapter Seven

Humility and Whiteness

*"How Did I Look without Seeing,
Hear without Listening?"*

Rebecca Aanerud

WHITENESS INTERRUPTED

It was just over twenty-years ago that Ruth Frankenberg's ground-breaking book *White Women, Race Matters: The Social Construction of Whiteness* was published. [1] Frankenberg's book significantly helped to mark the beginning of a new sub-field of race studies: whiteness studies. Frankenberg's goal was to complicate the race narrative in which "race" seemed to apply only to those who were not white, leaving white people somehow unmarked and oddly racially neutral. This seeming neutrality, so perfectly captured in Richard Dyer's phrase of "ordinary, inevitable way of being human,"[2] is of course the indicator of an ideological norm and as such signifies racial privilege and material power. [3] Frankenberg's book analyzed the discursive repertoires engaged by the thirty white women of her study. Through her analysis she highlighted various associations these white women had with whiteness, such as boring, cultural-less, superior, and bad. While whiteness was not articulated as a "problem" by her study participates per se, many of their comments suggested discomfort and ambivalence as they map their whiteness onto the histories of colonialism, Western imperialism, and white supremacist groups within the United States. Indeed, as one participant put it: "What is there to us? Besides the largest colonial legacy anyone has ever seen in history, and the complete rewriting of everything anyone else knows himself by?"[4]

Although Frankenberg's book was among the first critical analysis of whiteness by a white person, she was by no means the first writer to comment on and critique whiteness. Astute observations by W. E. B. Du Bois, Langston Hughes, bell hooks, and most notably James Baldwin tell the story of whiteness that is anything but "unmarked or neutral." In fact, the history of racism in the United States is accompanied by detailed knowledge about whiteness because as Mia Bay notes, "African-American discussions of whiteness are embedded within a larger story of black resistance to racism."[5] Yet, it remains true that many white people in the United States are woefully uninformed about whiteness as a site of structural racial advantage that carries with it ontological and epistemological implications. Certainly anyone who has taught classes on race and racism to white college and university students knows that familiar, predictable, and, in fact, thoroughly understandable moment when students begin to grasp the immense layers of violence done in the name of whiteness. All of a sudden the class moves from a place in which they have positioned themselves as the "enlightened" ones to a place in which now they are the problem—complicit with the very systems they wish to dismantle. This moment is best described as both a political crisis and a spiritual crisis for the students. In this chapter, I explore the pedagogical promise of this moment. I introduce a theoretical framework of humility as a means for understanding how we might help our students negotiate (not negate) this difficult reality of being a white problem. By humility I am invoking three key concepts: the attention to the limitations of knowing and a willingness to stay within the space of uncertainty, the ongoing need for accountability, and the inescapability of the interconnection of all things.[6]

BAD, SAD, AND MAD

There are very few classes I teach that do not engage race, racism, and whiteness, most typically through the lens of gender and sexuality. The white students range from those fairly sophisticated in recognizing that they benefit from whiteness even as they experience oppression on the basis of their gender or sexual identities to those generally unaware of whiteness as a structural site of power and privilege. Yet, despite this range, all white students take on the whiteness problem in three similar ways, which I will colloquially refer to as "bad, sad, and mad." Bad, sad, and mad represent three distinct responses or performances that privilege individual over structural responses. Bad is, of course, feeling bad about "being white." It is an ontological crisis that is best understood as "white guilt." White guilt, as James Baldwin suggests is motivated by "personal incoherence." Baldwin is referring to a particular story of entitlement that white Americans have told themselves in which they are the deserving recipients of material and social well-being. This story is set against a startling historical backdrop of racial exploitation, slavery, and murder. In a 1965 article, titled "White Man's Guilt," Baldwin writes that white people in the United States are "dimly or vividly aware that the history they have fed themselves is mainly a lie."[7] In the classroom, it is this awareness that propels white students into guilt or feeling bad. If guilt were somehow a productive psychological space, its occurrence could be welcome. But, it tends simply to reinscribe the centrality of the white subject, producing a self-serving paralysis. As Audre Lorde writes: ". . . all too often, guilt is just another name for impotence, for defensiveness destructive of communication; it becomes a device to protect ignorance and the continuation of things the way they are, the ultimate pro-tection for changelessness."[8] When guilt settles in, students move from en-gaging in full and meaningful understandings of race and racism to disengag-ing, looking for the closest escape route.

Sad, the second student response to the crisis of whiteness, has a different tenor from bad. Here students, not inappropriately, enter into a state of grief—grief for all the violence done in the name of whiteness and grief for the ways that racism has limited their own lives through misinformation and a rhetoric of difference rendered as fear and distrust. I often show my stu-dents a video on white flight in which the goal of town leaders is to create a fully racially integrated municipality. As more African Americans move into this town, white people move out. In one particular class after showing this video, a young white man exclaimed that he would give anything to live in that desegregated town. His overarching expression was one of sadness that his own upbringing had been largely monolithically white. He was taught, not overtly but in subtle and unspoken ways, to fear racial difference and assume superiority. He told me later that this video helped make Audre Lorde's words about difference come alive for him. Lorde writes: "Certainly there are real differences between us [. . .]. But it is not those differences between us that are separating us. It is rather our refusal to recognize those differences, and to examine the distortions that results from our misnaming them and their effects upon human behavior and expectations."[9] His sadness stemmed not just from the result of his upbringing, grounded in a particular pedagogy of whiteness, but that this pedagogy is itself so imbricated into a dominant narrative of Americanness for white people, that neither he nor his parents recognized its existence or its impact.

While bad, sad, mad are not developmental stages, in fact, white grief can fall into self-centered "woe is me" ontology, making it as useless as white guilt. White grief can also shift to whiteness as mad. For many of my stu-dents their most salient feeling is neither guilt nor grief, but anger. Whiteness as mad is an articulation of their frustration with racism—their own and that of others. It is also an articulation of the realization that racism is their problem as much as it is a problem for people of color. As I have written elsewhere, it was an unwelcome recognition that, despite what I had been taught by my white parents, racism was indeed my problem and one that I would need to grapple with for the rest of my life.[10] However, anger, more so than guilt or grief, holds the potential for transformation because, as Lorde has stated, anger is filled with information and energy. In an essay titled, "The Uses of Anger: Women Responding to Racism," Lorde explores the contours of anger. Recognizing that many people, particularly women, are taught to repress or deflect anger, Lorde offers a compelling argument for why anger is both a legitimate response to racism and necessary for bringing about change. She stresses that, "anger expressed and translated into action in the service of our vision and our future is a liberating and strengthening act of clarification."[11] Anger, for Lorde, unlike guilt or grief, holds the stronger possibility for transformation. However, like bad and sad, there is no auto-matic link between whiteness as mad and engaging in change. In fact, for some students, being mad inspires self-importance and impatience with oth-ers, reproducing the very same "enlightened" narrative initially disrupted by learning about the history of whiteness. Or, being mad can be a defensive response directed toward the fact of accountability itself.

PEDAGOGY OF HUMILITY

Regardless of whether the problem of whiteness is enacted as "bad, sad, or mad" by white students, the pedagogical approach must not be one of reassu-rance. Indeed the pedagogy needed at these moments is one that invites the white students to sit with incoherence; attend to its discomforting realities and personal vulnerabilities. I am not one who believes in "safe spaces" when it comes to pedagogy. I simply do not believe it is possible to learn how to grapple meaningfully with systems of power and oppression and have everyone, all students not just white students, feel safe all the time. I am not suggesting we seek to create antagonist classrooms, but I am suggesting that moments of tension and discomfort are moments of potential transformation, and we must learn to resist easy resolutions to these tensions—to the problem of whiteness. The goal is to help white students resist defensiveness by remaining present and intellectually and emotionally engaged. There are nu-merous ways to do this. For example, AnaLouise Keating suggests that one way to keep students from disengaging is to begin classes by "forging com-monalities." This pedagogy involves having students identify and draw from "complex points of connection" from which to shape discussions that "nei-ther invite nor permit students to assume that their experiences, histories, ideas, or traits are identical with those of others."[12] Such an approach positions all students to have a stake in the conversation and challenges them to be accountable to their interpretations.

I am interested in generating the same investments and accountability but do so through what I call a pedagogy of humility. Humility might seem almost antithetical to the academy; indeed, given that the academic currency is "certainty" and "knowledge" and the demonstration of certainty through one's knowledge, it is. However, I argue that humility, particularly when addressed to racism and whiteness, can inspire clarity and accountability, and we must not shy away from it. In an essay published a few years after *White Women, Race Matters,* Frankenberg examined the subtle workings of racism and self-delusion. In that essay she looked not to the words of other white women but to her own discourse and motivations. Interrupting an impulse to imagine that as an authority on racism, she herself was immune to its repro-duction, she highlighted the ways that she too must remain ever attentive to the complexities of racism, noting that "we are frequently complicit with racism even when we are absolutely confident that we are not."[13] Franken-berg insists that looking at one's racism takes as much "honesty and clarity as the ego can muster."[14] By humility I am not suggesting self-effacement or something akin to moral virtue; rather I am suggesting a conception of the self as accountable, interconnected, and open to cognitive uncertainty and mystery. Humility, I propose is an inescapable aspect or condition of an ethical social existence.[15]

For example, in "Retrieving Humility," Michelle Voss Roberts takes up the relationship between humility and accountability through an analysis of the writings of thirteenth-century Catholic mystic Mechthild of Magdeburg. As Roberts points out, Mechthild's rhetoric is almost comically excessive in terms of humility. Mechthild routinely refers to herself as a "lowly crow," as a "foul cesspool." At one point she moves to the abject stating that she wishes to dwell beneath Lucifer's tail. However, despite these rhetorical strategies, Roberts argues that Mechthild offers a complex and nuanced understanding of humility that provides a sophisticated analysis of power dynamics, hierarchical structures, and accountability. Mechthild was born into an educated German family. She was literate and familiar with court customs and literatures. She wrote extensively and was criticized for writing about spirituality given that she was a woman. She disregarded this criticism and continued writing throughout her life. Her location as simultaneously educated and marginalized, particularly as she aged, inspired her to more assiduously question hierarchical structures. As Roberts writes, "Mechthild would make everyone in positions of power (men, religious authorities, women with class or education privilege) receptive and accountable to those on the underside of the hierarchy."[16] Roberts suggests that Mechthild comes to this language of accountability through humility. For Mechthild, humility enabled her to reflect on power relations through the lens of compassion and difference. She recognized that her own class and education privilege created blind spots to the humanity of the Other. Far from rendering her silent, humility provided the foundation for her to question limitations of knowing that result from the power structures to which she both benefitted and suffered.

This attention to the limitations of knowing and a willingness to stay within the space of uncertainty is one of the key aspects of humility. A pedagogy of humility requires students to sit with two distinct but related premises. First, that what they have learned and think that they know will always be exceeded by the very limits of their knowledge and "uncertainty" is the constant reality.[17] Second, the narrative that suggests that they have earned what they have achieved is not completely but largely false. Of course many students recognize that there will always be more to know, but I am suggesting something slightly different. I am suggesting that mystery and uncertainty are necessary conditions for knowledge, particularly knowledge about race and whiteness. In her discussion about knowledge, feminist theorist Leela Fernandes offers the following challenge:

> Imagine, for instance, if we were to allow our understanding of knowledge to sit within a sense of mystery; this is in many ways unthinkable for even traditional disciplines in the social sciences, let alone the sciences. Yet it is precisely this sense of mystery, of the unknowable that permeated a great deal of recent feminist writing; the partiality of knowledge which feminist thinkers have talked about is not antithetical to universal knowledge, it is intrinsic to it.[18]

Arguing along similar lines, Immanuel Wallerstein writes that we must take "uncertainty as a basic building block of our systems of knowledge."[19] In doing so, we will be able "to construct understandings of reality that, albeit inherently approximate and certainly not deterministic, will be useful heuristically in focusing us on the historical options we have in the present in which we all live."[20] Following both Fernandes and Wallerstein, I argue that uncertainty is the ideal space for white students contemplating the problem of their whiteness because it challenges them to resist filling in their discomfort with a claim to knowledge. Asking white students to sit with uncertainty is designed to have them be, as David G. Allen has written, still in the face of their anxiety. This stillness is necessary because it is simply too easy to re-center whiteness in the guise of other discourses.[21] For example, when white students ask to hear from their classmates who are not white, ostensibly so they can better understand and know the effects of racism, it is important to analyze exactly what might be at play through this request. The request to "share experiences" repeats the classic move of asking students of color to educate white students only to have white students use these experiences not only as "spectacle," thus reinstating whiteness as a norm, but also as a means to underscore and defend their own innocence. That is, white students use the stories of their classmates as a means to reassure themselves that they have never engaged in racism. [22] Moreover, the request is often motivated by the desire to restore certainty and relieve anxiety rather than create less of the former and more of the latter. Clearly the ontological state informing the request cannot be dismissed.

"Stillness," in response to uncertainty can serve, as Fernandes has written, as a means to dis-identify with the power structures we are seeking to dismantle. Cautioning against the ego-oriented knower who fails to question her own motivations and limitations, Fernandes calls for a "radical humility." She reminds us "that it is usually easier to identify and condemn the error that others commit than to face our own." [23] Humility is about strength. It provides us with the ability to recognize that our knowledge is always limited, which is not a deficit but a crucial source of information. But it is information that we must be willing to access and act upon, which leads to accountability.

By accountability, I am speaking of a constellation of activities that involve Fernandes's inward process of self-examination, Frankenberg's invocation of as much honesty as the ego can muster, and the ability to (dispassionately) place oneself in historical legacies of structural privilege and oppression. A key aspect of accountability is the rejection of meritocracy or the idea that what we have is somehow earned. In her book, *Ontological Humility,* Nancy Holland draws from Heiddeger to explore this premise. She writes that ontological humility interrupts the idea of entitlement, through problematizing what has been "given to us by what Heiddeger calls 'Being.' We can believe that we deserve [what we have] because of some inherent or achieved virtue of our own, but, whatever we might have done to merit our success in any endeavor owes far more to chance . . . than it does our own efforts." [24] In my experience, students are able to comprehend that there is a certain "randomness" or chance to, in effect, being white (or male, or able bodied, or in a family in which basic survival is not a daily struggle), and some of them are able to connect this "randomness" to the powerful and ubiquitous narrative of meritocracy. [25] That is, they understand that being white is not at all incidental to life experiences and successes; it is fundamental to it. In fact, it is this realization that often inspires guilt. As I've discussed above guilt seldom leads to a commitment to social change. The task is to connect the randomness of being white to accountability, and this is where humility enters. As we saw above, for Mechtild the recognition of her own dual relationship to privilege and oppression brought her to a deep understanding of the need to resist and revise class and gender power dynamics.

For a more contemporary example, we can turn to the work of Minnie Bruce Pratt. One of the first works that I read about racism by a white woman was Pratt's "Identity: Skin, Blood, Heart." Pratt's essay provided a kind of road map for the internal work and brutal honesty needed as I learned how to confront my own racism (which is, of course, an ongoing process). Pratt posits a simple but powerful question that resonates with Mechthild's recognition of power relations and accountability. Having been raised in the Jim Crow South, Pratt struggles to face her reality, writing: "In this *world* you aren't the superior race or culture, and never were, whatever you were raised to think. When are you going to be ready to live in this world?"[26] For Pratt, to be ready to live in this world means being accountable to her whiteness and the class privilege that shaped her childhood. In a carefully delineated narrative Pratt uncovers the historical legacies of racism that inform, for example, the social relations between her and the black men she encounters on the street. Her goal is not to look for ways out of racism, but, to better understand and account for how racism resides in her. As Frankenberg will later put it, not only do we live in the master's house of racism, but by some architectural trick, the master's house lives in us.[27] Similarly, poet and essayist Adrienne Rich invokes humility as her path to accountability. She writes: "Marginalized though we have been as women, as white and Western makers of theory, we also marginalized others because our lived experience is thoughtlessly white . . ."[28] Rejecting earlier assumptions of universal "sisterhood" that served to mask Western dominance, Rich calls into question how she was blind to her own limits of understanding. Asking: "how did I look without seeing, hear without listening?"[29]

It should come as no surprise that when we begin to take seriously a deep commitment to accountability we encounter such questions; because, accountability requires that we attend to multiple and interlocking systems of privilege and oppression that inform all of our lives. As numerous scholars have demonstrated such systems, particularly systems of privilege work most effectively when invisible. "How did I look without seeing, hear without listening?" is the essence of humility. In her recent essay, feminist theologian Elizabeth Hinson-Hasty asks that we consider "the complex web of attitudes, systems, laws, and institutions created in the West to dehumanize, colonize, and enslave peoples in the Global South."[30] She continues: "Genuine humility must always be understood as a means of seeing oneself as part of the larger, interdependent earth, in relationship with the larger community, and as an integral part of transforming attitudes, structures, organizations, and institutions that marginalize people who differ from the dominant norms."[31]

It is this vision of recognizing one's self as part of a larger interdependent earth and in relationship with and to a broader set of communities that my argument for a pedagogy of humility is based. Humility is a recalculation of the scale of self-importance, not to self-deprecation but to a more sophisticated and accurate rendering of achievement. Let me provide two brief examples of this recalculation. In the first example the former chair of my department (Gender, Women, and Sexuality Studies), a white, straight man unpacks the "best man for the job" narrative employed to explain why he was chosen to lead our department. He analyzes his career path from young white kid growing up in Colorado to full professor in nursing and eventually chair of a women's studies department through the lens of meritocracy. He then reframes the narrative to underscore the many layers of privilege (race, class, gender) that guaranteed a small competitive pool through which he emerges on top. The first narrative chronicles the following key moments: Growing up in Colorado in family-owned home, post–WWII, attending college counseling session in seventh grade, attending college, working construction to cover tuition, avoiding going to Vietnam, attending graduate school, advancing through faculty promotions, and so on.

The second narrative does not deny any of the above facts, but, provides the context.[32] Homeownership in Colorado was predominantly available to white families, and the land was available because of a U.S. government violation of the 1868 Laramie Treaty. College-education was deemed a "natural fit" for a person of his race, gender, and class. The work to pay tuition was largely a function of hiring white men over men of color in a community that was hostile to anyone who was not white. Avoiding going to Vietnam was a function of being enrolled in college and graduate school, which are class- and race-based benefits. Career success was tied, in part, to being a man in a female-nominated profession.[33] I am not suggesting, nor would he, that he didn't work hard and wasn't qualified for his promotions and leading our department. But, as he would readily agree, from before birth onward, his way was paved and his chances of success increased by the exclusion of others.[34]

The second example is from my own life. As an undergraduate I was enrolled in an African American literature class taught by a well-known African American scholar. I had convinced myself that, given my whiteness, I would be at a distinct disadvantage in this class compared to my African American classmates. To my great surprise I received As on all of my papers. One day, while waiting in the hallway for office hours with the professor, I overheard her assisting one of my classmates, an African American man, who was an articulate and active member of our class. I was shocked to hear not a vibrant and dynamic conversation, but a person struggling with basic writing, grammar, and parts of speech. I left without meeting with the professor. As I tried to make sense of what I had just overheard, I realized that my whiteness (and class privilege) far from ill-preparing me for this class, overprepared me. It was the first time that I started to think through the profound impact my white upbringing played in my success. I grew up in a family with a father who had a job that allowed my mother to stay home, provide healthy meals, keeping us well fed and dressed. Both my parents (heterosexual and married) spoke English and were able to assist with homework or intervene on our behalf with teachers, when needed. My father's job provided housing stability and health care benefits. When I was sick I would be taken to the doctor, receive the necessary care, and be back at school relatively quickly. As I reflected on my upbringing, I realized I didn't do well in this college class despite my whiteness; I did well *because of* my whiteness. For me this was a transformative realization that didn't inspire a sense of guilt or shame but did inspire a repositioning—a humbling—of my understanding of self-achievement. It inspired accountability and a dismantling of a simplistic meritocracy. It helped me to see that my efforts, while legitimate and admirable, were part of a much larger constellation of forces.

Because meritocracy privileges self-achievement, it supports a false representation both of accomplishments and of so-called lack of accomplishments. The flipside of "the best man for the job" narrative of my former chair is, of course, "the lack of qualified women for the job" narrative. Meritocracy seeks to make invisible the reality that the very same conditions that advance certain people's material or social status, very often limit those of others. "It precludes our seeing ourselves, and what we do," writes Lata Mani, "as part of a broader and interconnected whole."[35] Helping white students see the subtlety with which meritocracy operates provides them with a complex lens through which to reflect on their lives as embedded within structural powers and calls into question "objective" standards of achievement measured by certain conceptions of "autonomy." As Mani writes, in a related context, the loss of this objective stance need not invite crisis but "lead instead to critical dispassion and humility."[36] As my ability to position my undergraduate achievements within that larger constellation of forces increased, my whiteness simultaneously came into greater focus, that is, I was able to see it with greater clarity *and* it became less all-encompassing. My critical dispassion enabled me to see whiteness as a mechanism through which I came to know myself and was defined, but its meaning was more fluid and the ways I chose to occupy it, more diverse.

As the best work in the field of whiteness studies has shown, there is nothing static or fixed about whiteness or being white. While white students tend to invoke bad, sad, or mad, there is no reason why they have to. Indeed, in many cases white students are aware that feeling bad, sad, or mad does more to maintain the power of whiteness, through paralysis and re-centering, than dismantle it. They are looking for a wider range of options. I know, for instance, that as a white woman, my students (all of them) look to me to model engagement and full presence. They see me as performing whiteness in a way that is not paralyzed by guilt, grief, or anger. They see me as a person able to invoke a critical whiteness discourse and critical dispassion that provides analytical clarity about the ways that whiteness operates in different settings and at different historical moments and yet remain open to my inevitable need for ongoing learning. It is my argument that a pedagogy of humility, grounded in the recognition of the inevitable limits of what we can know, a deep commitment to accountability, and a basic understanding of the interconnection of all things, provides students (all students, albeit in very different ways on the basis of race, class, sexual and gender identities, disability) with a more realistic rendering of their location within structural systems of power and oppression. The pedagogy is geared fundamentally toward an awareness that "bad, sad, and mad" are not only predictable performances that white students enter but that they keep white students from engaging with and critiquing the very systems that shape their whiteness.

CONCLUSION: THE NATURE OF CHANGE

Throughout this chapter I have posited three claims about humility. One, humility is about honesty and strength. Two, humility involves a recalculation of the scale of self-importance. Three, humility is an inescapable condition for an ethical social existence. In the context of race, racism, and whiteness, a pedagogy of humility provides white students with an avenue to remain present to the violence done in the name of whiteness and to take up a meaningful critical stance toward that violence. It invites and challenges white students to engage the meaning of their whiteness as a dynamic site of struggle and transformation. Further, a pedagogy of humility positions all students as part of that broader interconnected whole Mani writes of, by which I take her to mean our fundamental interdependency of and responsibility to each other. Such positioning moves us past a largely meaningless focus on individual blame and shame, what Fernandes refers to as "strategies of the ego" (75), and moves us toward a collective vision of and commitment to social change. This vision and commitment does not deny the history and ongoing legacy of whiteness as an exploitive system (or for that matter the histories of other exploitive systems such as heteronormative masculinity), but it does suggest that we are not completely and inevitably determined by that history. Change—both individual and collective—is possible, and in fact, unavoidable. It is the nature of that change, the direction it takes, to which the pedagogy of humility concerns itself. This pedagogy asks that we learn to welcome and sustain humility in ourselves, our students, and all who we encounter, to resist the desire to reassure ourselves of our benign innocence, and to honor that our very existence and growth is dependent upon each.

NOTES

1. The title of this chapter quotes Adrienne Rich, "Towards a Politics of Location" in *Feminist Theory Reader: Local and Global Perspectives,* eds. Carol R. McCann and Seung-Kyung Kim (New York: Routledge, 2003), 447-459.
2. "White." *Screen 29 4: 44–64.*

3. For the development of whiteness as a racial norm within US and European contexts see the following historical analysis: Theodore W. Allen, *The Invention of the White Race vol.1* (London & New York: Verso, 1994); F. James Davis, *Who is Black? One Nation's Definition* (University Park, Pennsylvania, 1991); Matthew Frye Jacobson, *Whiteness of a Different Color: European Immigrants and the Alchemy of Race* (Cambridge: Harvard University Press, 1998); David R. Roediger *The Wages of Whiteness: Race and the Making of the American Working Class* (London and New York: Verso, 1991). See also, Ladelle McWhorter's "Where do white people come from?": A Foucaultian Critique of Whiteness Studies" *Philosophy and Social Criticism* 31 (2005): 533–56, for a discussion of development of white racial subject positions within the context of Foucault's development of the biopower.

4. Ruth Frankenburg, *White Women, Race Matters: The Social Construction of Whiteness*, 169.

5. Mia Bay, *The White Image in the Black Mind: African American Ideas about White People, 1830–1925* (Oxford: Oxford University Press, 2000), 7.

6. As will become apparent, my points of reference throughout this chapter are drawn from feminist writings, which is why I often refer to this concept of humility as feminist humility.

7. James Baldwin, "The White Man's Guilt." *Ebony 20* (1964): 47–48.

8. Audre Lorde. *Sister Outsider* (Trumansburg, N.Y.: The Crossing Press, 1984), 130.

9. Lorde, 115.

10. Rebecca Aanerud, "Thinking Again: *This Bridge Called My Back* and the Challenge to Whiteness," in *This Bridge We Call Home: Radical Visions for Transformation*, eds. Gloria E. Anzaldúa and AnaLouise Keating, (New York & London: Routledge, 2002), 69–77.

11. Lorde, 127.

12. AnaLouise Keating, *Teaching Transformation: Transcultural Classroom Dialogues*, (New York: Palgrave MacMillian, 2007).

13. Ruth Frankenberg, "When We are Capable of Stopping, We Begin to See: Being White, Seeing Whiteness," in *Names We Call Home: Autobiography of Racial Identity, eds* Becky Thompson and Sangeeta Tyagi, (New York & London: Routledge, 1996), 6.

14. Ibid., 6.

15. I am grateful to Lata Mani for conversation on this particular articulation.

16. Michelle Voss Roberts, *Feminist Theology: The Journal of the Britain & Ireland School of Feminist Theology*, 18 no. 1 (Sep 2009): 69.

17. For a similar discussion of these limits framed as "opacity" see chapters 5 and 6 of George Yancy, *Look a White!: Philosophical Essays on Whiteness*, (Philadelphia: Temple University Press, 2012).

18. Leela Fernandes,, *Transforming Feminist Practice; Non-Violence, Social Justice, and the Possibilities of a Spiritualized Feminism.* (San Francisco: Aunt Lute Books, 2003) 99. See also, George Yancy, *Black Bodies, White Gazes: The Continuing Significance of Race* (Lanham, Md: Rowman & Littlefield, 2008), who identifies this domain of the "unknowable" as linked to the concept of "ambush."

19. Immanuel Wallerstein, *The Uncertainties of Knowledge*, (Philadelphia: Temple University Press, 2004), 3.

20. Ibid., 3.

21. See also Allen's "Whiteness and Difference in Nursing" *Nursing Philosophy, 7* (2006) in which he writes: "As nurses we need to be still during the anxiety this ambiguity triggers. For example, as soon as one mentions opening curricular goals and objectives for negotiation, educators typically raise the specter of licensing examinations and other constraints. This is a power move. We are already aligned with the values of those exams and constraints which are themselves culturally embedded" (73–74).

22. For a succinct example of this phenomenon see Ruth Frankenberg's "When we are Capable of Stopping, We Begin to See." In *Names We Call Home: Autobiography of Racial Identity, eds.* Becky Thompson and Sangeeta Tyagi, (New York & London: Routledge, 1996), 3–17.

23. Fernandes, 44.

24. Nancy J. Holland, *Ontological Humility: Lorde Voldemort and the Philosophers*, (Albany: SUNY Press, 2013), 2.

25. I place "randomness" in quotation marks to draw out various social histories and disciplinary technologies (such as anti-miscegenation laws and "race suicide" rhetoric) that, as John T. Warren has argued, predict that some bodies will be white. In addition to work by Warren, see also, my essay, "The Legacy of White Supremacy and the Challenge of Antiracist White Mothering" *Hypatia 22 no. 2* (spring 2007): 20–38. I am especially grateful to George Yancy for this insight on randomness.

26. Minnie Bruce Pratt, "Identity: Skin, Blood, Heart" In *Yours in Struggle; Three Feminist Perspectives on Anti-Semitism and Racism*, eds. Elly Bulkin, Minnie Bruce Pratt, and Barbara Smith, (Ithaca: Firebrand Books, 1984), 13.

27. This phrasing is in reference to Audre Lorde's famous essay, "The Master's Tools Will Never Dismantle the Master's House," in *Sister Outsider* (Trumansburg, NY: The Crossing Press, 1984), 110–13.

28. Rich, 451.

29. Rich, 454.

30. Elizabeth Hinson-Hasty, "Revisiting Feminist Discussions of Sin and Genuine Humility." *Journal of Feminist Studies in Religion*, 2012, 28(1), 112.

31. Ibid. 112.

32. See also Robert Jensen's discussion of re-contextualizing narratives of whiteness in his book, *The Heart of Whiteness: Confronting Race, Racism, and White Privilege, (*San Francisco, CA: City Lights, 2006).

33. See Christine L. Williams, "The Glass Escalator: Hidden Advantages for men in the 'Female' Professions" *Social Problems 39(3):* 253–67.

34. I would like to thank David G. Allen for sharing with me his unpublished lecture: "Best Man for the Job!: My Career as a Case Study in Diversity."

35. Lata Mani, *Sacred/Secular: Contemporary Cultural Critique,* (London & New York: Routledge, 2009), 177.

36. _____, *The Integral Nature of Things: Critical Reflections on the Present.* (London & New York: Routledge, 2013), 81.

Chapter Eight

I Speak for My People

A Racial Manifesto

Crispin Sartwell

I am a middle-aged, middle-class, rural, white, male heterosexual. I will refer to this constellation of identities—particularly the last three—as my "race." If you don't think that being a member of my race is a problem, you haven't been reading, for example, the *New York Times* op-ed page, where we are continuously excoriated—with, let me admit, some justice—as the most re-actionary and bigoted portion of the population, bent on maintaining our privileges against the tide of justice and demography. Here are some of our racial characteristics. We are opposed to science and are in general congeni-tally or perhaps willfully ignorant. We are what's the matter with Kansas. We are hoarding ammunition as we grow ever-more disgruntled. We despise the poor and blame them for their poverty, which is actually, of course, due to their exploitation by us. We think people ought to be allowed to starve so that we can save a few dollars on our taxes. We're the only reservoir of homophobia: bullies almost in virtue of our very identity. That may well be because we're actually closeted gay people, who must insulate our pseudo-masculinity in imagination from the awful drag queen within. We are bent on maintaining our control of the bodies of women by a thousand anachronistic mechanisms, from laws concerning abortion and contraception to our very glance, which carries with it the preternatural destructive power of the evil eye.

All of this is at least approximately true, and I think it is time we admitted it straight out: The history of my race is one of unremitting evil relieved only by spasms of hypocrisy. My people have visited every sort of disaster upon yours, from colonialism and the slave trade to capitalism, housewifery, and atomic weaponry.

My race lives at a deranged distance from nature, for we are the agents of technology and climate change. No doubt we hate our mother the earth just as we resent our real mothers, or any woman who seems to have any power over us, such as Hillary Clinton. We don't think Barack Obama is an American, because we are certainly Americans, and he is certainly not us, whoever in fact he may be. Deep inside, despite our huge flimsy compensatory egos and infinite capacity for self-deception, we know that we are over, and our every reflexive paroxysm comes from fear and resentment of this situation. We are always fighting a rearguard action against the forces of the future. We want time to run backward, against the great tide of freedom carrying you on.

In short, we are the inventors and perpetrators of all oppressions. Amazingly, we convinced ourselves at various times and in various ways that you wanted us to oppress you; you needed us to oppress you; we were oppressing you for your own good. I admit that was insane. We white male heterosexuals are a gutter race, irremediably flawed. When the Nation of Islam referred to white people as "devils," quite possibly it had a point. One might speculate as to the respective roles of genetics, environment, and blood guilt, but there is no denying that something has gone terribly wrong somewhere. My race has a streak of moral degeneracy, a counter-evolutionary tendency.

Some of my people once conceived "the Negro" as a problem or worried about "the woman problem," but everyone including me is now agreed on who the problem actually always was: me. Du Bois explored how it felt to be *regarded* as a problem; I am exploring what it means actually to be a problem, in fact to be *the* problem. Think about what sort of dilemmas this imposes on my people or what it's like to be colorless me. For example, most folks can vote in good conscience for their own self-interests, broadly construcd. No one blames black people for voting for black people in the interests of black people, or women for voting for women in the interests of women; people have become heroes by making that possible. But if white male heterosexuals vote for white male heterosexuals because they are white male heterosexuals and would defend the interests of white male heterosexuals—for example, gender hierarchy, heteronormativity, and white privilege—we are doing wrong. When you pursue your interests, your voice is a cry for justice. When we pursue our interests, we are doing real harm and real evil. Harm and evil *are* our interests.

Admittedly, my race has had some achievements as well, which we might be able to remind everyone about if we someday get our own history month. It is hard to tell, historically, who really counts as a white heterosexual male. But perhaps you could give us William Shakespeare, Isaac Newton, Ben Franklin, Napoleon, Vincent Van Gogh? (Wait, maybe Shakespeare was gay?) We could make some t-shirts. But it will be a long time before my race gets its history month. Expressions of white or male or heterosexual pride are

unbelievably problematic; no one articulates such things publicly except insane supremacists and hate criminals. We dare not, and indeed perhaps we
should not, speak frankly as ourselves or for ourselves. That is why so many
of the machinations by which we have retained power have been hidden,
even from ourselves.

I suspect that to take real pride in our identity, history, and customs—and
for us to rise to real racial consciousness and knowledge of self—the members of my race will have to pass through a subaltern or abject phase, a time
of trial in which we shall be humbled and brought low. Really, we have been
practically begging for it for centuries; we have irritated everyone when we
haven't actually profoundly compromised your life prospects. For our own
good, we need you to impose extremely aggressive affirmative action programs by which we could be systematically excluded from even a vestigial
grip on power. We are in any case ill-suited to mainstream education, cursed
as we are by congenital ADHD. We may need to live apart in ghettoes or on
reservations, where possibly we could be accessed for breeding purposes. All
the time we could be transforming our suffering into art, which would certainly be an improvement.

After that, we will need to undergo a Booker T/Mao stage of our racial
destiny, in which we learn the dignity of hard manual labor in the fields or
sweatshops. We must slowly establish that we are an industrious, sincere,
and above all a non-dangerous race, which may take some generations. At
that point we can generate a "talented tenth" or a racial intelligentsia, the
white male heterosexuals who are most like people of color, women, and gay
people. This cohort, I prophesy, could lead us toward integration into the
culture at large, and possibly even toward a measure of pride in some of the
achievements of the great white male heterosexuals of the past, if any. A
movement of pride and identity might then emerge that wouldn't carry the
full taint of our genocides. We might re-appropriate "cracker," "breeder,"
and "jerk" as honorifics, but I think we ought to stop short of white male
heterosexual nationalism. Nevertheless, our blood too might have a lesson, or
at least a cautionary tale, to teach the world.

It is far too early, then, to emphasize with a pure conscience the contributions of my race to the world. Nevertheless I would like to describe some of
them for future public service announcements. We are, I think, in a modest
way naturally musical, and even though Jimmie Rodgers or Hank Williams
are inconceivable without African American music, I think my people might
someday take pride in their achievements. Some elusive quality of whitema-
lestraightness, a font of ancestral creativity, emerges in their work. To take
another example, I'm not sure that the colored, female, and gay races have
produced cynics as magnificently destructive as H. L. Mencken or Ambrose
Bierce. Admittedly, their sheer assholery is characteristic of the whole de-
based history of my people; nevertheless, there is art in their prose, which

could be recovered as their actual political positions sink into historical oblivion. Ours is not the most athletic of races, but figures such as Lance Armstrong have carried forward the banner of my race with distinction, if also with our characteristic cheating. A certain rudimentary mechanical ability is native to my race, I believe, and for every semi-sane Tesla we have produced an eminently practical Edison. Admittedly, this racial tic has given rise to the weaponry by which we have dominated and infuriated the world. But it could in principle be turned to peaceful purposes.

It sometimes seems that being a straight guy like me is nothing but a set of exclusions and dominations. What, I often ask myself, is my straightness without homophobia, misogyny, and many other vicious prepossessions of which I may only dimly be aware? Also, it is certainly plausible to hold that the mating of a man with a woman is unnatural, a monstrous copulation between members of different species. But anyone should try to love anyone they want to try to love, and if heterosexuality could be relieved of its immense burden of normativity, it might be more fun. In other words, if I were just having sex with you and not also thereby oppressing you, we might both enjoy ourselves more, or at any rate be less angry at one another. That might be legitimate within a certain significant sexual sub-culture of the distant future, because there is something to be said for heterosexuality. Men and women are not the only sorts of people who fit together, but when we do fit together, we really fit together, if you know what I'm talking about, and this idea I feel could someday constitute (partly) a contribution of my race to mainstream culture.

Admittedly, my race has developed the narrow and idiotic normative standards of beauty that have become the mechanisms of your self-oppression. We made you conk your hair, starve yourself, bleach your skin, dress all fem or not fem at all. We made you try to produce yourself as the body we wanted to see. Partly, I would speculate, that is because members of my own race are not notably attractive. We are gross, actually, though occasionally we do throw out a Brad Pitt or other genetic outlier. We can distract you from that if we can make you focus instead on your own alleged ugliness. But even our bizarre standards of beauty might be incorporated into the mainstream if they were just part of the vast diverse tapestry of human aesthetic preferences. We could eventually reach a situation in which it was as permissible to prefer skinny or lingerie-model-type women as to prefer any other sort of otherwise weighted or gendered person. Some folks just have a type.

The political traditions and rhetorics of my race focus on autonomy, individualism, self-reliance, pulling yourself up by your own bootstraps, competition, and whatnot. We like to talk about individual rights rather than interpersonal connections. Now admittedly this ideology is a tissue of privileges, falsifications, and contradictions. No human being ever accomplishes anything by himself, but each of my people is trying to make himself an invulnerable autonomous being; we want to armor ourselves all in Kevlar. Putting it mildly, we need therapy. It must always be borne in mind that Emerson's composition of "Self-Reliance" was made possible by his wife and a small domestic staff; perhaps its composition didn't require Emerson at all. That Jefferson was a great defender of individual rights and was also engaged so multidimensionally in slavery shows the problem; his status as an autonomous gentleman required the constant labor of others and the erasure of the subjectivity of the people who performed it. He could at least have apologized. In industrial capitalism, the doctrine of individual rights becomes an ideology of oppression. The idea that a worker in a capitalist system is free because he can sell his labor on a contractual basis is just a rationalization of the most pervasive forms of economic exploitation, precisely those which benefit us and affront you.

Nevertheless, I think that there are elements of individualism that you might pluck from the flotsam after the wreck of my race's swagger. You might contemplate what happens when the human individual is actually regarded as in some sense unreal or not ontologically primary. One devastating effect is essays precisely like this one or the persona of the racial spokesman. Also, it is a very short trip from unrealing individuals to liquidating them for the collective good, as many collectivist regimes have actually done. I would suggest that a version of Jeffersonian or Thoreauvian suspicion of centralized power might be worth retaining in a library somewhere just in case. Our elders have set it down as part of our traditional lore that a government that provides your food tells you what and whether to eat. Well, you can take or leave that, but you might end up finding it useful.

And so as we recede from history, we bid you a semi-fond adieu. We certainly created many psychological and practical difficulties for you, but I'd be lying if I said we didn't enjoy our time atop the pinnacle. With tremendous gratitude for all the collusion you gave us, we now step aside to spend more time with our disintegrated families. As we exit the stage, we acknowledge that we got pretty much everything wrong. We leave you with our sincerest apologies and not a dime in reparations.

Chapter Nine

Being a White Problem and Feeling It

Bridget M. Newell

To the real question, "How does it feel to be a problem," I answer seldom a word. And yet, being a problem is a strange experience—peculiar, even for one who has never been anything else save perhaps in boyhood and in Europe."—W. E. B. Du Bois[1]

In the early 1900s, W. E. B. Du Bois explored what it meant and how it felt to be seen as a problem due to his race.[2] Now, little more than a century later, I have been asked to "flip the script," to consider what it means to be a problem due to *my* race. What, from my perspective, does it mean and how does it feel to be a white problem?

For a long time I considered various ways to approach this question, and I grappled with the important, yet daunting request that I include in my response—as Du Bois did—some of my own personal history in coming to see whiteness, including my own whiteness, as a problem. Like any academic, as part of my planning process, I went to the source, Du Bois's own words. I was struck by the fact that I and many other white people could begin the conversation using the exact same words as Du Bois. To the question, "How does it feel to be a white problem?" I, like many whites, "answer seldom a word."

Of course, this question is not usually posed in such an explicit fashion to white people, but it does arise in multiple forms, and when it does, we whites are often silent. *We* answer seldom a word. We *cannot* or *do not want to* answer. Unlike Du Bois, however, we whites do not live with constant reminders that we are seen as problems due to our race. We do not usually explore how it feels or what it means to be white or "have" a race. When we do address race, the focus is on people of color. That is, race is about black people, or Latinos, or . . . it is not about whites. Moreover, within the context of racism, if the idea of whites or whiteness arises, we focus on other whites—those racist whites—but not ourselves.

Given this, *we* "say seldom a word" because the idea of having to explore our own whiteness, let alone the idea that we ourselves might be a problem due to our race/whiteness, does not occur to us.

DUCKING THE QUESTION

We face other difficulties when the question *is* understood to apply to all whites. When it is understood that the question comes from a perspective that suggests that—due to the pervasive, systemic, and interconnected natures of white privilege, white ignorance, racism, and George Yancy's concept of white opacity—*all* whites *are* racists, one *still* may "say hardly a word." Rather than responding, one might either deflect the question and instead discuss one's own commitment to a colorblind, race-free, or nonracist society, or one might continue to defend oneself against claims of racism, thus saying hardly a word in response to the actual question.[3]

In other cases, whites may say hardly a word because we cannot quite figure out what to say or because we may not *want to* answer. When we cannot figure out what to say, we may understand what white privilege is and how it works conceptually and in the world. And we might know that we are part of that system that is the problem, but we may not understand or see the linkage to ourselves. A move from the theoretical to the concrete and personal hasn't occurred. Thus a white person might find herself saying, "I 'get it' on some level, but I really can't say how I am *personally* a problem." This signals an attempt at understanding that could lead to an answer, but not yet.

At the level of understanding whiteness and white privilege in which one sees herself as part of and complicit in the system of white supremacy and feels responsible for doing something about white privilege, one may *still* say hardly a word for a variety of reasons. Some may feel overwhelmed by white guilt or shame and be at a loss for what to say about being a white problem. This silence occurs because a person is lost in his or her own feelings. In other cases, silence could be a strategic effort either to avoid the appearance of being un- or underinformed or to avoid saying "the wrong thing," the "thing" that would illustrate just how much of a problem she is. In either case, the silence is reflective of an effort to avoid vulnerability and to remain in control. This effort, of course, can also be ascribed to whiteness and white privilege.

A more generous reading of the silence or question-ducking would simply be that conversations about our own implications in systems of privilege and power occur very rarely, if ever, among white people. We rely on people of color to teach us about racism, so we have little practice or skill in discussing how it feels to be a white problem, even if we do know how it feels. We whites are not ready or able to engage in the discussion, and so we remain silent. *We say hardly a word.*

I begin with this discussion of why and how whites are often silent on the problem of whiteness to illustrate the many barriers to solid and personal conversations about whiteness and about being a white problem in a literal sense. This silence only adds to the problem. It leaves people stranded, with issues (and tensions) hanging in the air. The silence is left "out there" to be interpreted—Do they not care that they are a problem? Does the silence mean "Tough luck for you; my life is fine"? Does the silence tell me I'm wasting my time discussing whiteness and white privilege and racism? Does the silence indicate that you have been caught off guard and are processing information? How is anyone to know what our silence means when it can mean any of the above and more?

ADDRESSING THE QUESTION

Given this—and if we recognize the difficulty and value of addressing the question, "What does it mean to be a [white] problem?"—each of us must try to break free of the pattern of silence, to speak, and to share what occurs to us without keeping the discussion wholly at a distance, on a purely abstract or theoretical level.

So, where am I in this conversation? I have taught about whiteness in my philosophy classes, and I have engaged in various conversations about whiteness. Diversity work is my focus, yet I have not spent much time *making my own whiteness part of the conversation*—spoken or written. I have reflected on it a great deal. Like all whites I have lived the experience of being a white problem, but I have avoided injecting my personal story into discussions of whiteness. Mainly, I have been concerned that any attempt at making personal explorations public would result in the construction of a "too-neat" narrative rendition of the difficult, complex, and ongoing process of exploring, learning, and grappling with what it means to be a white problem both conceptually and personally. But also, and just as importantly, I have been concerned that a more personalized discussion would shift the focus to me, as if I am holding myself up as a "knowing white" who has grappled with her whiteness, who claims to have a much better perspective than other whites, who is finished with her work, and is sharing her wisdom. That is definitely not the case.

I understand the value of exploring questions of identity in a personal manner. I have often learned from others who have shared their experiences related to issues of privilege, power, and oppression, so I will share as well.

My account is about how I have come to answer the question, "What is it like to be a white problem?" at this point in time.

To begin with, I want to "unpack" the question. From there, I will briefly explore some of the salient problematic aspects of whiteness as I understand them, and then explore three interrelated answers to the question, "How does it feel to be a white problem?" Although the three answers I provide can be reflective of a developmental process, I do not understand them as part of a simple linear process. Combined, they are more like attempting to climb a steep mountain that no one has conquered—one makes progress, loses ground, struggles back up again, and continues. Progress requires deliberative movement and effort toward the goal if one wishes to "minimize" (to the extent possible) the level and kind of white problem one is. I end not with a solution to "being" a white problem but rather with an approach centered in "tough optimism," to borrow a phrase from Sartre. I believe it can help one avoid the silence and inaction that result from guilt or other unproductive responses to recognizing "I am a white problem."[4]

UNPACKING THE QUESTION

The elements that I focus on when considering what it means to be a white problem include white privilege, white ignorance, and the resulting inability of whites to detect the extent to which they are impacted by systemic privileges and power associated with whiteness:

1. Whites are systemically granted unearned advantages and privileges simply because they are (or appear) white. As Peggy McIntosh notes in "White Privilege and Male Privilege," these privileges allow us to feel comfortable in the world, see ourselves as good people if we are not overt racists, and grease the path toward achievement.[5]
2. These advantages are seen by whites as part of everyday, normal human experience for all, a view reinforced by a number of things, including: pervasive notions of meritocracy, the belief in the American Dream, the hyper-visibility of exceptional people of color, claims that we live in a colorblind and post-racial society, as well as the facts that whites participate in and perpetuate an epistemology of ignorance in regard to white privilege, racism, and race relations.[6]
3. The system of white privilege results not only in whites' experiences of feeling welcome in the world but also in a lack of awareness and understanding of the experiences of those without white privilege—a sense of arrogance, obliviousness, and a lack of compassion and worse toward those who are not white.[7]

4. The "flip side" of systemic privilege is systemic racism. The advantages I gain through systemic white privilege are reflected in and reinforce a person of color's disadvantage, perhaps not always one-on-one, but the systemic link exists.
5. The limitations of humans' abilities for self-awareness and self-understanding as well as the "invisibility" of privilege make it impossible for whites to completely know, let alone eradicate, the extent to which racism and privilege shape who we are and how we think.[8]

McIntosh likens white privilege to an invisible knapsack with maps, compass, and so on, that help whites more easily navigate the world. Alison Bailey refers to a model of a computer with already-established default settings, and Beverly Tatum uses the illustration of an automatic sidewalk.[9] Each of these perspectives has influenced my own.

I have sometimes described white privilege as likened to a magic coin possessed only by a specific group within a society in which automatic doors are a central component. In this society, all important structures have been designed with automatic doors. The coin activates the doors so they open automatically when the coin is close to the door. Those with the coin see and understand reality as one in which doors open when one gets close enough. Sometimes the doors open more quickly or more slowly than they have in the past; infrequently the doors get stuck, but eventually they open for those with the coin.

Those without a coin walk among the same structures, but the doors don't open automatically. Due to the fact that they were not created for manual opening, the doors are very heavy and hard to pull open. Manual opening usually requires two hands, so those without the coin need to put down whatever they are carrying to open the door. Once the door is open, the person without the coin must prop the door with one leg, retrieve the items she was carrying, and walk through the door before it shuts.

Those with the coin have little to no idea of what life without the coin is like. They wonder about and scorn those without the coins: "What is wrong with them? They are taking *forever* to get here. Can't they just walk on pace?" At school, students learn about the structures—they are so well designed and effective—the best in the world. They are for everyone; they are clearly marked with "welcome" signs. If a person works hard to walk well, the doors open. If a person walks off path or doesn't pay attention, the doors won't open.

Coinholders recognize the trouble some have with the doors, so special programs are established for those who have to open the doors on their own. (There was a time when they were not allowed through the doors, but that is in the past. Now they are very welcome, but they have trouble with the doors.) As a sign of "progress," society has established strength-building programs, lessons in fast walking, and classes that teach door-opening skills to help those without the coins get to where those with the coins are. If they do enough training, then people without coins will get through the doors just like those with coins do. They reflect on their situation, saying, "I must have a natural gift for walking between the structures because I don't need so much walking or strength training. It does come in handy sometimes when the doors are stuck, though. But mainly I just walk through."

The system was built for and by those with the coins, and despite the problems some have with the doors, those with the coins don't really think there is a need to change the system. They walk through the doors and are rewarded for their progress. They pay taxes that maintain the system. Each time those with the coin walk through doors with ease, the notion that others are slow and need training is reinforced. As with any society, resources and opportunities are limited. So those who arrive first get the rewards. They are "simply at the right place at right time." Others must settle for what is left or go without. All participants can get through the doors, so it is argued that all have an equal opportunity to receive rewards.

A by-product of living with a coin is that its constant use results in the development of blinders on coinholders. They are so caught in reciprocity between themselves and the system that works with them that they cannot see the wider world around them. They do not see the system as a human construct; to them, it is reality as such, something existing independently of human action, and the coin becomes almost invisible to them. Additionally, they are blind to the perspectives of those without the coin. They view those without the coins as needing help or as lazy. ("Just take the classes already!") Some coinholders do see the system for what it is, but they haven't changed it.

ANSWERING THE QUESTION: HOW DOES IT FEEL TO BE A WHITE PROBLEM?

So, how does it feel to be a white problem? I will explore three answers: (1) It feels fine. (2) It feels embarrassing, painful, frustrating, daunting. It feels like I have lots of work to do. (3) It feels OK.

Answer 1: It Feels Fine.
Of course, some white problems know they are white problems, and if asked how it feels, they would say, "It feels fine!" They know what the "PC police" think, and they don't care. They are explicitly racist. They tell racist jokes and make racist comments and intentionally block progress on racial equality because they think it's wrong. Some are members of organizations such as the KKK. Many others are subtler about their views. They say they are "just

joking" if someone calls them on it, but that's just to "keep people off their backs." Some present arguments in support of their views that whites are superior. Some share their position publicly; others do so out of view of the public, with their friends, family, or acquaintances they believe align with them. They are white problems, and it feels fine. I won't spend much time on this group.

While there is much that should be said about and to this group, their response to this particular question is simple (in more ways than one) and it is widely accepted that such are a white problem. They are not, however, the only whites who present a problem, and these others are the ones who are of interest within the context of this discussion.

Because of the pervasiveness of white ignorance and understandings of racism that are limited to such overt or extreme forms of racism, it's not uncommon for other white people to be unaware of the fact that they are a white problem, too. From their flawed perspective, if one is not actively thinking racist thoughts or (knowingly) engaging in racist acts, then one is clearly not a racist. This lack of knowledge and the accompanying assumption that one actually does know what one does not know serve to insulate many whites from an awareness of their role in the perpetuation and maintenance of systems of white privilege and racism.[10] They see themselves as knowledgeable about race and racism, as nonracists, and as Applebaum notes, as morally good white people.[11] These good whites are white problems who are oblivious to the fact of being a problem. They don't know themselves (as white problems). Unfortunately, ignorance precludes many "good hearted" whites from effective antiracist work. Such ignorance also ensures that the white person "feels fine" about being a white problem. In this case, she feels fine because she *is unaware of* the fact that she is a white problem. Ignorance is bliss.

I sometimes refer to the combination of white privilege and white ignorance as the "Look Here, Not There Problem" of how whites usually educate and are usually educated about race, and therefore how whites often approach discussions of racism. When learning about race and racism, white lessons often highlight the *past* oppression of blacks, slavery, and the civil rights movement; explicitly or implicitly, they point to progress already made and reinforce the idea that racists and racism are things of the past and take (very) blatant forms. In addition, many discussions about race and racism explicitly focus on only one side of the issue—racism, oppression, people of color (mainly black people), but not the other side—white privilege, current racism, and covert, systemic, and institutional racism. By avoiding more contemporary and covert forms of racism, while highlighting examples of progress and overt forms of racism, the general message we perpetuate (and seek) is that "we have taken care of the problem of racism." In addition, as we perpetuate the myth of the American Dream—anyone can succeed, move from "rags to riches," if she just works hard enough—and, as McIntosh notes, emphasize that the United States operates on a fair meritocracy, we maintain and perpetuate limited, flawed, and ultimately damaging "knowledge" about contemporary racism, systems of privilege, power, and oppression.

In some cases in which a deeper level of awareness about whiteness and racism becomes a possibility, some white problems still feel fine about being white problems. They may have heard or learned about white privilege, but they don't buy it. In their view, everyone has difficulties, and some people of color have more privileges than they do. They themselves don't see color, they experience ours as a post-racial society, and they are sorry about or impatient with the fact that others cannot just move on and live in the present. In their opinion some extreme forms of racism may exist in pockets, but the problem is minimal. *That* racism, which they are not a part of, is the problem. They—those white problems who have learned about but don't believe in white privilege—are also white problems, but they don't know it. They feel fine.

Because of the pervasive nature of white privilege and the fact that living with and in it is part of the "invisible norm" of white people's lives, even those who understand and accept that they experience and are complicit in systemic white privilege, white ignorance, and racism can slip in and out of awareness of it and feel fine in those moments. As McIntosh notes in "White Privilege and Male Privilege, "when discussing the list of white privileges she experienced:

> I repeatedly forgot each of the realizations on this list until I wrote it down. For me white privilege has turned out to be an elusive and fugitive subject. The pressure to avoid it is great, for in facing it I must give up the myth of meritocracy. If these things are true, this is not such a free country; one's life is not what one makes it; many doors open for certain people through no virtues of their own.[12]

Certainly this "repeated forgetting" is not unique to McIntosh. Keeping white privilege and the fact of one's being a "white problem" at the forefront of one's mind requires active practice, intentionality. Add to this the fact that we are not able to see the multiple ways racist biases and assumptions slip into our understandings of, and actions in, the world, it is not unusual to work against, slip back into, and completely miss the ways we ourselves are white problems. At these times, even the "best" antiracists are problems, and it feels fine.

Turning to my own experience, I have seen all of this play out in my own life, despite being on some level aware of issues of race and ethnicity, class, and gender from a fairly early age. Growing up and through my college years I was fortunate enough to experience what might now be termed "diversity experiences" that positioned me for growth and learning across differences in age, ability, class, national origin, race, and ethnicity. Hanging out, playing, becoming friends with people who came from social groups that were different than my own positioned me to notice fears, inequities, hierarchies, and privileges based on class, race, gender, ethnicity, among others—although I did not have the language or level of understanding to name it or discuss it very well. I pretty much knew every racial slur in middle school, so I'm not reporting that I lived in a world of racial harmony. I lived in a world where race and other differences were "out there" to be seen, known, learned about (for good or bad). Simply spending time in activities of common interest with or going about day-to-day activities among people who were different than me in significant ways helped me to develop a slight base in what I would now call cultural competency and awareness. [13]

I provide this context not to say that I was special, or that I thought these experiences made me immune to racism, classism, sexism, homophobia, and so on. (I did, however, think that the fact that I did not and would not use racial slurs or engage in other overt acts of racism [after all, what other forms were there?] showed that I was not racist.) Rather I share this information to say that I felt comfortable with and was aware of gaining insights from various interactions and friendships across difference. This was mainly through the "osmosis" of hanging out; there was nothing intentional in it. As I got older and went to college, I learned a bit about white ignorance, race, and class privilege, inside and outside of the classroom. These experiences and my reflections on them did not prevent me from being a white problem.

* * *

The following examples illustrate my own "feeling fine" as a white problem: One of the first times I went to a predominately black party in college, I was surprised to notice that I felt uncomfortable even though I was invited by and went with two black friends, and I knew I would know at least some of the other students at the party. I had not in the past been uncomfortable if I was the only white person sitting with black students in the student union (a larger white context—which I didn't reflect on at that moment), so I was surprised by how uneasy I felt. I am slightly shy around strangers, but I knew this feeling of unease was different. I was wondering if the people throwing the party—who I didn't know—would wonder why I was there, at *their* party. I was wondering whether I was welcome despite the fact that my friends invited me. For one of the first times, I was walking in a world that was not completely mine. I felt like an outsider, and I didn't know what to do with that. In my few moments of feeling like an outsider, I explicitly wondered about the experience of the two friends I came with: Did *they* ever feel this way when they went out to the bars with me in the predominately white town that our predominately white college existed in? I was heading toward empathy, but I quickly concluded that they did not feel the discomfort I felt because they were used to it. I was very confident about that conclusion. I moved on, confident that my experience was more uncomfortable than theirs. I was not only an expert on my experience, but also on theirs—it did not occur to me to ask them how it felt.[14] *How does it feel to be a white problem? It feels fine.*

Another time, I was having a conversation with a black friend when the topic of racist stereotypes arose. During the conversation he asked if I knew of this stereotype or that stereotype. I had never heard of them, and I said so. I remember thinking somewhat proudly that my lack of knowledge of several stereotypes served as proof that I was not racist. *How does it feel to be a white problem? It feels fine.*

Even after having developed a more critical consciousness, I can still slip into habits I know (but forget in the moment) are reflective of white privilege. I move into a new, predominately white community and feel fairly comfortable, despite the fact that I had reservations about living in such a homogeneous community. I find myself saying the community was so welcoming (to whom?) and felt so comfortable (to whom?). *It feels fine.*

I may find myself in a conversation in which a colleague of color tells me about an encounter with a white colleague. Unthinkingly, reflexively—and thankfully infrequently—I jump to wanting to smooth things over. "Maybe she didn't mean it that way," I start off, *feeling fine* and I engage in micro-invalidation. On a good day, I stop myself at that point.

In these examples in different ways, I was a white problem, and I felt fine until I recognized what I was and was doing. When I do recognize such behaviors for what they are, I move to a different, improved response to the question.

Answer 2: It Feels Embarrassing, Painful, Daunting . . . It Feels Like I Have Lots of Work to Do
The move from "it feels fine" to "it feels embarrassing, painful, daunting, etc.," requires raising of one's critical consciousness. For me, the development of my critical consciousness and my commitment to being and becoming an antiracist came through the combination of a number of factors, including: (1) lived experience; (2) academic experiences that provided theoretical frameworks for understanding that lived experience; (3) pointed, intentional self-reflection; (4) listening; and (5) honest conversations with friends and colleagues. This consciousness-raising and development was and continues to be an ongoing, recursive, nonlinear process. While I saw, thought about, or experienced some inequities related to race, class, and gender growing up, I feel fortunate that the initial sharpening of my critical consciousness began early in my college years—given that young adulthood

is often a time for seriously considering who one is and who one wants to be. In many important respects, the raising of my critical consciousness in relation to gender and race issues prompted me to think seriously about who I was and what I stood for.

My lived experienced helped me to accept—as well as motivated me to seek—conceptual and theoretical understandings of race, racism, privilege, and so on. Theory gave me the words to describe, as well as the framework for understanding, some of what I noticed, and it helped me to notice much more. In college I was very aware of the fact that I was gaining insights on race from various perspectives. As a white woman who spent time with friends who were white and friends who were black, I felt (and was) at times hyperaware of race. At times I found myself faced with surprising questions and comments about black people from white friends or acquaintances. "Is that girl black?" "What do you think of . . .?" "Is it true that . . .?" I did not anticipate or know where the questions were coming from.

At times I felt judgment in the questions, and I started to seriously wonder what was wrong with some white people. Why don't they just pay attention? I thought that they would know a lot more if they just observed and listened. I began to distance myself from "those white people" who were so clueless. I did not think I was an expert on race, but I believed I knew more than they did, and I definitely did not think I was racist.

Motivated in part by experience but also by the sheer luck of having some professors and classes that addressed issues of race (and gender), I began to pay more attention to and sought to learn more about race and racism. But I didn't interrogate myself.

Over time, pieces started to fit together. Academic readings helped me to reframe, validate, and/or more deeply understand some lived experiences. Lived experiences provided me with examples that helped me to accept and seek out understandings of race, racism, privilege, and so on. Much of the time this new kind of engagement was energizing; I was learning about something that mattered to me, that helped me to make sense of the world, and that opened my mind. Somewhere along the line I read or heard an argument that suggested that it makes sense to assume that anyone raised in a racist, sexist, homophobic culture would be racist, sexist, and homophobic themselves. That made sense to me.

An initial connection of this theory to myself occurred in relation to gender. Through learning about feminism, I saw how I had internalized numerous sexist messages and was unwittingly complicit in systemic sexism. This was a surprising and somewhat painful lesson to learn but not one that was hard to accept. So applying the same line of thinking to racism and other "isms" made perfectly *logical* sense to me. I could think of concrete ways I had been influenced by and perpetuated sexism, so I assumed that would also be the case with racism. I did not, however, dig deeper to identify exactly how I had done that, though. My acceptance of this was rational and theoretical. It seemed like a good idea to progress *as if* I am racist, sexist, homophobic, classist, ableist, and so on.

Later, learning about white privilege, I connected the examples and concepts in McIntosh's "White Privilege and Male Privilege" to what I had seen or experienced in the world. I had never seen "nude" pantyhose or crayons that weren't focused on whiteness; I had difficulty trying to buy a card for a friend of color who had a new baby because all the babies on the cards were white. My history classes in grade school and high school focused on white people, except perhaps the special topics that were addressed in the shaded blue boxes. As I read I thought, "Yes, this notion of white privilege makes sense. I see it." I remember trying to go through as many examples as I could think of and identify something from my life that connected.

McIntosh lists forty-six different privileges she experienced. In places on that list, I found myself.

- I can if I wish arrange to be in the company of people of my race most of the time. (#1)
- I can avoid spending time with people whom I was trained to mistrust and who have learned to mistrust my kind or me. (#2)
- I can arrange to protect my children most of the time from people who might not like them. (#14)
- I do not have to educate my children to be aware of systemic racism for their own daily physical protection. (#15)

Thinking about these examples in addition to McIntosh's qualification, "I now think that we need a more finely differentiated taxonomy of privilege, for some of these varieties are only what one would want for everyone in a just society, and others give license to be ignorant, oblivious, arrogant and destructive,"[15] prompted me to flash back to experiences with my friends. *I* had been oblivious/arrogant to assume that I knew whether and to what extent my black friends felt comfortable at predominately white bars at a predominately white college based on my own experiences. What kind of friend was I? I thought I had been a person who considered my friends' feelings and experiences and was fairly well aware of race and racial issues. But clearly I was wrong about myself. I thought I was more aware than I actually was.[16] In terms of my lack of knowledge of racist stereotypes, I was *not* "not racist" because I lacked that knowledge; that ignorance simply demonstrated my white privilege.

When these revelations occurred, I was by myself thinking about McIntosh's work, and I felt horrible. I was embarrassed and ashamed. My rational, theoretical acceptance that I was (likely) a racist was transformed. I was clearly a white problem. *It felt embarrassing, painful, daunting. It felt like I had a lot of work to do.*

I had never conveyed my assumptions about how my friends felt, nor had I discussed my positive assessment of my lack of knowledge of racist stereotypes to my friends, so my shame and embarrassment was not related to a need to save myself via retraction. I was weighted down by the realization that I was not the person I thought I was. I wondered what else I might have thought or done in ignorance.

The fact that the friendships had continued did not mitigate the feeling—I did not assume that, because the friendships continued, everything was fine, so I didn't have to worry about it. While I thought about bringing up the issue and apologizing, I did not do that. I wasn't sure what my real motivations were. Would I be doing this to prove just how aware I am now, and somehow gain more favor in my friends' eyes? That seemed wrong. Would I be doing this to position my friends to say, "Don't worry; it was nothing," and therefore absolve me, make it right for me? That seemed wrong. Would I be doing this assuming that they didn't already know I was not as aware of race and racism as I thought I was? That would be a bad assumption. In addition, I was ashamed and probably a bit of a coward.

I had had this happen before—when through developing a feminist critical consciousness, I recognized that some of my actions that I thought were fun or empowering actually contributed to my own objectification. Reading Herbert Marcuse's *One Dimensional Man* for class led me to realize just how much I *didn't* know. Philosophy—theoretical exploration—had "done this to me" before, and I had grown from it. Wallowing in embarrassment accomplished nothing; using the new insights could be helpful.

Years later when I read Alison Bailey's "Despising an Identity They Taught Me to Claim" her assessment of white peoples' responses to their recognition of white privileges resonated with me. She describes two approaches many of us have seen: "reinventing oneself as black—'I feel like a black person inside'"[17] and "detours into one's own ethnicity"—'I'm Irish, my people have suffered too,'[18] noting that they trivialize the experience of those who are oppressed[19] or are "tied to selfishness and escapism."[20] These approaches to the painful experience of coming to know one's own white ignorance and complicity in the interconnected systems of privilege and oppression are, at bottom, unproductively "all about me."

I would like to say that my decision to "do" something with the shame or embarrassment associated with seeing myself more clearly came from a desire to avoid selfishness, but I cannot say that for certain. Mainly, being stuck in, and struck by, discomfort and ungroundedness positioned me to ask, "What now?" I could not pretend to not know what I now knew, and I could not assume that I knew as much as I had thought I knew about race, racism, privilege, or my own self.

To quote one of my students after she had grappled with a semester's worth of philosophical discussion, including discussion of race and whiteness, "I was slapped in the face with a hard dose of wisdom." The sting of wisdom can be powerful. On some level, I realized that all I could do was to use the sting as motivation to learn more and to practice critical awareness in daily life.

So returning to that example, when I begin to tell a colleague in response to his concern, "maybe she didn't mean to . . ." *if I'm paying attention* I catch myself—I know and feel it. *It feels awkward, embarrassing, like I have more work to do.* I apologize, and then move to a better response, one that does not invalidate.

Answer 3: It feels OK.

While the shame, embarrassment, or discomfort accompanying awareness of being a white problem is daunting and can "freeze a person" in her tracks, shaking her sense of self, it can also serve as an impetus for attentiveness, growth, and a clearer (although not perfectly clear) sense of self. As we know from Plato's *Apology*, Socrates spent much of his time engaging with self-proclaimed experts in an attempt to persuade them to pay attention to the kind of people they were. His interlocutors were often left in a state of discomfort, doubt, confusion, or even anger. They learned that they did not know what they thought they did. This uncomfortable state might motivate a person to retreat (*Euthyphro*), giving up on the discussion altogether; however, it could also prompt deeper and more complete examination that might allow for a clearer understanding. In the latter case, the shame or discomfort associated with recognizing that one does not know what she thought she knew is actually valuable. Given this, at his trial, Socrates argued that the discomfort he caused in others was invaluable:

> [I] am a sort of gadfly, given to the state by the God; and the state is like a great and noble steed who is tardy in his motions owing to his very size, and requires to be stirred into life. I am that gadfly which . . . all day long and in all places [is] always fastening upon you, arousing and persuading and reproaching you. . . . I dare say that you may feel irritated at being suddenly awakened when you are caught napping; and you may think that if you were to strike me dead, . . . then you would sleep on for the remainder of your lives. [21]

We could liken the experiences of coming face-to-face, so to speak, with our own complicity in the intertwining systems of racism and privilege to being painfully awakened by a stinging bug when we were napping. At these times, we face the choices of (1) waking up and trying to stay awake, (2) killing off the pest and going back to sleep, or (3) focusing on how the pain of the bite feels to us and how tired we are because the pest woke us up. This, of course, is the choice among (1) facing the fact that I am a white problem who is engaged in antiracist work and grappling with how to negotiate that, (2) opting out and returning to the obliviousness of white ignorance, or (3) wallowing in white guilt and shame.

While the pain of the moment may invite us to pursue the third option, especially when the pain is too severe to allow one to go back to sleep, in the end, this is not a productive response: one remains inactive and self-centered. It is necessary, then, to get beyond the pain and discomfort and take either corrective or preventative measures. But, what does that look like? How does one make a start?

When dealing with the sudden realization of my own hidden racism, I recognized that I could do nothing about the past, but I could use this new level of awareness and the discomfort that accompanied it for the future. At this point, recognizing oneself as a white problem presents an opportunity (a) to "get better at" antiracist work, (b) to be a more responsible antiracist, or (c) to be more attentive to the ways we might be deceived about ourselves. If I more deeply understand and accept the assumption that all whites are racists, I can begin to use it, not as something I think of every moment of the day, but as a "self check": what am I missing? What do I think I know? Am I listening, paying attention? How else can I learn?

This does not, however, carry with it the idyllic assumption that with more effort one will completely rid oneself of one's racism or complicity in the pervasive system of whiteness—privilege, power, ignorance—and be/ become the exceptional white person who is not racist. That is impossible.

A recent reading of George Yancy's, *Look, a White!* provided a powerful framework for more deeply understanding this impossibility—if that even makes sense. His discussion of "the opaque white racist self" addresses this impossibility:

> The white self that attempts to "ascertain such limits" [of one's own racism] has already arrived too late [here he cites Judith Butler] to determine the complex and insidious ways in which white racism has become embedded within her white embodied self. It is not that there is no transparency at all, that one is incapable of identifying various aspects of one's racist/nonracist white self. Rather, the reality of the sheer depth of white racialization is far too opaque.[22]

I cannot get at how deeply systemic white racism, privilege, and ignorance are ingrained in me. I can, however, strive to be "consistently conscious"[23] in an attempt to not live and behave in a "racially reckless" manner. Can I guarantee that I will evolve into a nonracist self? No. Can I guarantee that I will always catch myself when I enact what Bailey refers to as "whitely scripts"?[24] No.

My life-long lessons of what it means to be a "good white woman" are ingrained. The earlier example of micro-invalidation illustrates that I learned well the lessons of whiteness—what we whites refer to as "politeness," "morality"; keeping the "peace," "smoothing things over," and so forth. These influences are powerful and I must remain attentive to how they can work to silence and diminish.

The impossibility of "getting to the bottom" of one's racism may also induce one to stop trying, to return to self-pity, or to turn one's attention elsewhere entirely, but such responses fail to appreciate what's at stake and fail to take advantage of the progress that can be made. This positions us to recognize more fully our complicity in the intertwined systems of privilege and racism and "deal with" or learn to live with the discomfort. This white problem becomes comfortable enough with her discomfort that it does not freeze her in her tracks, but not so comfortable that it becomes part of the unnoticed background of her world. She sees the discomfort as valuable in limiting—as much as possible—self-deception as she continues to strive to live as an antiracist. The discomfort can help keep a person honest/grounded as they engage in antiracist work.

The realization itself positions one to take responsibility to learn more about racism and whiteness—accepting the wisdom and experience of others but not passively waiting for others to impart wisdom or to teach her. For example, as illustrated in this discussion, I have found a number of contributors to be extremely valuable in better understanding how to talk about, teach, and—importantly—self-reflect on being a white problem. [25] For example Applebaum's discussions of white complicity, evasive strategies, and the importance of listening and vulnerability as strategies of engagement; McIntosh's, Bailey's (and others') discussions of white privilege, [26] and Yancy's discussion of the opacity of whiteness. Exploration of epistemologies of ignorance was extremely helpful in illuminating aspects of inequities that I had not considered. Additionally, discussions of ally work also helped to illustrate the way an antiracist [27] might engage in her work.

In "Interrupting the Cycle of Oppression," Andrea Ayvazian discusses what it means to be an ally, [28] noting that there is "no such thing as a perfect ally. Perfection is not our goal. . . . When I asked my colleague Kenneth Jones what stood out for him as the most important characteristic of a strong ally, he said simply: 'being consistently conscious.' He didn't say 'never stumbling,' or 'never making mistakes.' He said, 'being consistently conscious.'" She continues, "These issues are too complex, too painful, and too pervasive for us to achieve a state of clarity and closure once and for all. The best we can hope for is to strive each day to be our strongest and clearest selves." [29]

While these passages address the inevitability of getting it wrong, at times—including getting ourselves wrong—they don't provide excuses and they don't allow for recklessness. Rather they stress that careful attentiveness is essential for honestly grappling and living with awareness of being an ally, a white problem who is antiracist.

At this point, I understand that I'm a problem; I know that I need to remain aware of and vigilant about my ignorance and blind spots. As much as I'm striving to learn through lived experience, study, dialogue, and reflection, I won't free myself from being a white problem. I accept and continue to work on my limitations. I'm committed to trying to keep the pesky gadfly around despite the discomfort it brings, because I know it helps me see what I haven't before—or at minimum, it helps me remember that I am not seeing clearly. This strategy can stop me from being reckless, or careless; it won't guarantee perfection, but it should not stop me from action or cause me to give up.

I've become "OK with" an awareness of the complicated and messiness of these contradictory aspects of who and what I am. I am not complacent. I accept discomfort as part of the work of a white problem antiracist. It does not prompt me to opt out or to be reckless. Being "OK" is not a fantastic state to be in, it would *feel* better to "feel fine," but it would not *be* better to settle back into that state of ignorance. Being "OK" leaves me wounded and looking less pretty than I did when I "felt fine," but it also enables me to pick myself up and struggle forward, even if, at times, I am unsure of my bearings. One must seek a state of mind that allows one to get beyond "feeling fine" or "feeling bad about oneself," and so allows one to carry on, flaws and all. This is what I call "being OK" with being a white problem.

The movement from "I feel fine" to "being OK" can certainly be seen as a developmental process, but it is not a neat, linear process. It is messy. Because of the pervasiveness and impenetrability of white privilege and white ignorance, I will fall back into "I feel fine" and be jarred awake again into "I feel uncomfortable," but I hope my attentiveness to the possibilities for this will limit the time spent wallowing in the shame or discomfort that accompanies my awareness of returning to "I feel fine" and will position me to feel and consider the discomfort in the following ways: What and how can I learn from this? Where do I need to continue my own awareness work? Now, how do I get back on track in my antiracist work?

Given the pervasiveness of white ignorance, I cannot avoid slipping "back" into "it feels fine" and feeling the subsequent shame, but I can work to reduce the number of slippages and accept my limitations and try to move forward with knowledge of them. I think that's the best I can do.

HOW'S IT FEEL TO BE A WHITE PROBLEM?

It does not feel great. It does not feel fine. It does not feel so uncomfortable that I am stuck and wallowing in shame or guilt. I've accepted and expect a level of discomfort.

It feels OK . . . then it feels fine . . . then it feels embarrassing . . . then it feels OK again . . .

NOTES

1. W. E. B. Du Bois, *The Souls of Black Folk*. New York: Cosmo Classics, 2007, 1.

2. W. E. B. Du Bois, *The Souls of Black Folk*. New York: Cosmo Classics, 2007.

3. See Barbara Applebaum, White Ignorance and Denials of Complicity. *The Center Must Not Hold: White Women Philosophers on the Whiteness of Philosophy*. Ed. George Yancy (New York: Lexington Books, 2011), for a more extensive and substantive discussion of distancing strategies, 10–11.

4. This reference to unproductive responses brings to mind Alison Bailey's "Despising an Identity they Taught Me to Claim" (*Whiteness: Feminist Political Reflections*. Ed. Chris Cuomo and Kim T. Hall. NY: Roman & Littlefield, 1999: 85–104) where she discusses "detours" from white privilege that serve to center the focus on oneself and "fail as strategies for social justice"(93).

5. Peggy McIntosh, "White Privilege and Male Privilege: A Personal Account of Coming to See Correspondences through Work in Women's Studies." *Oppression, Privilege, and Resistance: Theoretical Perspectives on Racism, Sexism, and Heterosexism*. Ed. Lisa Heldke and Peg O'Connor. Boston: McGraw Hill, 2004, 322–23.

6. McIntosh "White Privilege," 319, 322; Applebaum "White Ignorance," 4–5.

7. McIntosh "White Privilege," 323.

8. In *Look a White!* Yancy provides a much more in-depth discussion and refers to this as "the opaque white racist self" (168).

9. Beverly D. Tatum, *Why Are All The Black Kids Sitting Together in the Cafeteria? And Other Conversations About Race*. New York: Basic Books, 1997.

10. Applebaum "White Ignorance," 6.

11. Barbara Applebaum, Barbara. *Being White, Being Good: White Complicity, White Moral Responsibility, and Social Justice Pedagogy*. Lanham, MD: Lexington Books, 2011, chapter 1.

12. McIntosh "White Privilege," 322.

13. This does not mean that I was not a racist "because I had black friends" or friends of other races. The superficiality of that view was apparent to me because I knew plenty of people who were clearly racists (and made little effort to hide that fact) and who spent time among the very same people that I did. "Having black friends" can provide insight, and may, for some, be a start towards an anti-racist stance, but, in and of itself, it proves little or nothing.

14. This was the case despite the fact that many times while walking across campus I had thought about how uncomfortable it might be for black students because they were such a small percentage of the whole student body.

15. McIntosh "White Privilege," 322–23.

16. Much later, as I interrogated my feelings of discomfort, I had to conclude that some—all?—of that discomfort stemmed from racist messages I had unknowingly internalized.

17. Alison Bailey, Despising an Identity They Taught Me to Claim, In Chris Cuomo and Kim T. Hall (Eds.) *Whiteness: Feminist Political Reflections* (NY: Roman & Littlefield, 1999), p. 90.

18. Bailey, Despising an Identity They Taught Me to Claim, 91.

19. Bailey, Despising an Identity They Taught Me to Claim, 90.

20. Bailey, Despising an Identity They Taught Me to Claim, 92.

21. Plato. The Apology. Benjamin Jowett, trans. http://classics.mit.edu/Plato/apology.html. Retrieved November 4, 2012.

22. George Yancy, *Look, A White!* Philadelphia: Temple University Press, 2012, p. 168.

23. See Andrea Avyazian, Interrupting the Cycle of Oppression: The Role of Allies as Agents of Change. In Paula Pothenberg (Ed.) *Race, Class, and Gender in the United States: An Integrated Study, 5th ed.* Worth Publishers, 61.

24. Bailey, Despising an Identity They Taught Me to Claim, 96.

25. However, I have never used the terminology "white problem" before.

26. Alison Bailey, Privilege: Expanding on Marilyn Frye's "Oppression." *Oppression, Privilege, and Resistance: Theoretical Perspectives on Racism, Sexism, and Heterosexism.* Ed. Lisa Heldke and Peg O'Connor. Boston: McGraw Hill, 2004. 301–16.

27. Or " antiracist racist" as Yancy suggests in *Look, A White!*, 175.

28. An ally is a member of a privileged group who attempts to use her privilege to undermine the system of privilege she benefits from. See Andrea Avyazian, Interrupting the Cycle of Oppression: The Role of Allies as Agents of Change. In Paula Pothenberg (Ed.) *Race, Class, and Gender in the United States: An Integrated Study, 5th ed.* Worth Publishers, 609.

29. Avyazian, Interrupting the Cycle of Oppression, 615.

Chapter Ten

Keeping the Strange Unfamiliar

The Racial Privilege of Dismantling Whiteness

Nancy McHugh

And yet, being a problem is a strange experience.—W. E. B. Du Bois [1]

Early in *The Souls of Black Folk*, W. E. B. Du Bois articulates this epistemically embodied experience of what it is like to be a "problem." For Du Bois, there is a bit of irony, because, as he points out, except as an infant and when in Europe, he has had few moments in which he has "never been anything else" but a problem. [2] Even though this experience is the norm for Du Bois and other African Americans, it is still a norm that never becomes comfortable. There is always an epistemic and embodied disjunct between what Du Bois knows his self to be and how whites see him. The irony goes even deeper because even with a cursory reading of these first few pages of *Souls* it becomes obvious that Du Bois is not really the "problem"; his white questioner is. Yet the white questioner never experiences the cognitive and visceral disorientation of being a problem. His questioner's entrenched privilege and ability to remain ignorant when he thinks he is acting "compassionately" or "curiously" precludes him from having the "strange experience" of being a problem. [3]

Though Du Bois's supposedly sympathetic white questioner never experiences himself as a problem, some whites do have this strange experience of what it is like to be a problem. For many of us it comes along with a developing awareness of ourselves as raced and of ourselves as having privilege in virtue of being white. [4] It also comes through with the awareness that (like Du Bois's questioner) even though many whites like to believe that we are not racist, we in fact are. I frame this chapter through three teaching moments, painting a picture of my struggle with working to understand, articulate, and embody what it means to be a problem and the challenges that I have had in having my students join me in this struggle. I hope to articulate that part of the process of coming to terms with one's white privilege and racism is recognizing that as a white woman in a racist culture that I am always going to be a problem and that being troubled by this, while at the same time working to create change, is a valuable epistemic and practical location.

FRAME #1: GETTING AT ME FROM THE INSIDE-OUT

In the spring of 2010, I attended an Inside-Out Prison Exchange Training Institute at the University of Michigan Dearborn and Ryan Correction Facility in Detroit, Michigan. I first learned of the Inside-Out Program when I was in a visiting position in 1998 at Temple University where Lori Pompa founded the program. Twelve years later, I decided that I was interested in working in an academic setting with traditional college students alongside youth that are detained. An Inside-Out classroom experience ideally consists of fifteen "inside students," those that are detained and usually adults, and fifteen "outside students," students enrolled in college and living on the "outs." My plan was to teach a course called "The Art of Living Ethically" at the Clark County Juvenile Detention Center in Springfield, Ohio. The training consisted of sixty hours of training with about thirty-five hours in Ryan Correctional Facility. I was trained by a group of men that called themselves the Theory Group. The training was a once-in-a-lifetime learning experience that I feel very privileged to have had. The men in this group were excited that I planned to work with youth that were detained. The members of the Theory Group repeatedly told me that if they had this kind of opportunity when they were teens that maybe their lives would be different. I left the training feeling excited and inspired to be teaching in an environment designed to feel like a college classroom but in such an utterly different setting.

Five months later, we are six weeks in to our Art of Living Ethically course. All of the students are sitting in a circle in Clark County Juvenile Detention Center's gym. There are fourteen "outside" students, Wittenberg University College students, and twelve "inside" student, youth that are detained in the detention center. One of the readings for this week was the first chapter of *The Souls of Black Folk*, "Of Our Spiritual Strivings." Most of the students, inside and outside, have never read Du Bois. I try to prepare them for him by working up to Du Bois and to the discussion of race through a series of readings that included Peggy McIntosh's "Unpacking the White Knapsack of Privilege,"[5] poetry by A. Van Jordan,[6] and by reading something about Du Bois's life.[7] After a discussion of the terminology in the text, such as "veil" and "second-sight," I turned to the question that Du Bois broaches on the first page of "Of Our Spiritual Strivings." The question is: "How does it feel to be a problem?"[8] The students focused on the question readily with both inside and outside students bouncing ideas off of each other and getting at the heart of what Du Bois was trying to articulate. They talked about race and class issues rather comfortably, then moved to discuss how people say one thing but really mean another when it comes to race and class.[9] As the discussion slowed down, I changed the question up. I asked the class what does it feel like for *You* to be a problem. As Du Bois points out, this is the question that was really being asked of him.

Obviously, this was a very different question for the inside students than it is for the outside students. College students can certainly be a "problem," but the inside students, the youth that are detained, for much of their lives, like Du Bois, have been considered to be *the problem*, representing the failure of U.S. education and the "nuclear family," a blight on their communities, users of valuable taxpayer money and time, and, even worse, future "criminals." In other words, like Du Bois, these youth represent what we don't want to see, what we want to obscure, whose lives in many ways say more about our failures as a society than it does about them. The pause after this question is painful. All teachers know this feeling in a classroom, when you go from the discussion that gets everyone really excited to the question that shuts everything down. I decided to let us stay in that painful moment, hoping that the tension would lead to something fruitful. One inside student raised his hand and said, "I don't want to talk about this question. I don't want to have to repeat the obvious, that everyone sees us as the problem. Du Bois is dead, but I live with this, dreading this question every day."

At that moment I went cold inside. I realized that I was the problem. After all, how could I naively go in and ask a question in an academic framework and assume that it could be all academic, without emotion, without stirring things up, and without putting people in a situation in which they had to talk about themselves in a way that doesn't make them feel good? Just like Du Bois was put in a situation that was unfair to him and reified the racist asymmetry that he experienced every day, I, too, did the same thing to these students. I took them from the space where they were just students back to the space where they were incarcerated youth. In Du Bois's situation, he wasn't really the problem, the white questioner was. Similarly, the students in the classroom, inside or outside, were not "a problem," I was. I was "a problem" not only because I thought this question was a reasonable one to pose in this setting but because I failed to realize, as a *white* professor, the power I had in this situation to ask the question. My students, inside or outside, would never have posed that question to me. They would never have been that disrespectful, because they, especially the inside students, have a sense of what is at stake in the response to the question. Yet, I remained ignorant of the nuances in this setting vis-à-vis that question.

The chill that went through me was one that I had felt before when I became acutely aware that I was a problem in this Du Boisian sense. As he said, "being a problem is a strange experience"; it is one that once you have the experience is hard to shake.[10] Frequently, these moments do come up in the classroom when I, as a *white* professor, teach texts that engage race, especially texts that don't try to soften the blow of what it means to have racial privilege.[11] This is especially the case given that I teach at a predominantly white institution with students that have been habituated or, to use Shannon Sullivan's words, "seduced" into whiteness such that they don't see their own privilege.[12] Yet, these moments can highlight one of the things that I love most about teaching philosophy—the moments when I am forced to confront myself at the same time that I am asking students to do the same thing.[13] These rare moments of symmetry in the classroom in which we all are uncomfortable, on edge and have the opportunity to be, as George Yancy argues, "ambushed" by our whiteness.[14]

FRAME #2: THE WORDS I CAN NEVER TAKE BACK: CONFESSIONS OF AN ANTI-RACIST RACIST[15]

During the fall of 2010 I was teaching an upper-division undergraduate philosophy course called "Knowing Bodies." I describe the course as a study in the epistemology of the body. The class consisted of all philosophy majors, many of whom I knew very well. One student was black, and the remaining students were white. One of the early texts that we read was George Yancy's *Black Bodies, White Gazes,*[16] and Dr. Yancy was coming to our campus as part of our department colloquia. All of the students had readily engaged Yancy's text, seemed to understand and be persuaded by his arguments. But as we approached Yancy's visit and the final chapter in the book, "Whiteness as Ambush and the Transformative Power of Vigilance," I knew that we had not gone far enough with the text. We had engaged the ideas, but we had not embodied the arguments. This final chapter is especially challenging because in order to really take it on in the way that Yancy asks us to—as white readers we have to become aware of being "ambushed by our whiteness" and how whiteness is embodied and habituated to the point that we can deny its local (intrapersonal, interpersonal and community) and global reality.[17] But to be honest, I hadn't taken the text up sufficiently either. Most of our discussions had been academic. If I wanted them to take up Yancy's call, then I had to be willing to do it myself. I couldn't expect students to discuss coming to awareness of the ways they were ambushed by whiteness unless I was willing to share how I had been ambushed by my whiteness. But doing so was going to be painful, shameful, and make me vulnerable in a way that I was deeply uncomfortable with.

So I recounted an experience that I am deeply ashamed of, one that I had never shared with anyone in the twenty years since it happened. The incident was a small one but a telling one. During the summer before my second year of college when I was nineteen I spent a fair amount of time hanging out with my high school friends in Baltimore. One night we were driving around the city and there were black families sitting on their porches. Under my breath I muttered, "Porch monkeys." A friend in the car with me said, "Nancy, I didn't know you were like that!" My response was "like what?" "Racist," he replied. "That's not racist!" I said. For years I told myself that I didn't know what porch monkey meant, that I didn't know it was a racist term, that I thought it referred to anyone hanging out on his/her porch, not a derogatory term for black people living in the city. In my head, I told myself that I wasn't a racist. But, of course, it was and I was.

At my university I am thought of as one of the white faculty members that actively and verbally points out and resists racism. All of my classes engage race at some level. Even in my "Modern Philosophy" class we read Charles Mills's *Racial Contract* and talk about the role of race and privilege in the modern period and how that extends into current systems of oppression. Yet, that doesn't give me a clean slate or free me from the deeply embodied white privilege that is part of who I am. Admitting to my racist act and my racism was incredibly hard for me. On one level, I worried that talking about this incident (and surely there are more of these in my life—one doesn't utter "porch monkey" and not have committed other equally or more offensive racist acts) would make the students think less of me. I was worried that the students in class would be as disgusted with me as I was with myself. I also was concerned about the effect it would have on my relationship with the African American student in the class with whom I was close. Would it confirm what he probably suspected about me, that like all white people I too am racist? Even worse, how would it make him feel to hear those words even though they were not being said to him but obviously implicated him in some negative way? But I also knew that there was no way that we were going to really get at the heart of Yancy's argument without us having this frank and painful conversation.

As I recount this story with a voice thick with shame, I see the white students nodding their heads in understanding. I see the black student shaking his head in disgust, looking down at his book, doodling on his note pad. When I finish, he looks up at me and says, "You knew didn't you? You knew it was racist, didn't you?" And of course he was right. I knew twenty years ago and I know now. The evidence was right in front of me. If I didn't know, why did I not ever recount this story to anyone before? And why is it that everytime I thought about it did I feel a deep, sick shame? Why did it feel like my big racist secret? Because that is exactly what it was. I was ambushed by my whiteness, and yet it took me twenty years to be willing to admit this.

And that in part is where the shame and the problem lies. The denial runs so deep that even when I was ambushed by my whiteness, the protective layer of white skin cognitively protects me from what I should be admitting to myself. I have always wondered if the three men in the car with me, who also are white, remember this incident. I suspect that two of them do not, but I suspect that one of them does, in fact, remember. Here I am thinking about the one that told me he didn't know that I was a racist. He has converted from Judaism to Islam, is married to an African American woman, and has two beautiful children. He is a jazz musician who, through his music, works to resist racism and other types of oppression. He recognized that I was a problem long before I did.

In recounting this event to the students and being honest about my deep sense of shame and working to engage the legitimate disgust of the black student in my class, we did form a space in which the white students could have an honest discussion about how they were ambushed by their whiteness and the black student was able to talk about what it was like to hear us talk about our racism. None of this felt good to any of us. It involved tears and shame and many long uncomfortable pauses in the class over the course of several days. I think when we were done we had gotten closer to the point that Yancy asks us to reach. I know that we felt closer to each other as if we had struggled through something and came out still respecting and caring for each other. Yet, in spite of our increased awareness, we are all still works in progress. The point that Yancy really wants whites to reach is to understand that in a racist world we will always be a problem and that we must be vigilant about our own racism and the larger structural racism that as whites we benefit from. I can't stop being white, but I can start trying not to accept or exercise the privileges that come with my whiteness. I can begin to refuse to be ignorant of what it means to be me in a racist world.[18] Ignorance is where my next story moves.

FRAME #3: ON BEING IGNORANT: GETTING AT THE HEART OF WHITE DENIAL

Like many people who see themselves as part of the anti-racist struggle, I have had many moments during my life where I had these pin pricks of awareness of the ways in which I was a white problem. But like most white people, I had the privilege of choosing not to take these up and work through them. This is part of being a white problem, that is, part of a racially privileged group. I can choose to "dismantle" myself when I want to, on my own schedule and not at the demands of a group with more power.

The texts that initially forced me to confront my own white privilege and to understand the ways in which I was a problem are Charles Mills's 1999 text, *The Racial Contract* and Marilyn Frye's 1983 essays "On Being White" and "To Be and Be Seen" in *The Politics of Reality*.[19] These texts ask whites to understand how they have participated in active ignorance, refusing to see what is immediately in front of them and what they participate in on a daily basis. Mills argues that all whites are beneficiaries (many, if not most, are also signatories) of the racial contract. The racial contract is a collective agreement to "*mis*interpret the world" that is underlined by the confidence that this misinterpretation will count as "the true" account of the world by the beneficiaries/signatories of the account, whites.[20] This misinterpretation is an "*inverted epistemology, a epistemology of ignorance, a particular pattern of localized and global cognitive dysfunctions (which are psychologically and socially functional), producing the ironic outcome that whites will in general be unable to understand the world they themselves have made.*"[21] Ignorance is experienced as knowledge because it supplies a view of the world that is cohesive ("psychologically and socially functional") with whites' expectations. Whites think they "know" when in fact they do not. Furthermore, this ignorance is actively constructed—it is "in no way *accidental*, but *prescribed* by the terms of the Racial Contract, which requires a certain schedule of structured blindness and opacities in order to establish and maintain the white polity."[22]

Marilyn Frye's essays "To Be and Be Seen" and "On Being White" in *The Politics of Reality*[23] analyze of the role of ignorance in the construction and maintenance of power. Like Mills, Frye takes ignorance to be an *active* refusal to know. She argues, "[i]gnorance is not something simple: it is not a simple lack, absence or emptiness, and it is not a passive state. Ignorance of this sort—the determined ignorance most white Americans have of American Indian tribes and clans, the ostrichlike ignorance most white Americans have of the histories of Asian peoples in this country, the impoverishing ignorance most white Americans have of black language—ignorance of these sorts is a complex result of many acts and many negligences."[24] According to Frye, at the heart of knowing lies attending to something. Thus, the "mechanisms of ignorance" are the result of choosing not to lend attention to something. Attention is not given to something either because one is focusing on something else, for example making the focus men, when it should be women,[25] or because one refuses to see, to hear, to acknowledge what is right in front of them, for example, attacking university affirmative action but refusing to acknowledge the much broader pervasiveness and effect of unequal legacies.[26] For Frye, masculinist ways of "knowing" and white reality (which are really sites of not knowing) prevent seeing and knowing while actively constructing ignorance. Because these sites of power present illusory claims to "truth" and "knowledge" and have the power to maintain this illusion, ignorance creates "the conditions that ensures its continuance."[27]

It is this ignorance (that Mills and Frye describe) that makes it such a challenge for whites to face the fact that we are a problem in the Du Boisian sense. We have constructed a world in which we have learned to see people of other races or ethnicities as a problem, and we have the privilege to maintain our ignorance of the ways in which we are a problem. Whites, including myself, have refused to see what is right in front of us because doing so says so much about who we are and the actively constructed asymmetries that we have maintained. Thus, our ignorance is not just blissful; it is insidious.

I love teaching these texts in part because they have meant so much to me but also because I see such a transformation in students when they get the argument and its social and existential implications. It is one of those moments when something really clicks for students and you see in their faces and bodies that they have acquired a way to see the world that they didn't have before. When I teach "Logic and Critical Reasoning," I teach the critical reasoning portion of the course through epistemology of ignorance. Mills's definition of epistemology of ignorance as a cognitive dysfunction that feels psychologically and socially functional[28] is much like a standard definition for informal fallacies of relevance, in which premises feel strong because of their emotional or psychological appeal but in fact are cognitively/logically irrelevant or just plain wrong.[29] Having students think critically about oppression and ignorance in a course that was preceded by seven and a half weeks of sentential logic is a bit of a challenge, but I think it is the most important part of the course, especially as we spend the next seven and a half weeks discussing oppression, ignorance, and the active construction of false knowledge. I have the students begin this section of the course by reading the first forty-one pages of *The Racial Contract*. These pages, titled "Introduction" and "Overview," are hard hitting, laying out Mills's argument and terminology as well as providing a scathing history of the United States as founded on white supremacy. Many white students are put off by this text. First, it doesn't fit with their twelve or more years of prior education, which told a psychologically and socially comforting story of the colonization and development of the Americas. Second, it directly implicates them in maintaining the current reality of this history. Third, it points to them as at best beneficiaries of the racial contract, if not also signatories.

In this situation, the students see me as a problem in a different way. I am making them uncomfortable in their own skin, literally. Most white students have never really thought of themselves as having a racial identity. Some view themselves as having an ethnic identity, such as Irish or Italian, but not as belonging to a larger racial grouping referred to as white. And even when they think of themselves as "white," they don't see themselves as "raced." They hold on to their Irish or Italian ethnic identities but would never conceive that their black counterparts could also have historical ethnic identities like Congolese or Kenyan. Nor do they consider that their African American fellow students may have a longer historical heritage in the United States than they do as white Americans.

Asking white students to understand that they are part of a racially privileged group that has participated in and benefited from the racial contract evokes many confusing emotions that they don't usually experience in the classroom, especially in "Logic and Critical Reasoning." Many of them will talk about the mistakes others made in the past but situate these mistakes as those that don't apply to them, problems that are not their own. Indeed, they maintain that such problems no longer exist, are problems of the past, and that things are different now. Mills, of course, doesn't see it this way, and their implication in the current racist structure is painful and disconcerting, that is, the reality that Mills provides is not psychologically and socially comforting in anyway. I don't try to ease their discomfort but try to use it as part of a larger constructive classroom space. I ask them why Mills's terminology and argument are upsetting to them. Does his reading of U.S. history seem really all that inconsistent with what we know, or is he putting the pieces together in such a way that we are forced to see what we hadn't seen before? What examples from contemporary culture fit the argument he is making? Are there counter-examples to these?

Once I get them to the point that they can come up with examples, they readily begin to come up with them, and their heads go from hanging down to engaged. I'm still a problem, an agitator, but many of them begin to see an opening that they hadn't seen before. As Mills argues, at some level whites know that they are beneficiaries, and frequently signatories, to the racial contract, but they choose to ignore this reality. Many of the students begin to see that acknowledging that at minimum they are beneficiaries of the racial contract gives them the potential to choose not to be ignorant and to choose to live differently, even as the problem of whiteness will require more work, greater vigilance from them. For a twenty-year-old white student, this is an epistemically empowering place to be and it is the place that Mills asks whites to start from, to begin to acknowledge our ignorance and to begin to think about how to create a world in which we can all live differently. I am not naïve enough such that I fail to recognize that some of this is self-serving on their part and my part—white guilt can be a powerful motivator. As Robert Jenson argues, guilt is one of the emotions of white supremacy.[30] White guilt is a starting point, an opening because it "implies responsibility."[31] If it remains abstract, then all it serves to do is to reify the privilege of white supremacy because one has failed to act upon his/her responsibility. Thus, as we talk about guilt and knowledge, we also talk about action and change. What can we do differently, as white individuals and as part of a larger community? How do we fulfill our responsibility? Not surprisingly, there are varied responses to these questions and variations in students' willingness to enact change.

Students will tell me later how angry I made them, how disorienting the reading was and how angry Mills's language made them. They also thank me and tell me how often these concepts have helped them in other classes or with other interactions they have had. They also share how their discomfort got them to a point that an easier discussion never could have. Indeed, I had one student email me five years after he graduated to tell me that in the class that he took with me he learned "lessons for life, not for a day." At the end of the *Racial Contract*, Mills asks his readers to refuse to not know "where the bodies are buried" and to be willing to do some digging to excavate what we should have been seeing all along; these students are taking that first step in choosing not to be ignorant.

THE FINAL FRAME

There is a sense that being a white problem is an easy place to be compared to the position that Du Bois and other people of color face. To have most of your country view you as a problem and to have this deeply, culturally embodied in terms of what it means to be you, is very different from the privilege that I have to recognize myself as a problem. I can choose to experience this "strangeness." I could go through my whole life without ever being ambushed by my whiteness. I can choose to open up to being ambushed and the strangeness of being a "problem." For me, this process is bittersweet: in choosing to challenge and to work to dismantle my whiteness, to be willing to feel this "strangeness," I at the same time am exercising a privilege of being white. I am not sure how to wrap my head around what it means to exercise privilege in this sense. Yet, as many writers on whiteness articulate, this dismantling must occur. [32] So I continue with the process and hope that I continue to find it a struggle, for it to be strange. For once it becomes familiar and safe, then I am pretty sure that I am back to where I started—driving around Baltimore with three friends.

NOTES

1. W.E. B. Du Bois, *The Souls of Black Folk.* (New York: Penguin Books. 1989), 4.
2. Du Bois, *The Souls of Black Folk,* 4.
3. Du Bois, *The Souls of Black Folk,* 3.
4. See, for example, the whiteness readings in George Yancy (ed), *White on White, Black on Black* (Lanham, MD: Rowman and Littlefield. 2005), Shannon Sullivan, *Revealing Whiteness: The Unconscious Habits of Racial Privilege* (Bloomington, IN: Indiana University Press, 2006), Tim Wise, *White Like Me* (Berkeley, CA: Soft Skull Press 2008).
5. Peggy McIntosh, "White Privilege and Male Privilege: A Personal Account of Coming to See Correspondences Through Work in Women's Studies," 1988.

6. A. Van Jordan, *Quantum Lyrics: Poems* (New York: W. W. Norton & Company, 2009).

7. David Levering Lewis, *W. E. B. Du Bois, 1868-1919: Biography of a Race* (New York: Holt Press, 1994).

8. Du Bois, *The Souls of Black Folk*, 3.

9. The majority of the detained youth in the Clark County Juvenile Detention Center are white, grew up in poverty and many have been in the foster care system for much of their lives.

10. Du Bois, *The Souls of Black Folk*, 4.

11. Anna Stubblefield in her book *Ethics Along the Color Line* (Ithaca: Cornell University Press 2005) and in "Meditations on Postsupremacist Philosophy" in Yancy, *White on White Black on Black* does an excellent job discussing the challenges of white professors teaching race theory and Africana philosophy.

12. Sullivan, *Revealing Whiteness.*

13. They also can haunt me as they did with my Inside-Out class where I know that I have "wronged" my students in a particular way.

14. George Yancy, *Black Bodies, White Gazes* (Lanham, MD: Rowman & Littlefield Publishers, 2008), 229.

15. Yancy 2008 argues that even the best intentioned whites can at best hope to be anti-racist racists, that is, actively opposed to racism, but because of white privilege and the embodiment of Whiteness can never be truly free of racism. He also argues that at best men can be anti-sexist sexists.

16. Yancy 2008.

17. Yancy, *Black Bodies, White Gazes,* 230

18. Nancy McHugh, "Telling Her Own Truth: June Jordan, Standard English and the Epistemology of Ignorance." in *Still Seeking an Attitude,* Kinloch, V. and M. Grebowicz. (Baltimore: Lexington Books, 2004).

19. Marilyn Frye, *The Politics of Reality: Essays in Feminist Theory.* (Trumansburg, NY.: The Crossing Press, 1983).

20. Charles Mills. *The Racial Contract* (Ithaca, NY: Cornell University Press. 1997), 18.

21. Mills, *Racial Contract*, 18. Italics in the original.

22. Mills, *Racial Contract*, 19.

23. Marilyn Frye, *The Politics of Reality: Essays in Feminist Theory.* (Trumansburg, NY.: The Crossing Press, 1983).

24. Frye, *The Politics of Reality*, 118.

25. Frye, *The Politics of Reality*,121.

26. Legacies are the children or relatives of alumni that are given preferential admissions because of their relationship.

27. Frye, *The Politics of Reality*, 120.

28. Mills, *The Racial Contract*, 18.

29. For example, see Hurley's *Concise Introduction to Logic*, p. 116. 10th edition Thomson 2008 Belmont California.

30. Robert Jenson, *The Heart of Whiteness: Confronting Race, Racism and White Privilege*, San Francisco, CA: 2005.

31. Jenson *The Heart of Whiteness*, 47.

32. George Yancy (ed), *White on White, Black on Black* (Lanham, MD: Rowman and Littlefield. 2005), Shannon Sullivan, *Revealing Whiteness: The Unconscious Habits of Racial Privilege* (Bloomington, IN: Indiana University Press, 2006), Tim Wise, *White Like Me* (Berkeley, CA: Soft Skull Press 2008).

Chapter Eleven

Cornered by Whiteness

On Being a White Problem

David S. Owen

THE DOUBLE BIND OF WHITENESS

I have previously argued that in *The Souls of Black Folk* Du Bois accomplishes several tasks when he describes how there is ever the unasked question between himself and white people, that of "How does it feel to be a problem?"[1] He situates his own phenomenological analysis of race within the context of whiteness by focusing the reader's attention on the unnamed normative framework constituted by whiteness. However, Du Bois does more than highlight whiteness, as important as this is. In articulating the "ever unasked question," Du Bois is also clearing a discursive space for his own description and analysis of the racial lifeworld from (obviously) the perspective of the black experience. By doing this he explicitly rejects whiteness as a legitimate, unnamed interpretive framework for understanding how race operates in social life. He brilliantly does this in a way that does not directly and explicitly accuse white readers of some moral infelicity, thereby challenging and engaging these white readers at the same time.

This volume asks the question: what would it mean to invert Du Bois's question, to put it "right side up" in order to identify the rational kernel at the core of the question? It may be useful to begin by conducting a counterfactual reading of this passage in Du Bois *as if* the question were being posed to white people (rather than to himself). Such an exercise may provide some insights into what it would mean to pose the question, "how does it feel to be a problem?" to white people.[2]

In the opening sentence, Du Bois notes that the question is "unasked by some through feelings of delicacy; by others through the difficulty of rightly framing it."[3] So perhaps we can say that whiteness is not mentioned openly as a problem because of both feelings of delicacy and the difficulty of framing it. White people tend to be rather sensitive when it comes to the matter of their own complicity in the system of racial oppression—and I'm not immune from an instinctively defensive reaction. It's a subject whites would prefer to ignore as much as possible. I once was invited into a colleague's course to discuss white privilege, and I began with the privilege walk exercise. In the course of debriefing the exercise, one white female student asserted, "You just want us to feel guilty for being white." At first, I was taken aback by the certainty with which this was expressed (the certainty of the expression reflecting a degree of white privilege). Guilt is a stage in the racial identity development of whites, and so the implication that this student was feeling at least a bit guilty was a sign that she had been dislodged (at least momentarily) from her previous level of racial identity.[4] But the second half of Du Bois's sentence, I think, is even more significant. For here, the problem of right framing of the question reduces to possessing an adequate set of theoretical principles and terms for explaining whiteness. Asking white people "How does it feel to be a problem?" will result in a wide range of reactions from earnest expressions of empathy, to befuddlement, to failures to understand the coherence of the question, to expressions of guilt, and to outright hostility. A significant challenge underlying the asking of this question to whites is that there is a radical paucity in the publicly available theoretical and discursive resources for understanding the question and to begin an earnest engagement with it. Thus, I think an implicit message contained in Du Bois's *The Souls of Black Folk* is to challenge whites and blacks to unmask and theorize whiteness, to develop some resources by which we can better frame and understand our shared racial context.

Another virtue of *Souls* is how Du Bois exposes the inherent contradictions in the system of race.[5] His Hegelian training provides the methodological orientation for seeing racial oppression as a system of contradictions that situate inhabitants of that system in pervasive and persistent double binds. Marilyn Frye has explicitly analyzed how oppression functions to generate double binds for those who are targeted by the system: "One of the most characteristic and ubiquitous features of the world as experienced by oppressed people is the double bind—situations in which options are reduced to a very few and all of them expose one to penalty, censure or deprivation."[6] Frye's analysis shows how members of targeted groups face double binds where all options generate some form of harm. Iris Marian Young defines oppression as

> systematic institutional processes which prevent some people from learning and using satisfying and expansive skills in socially recognized settings, or institutionalized social processes which inhibit people's ability to play and

communicate with others or to express their feelings and perspective on social life in contexts where others can listen.[7]

As a complex set of processes that shape both shared practices and institutions,[8] oppression is defined by those patterns or structures that generate both harmful and beneficial consequences. We often think of only the targets of oppression, but oppression, as a structuring property of the social system, also generates beneficiaries. Thus, I suggest that a consequence of racial oppression is that white people also face double binds. To be sure, it appears to be a contradiction to say that white people both benefit from the system by being the beneficiaries of white privilege, and at the same time we experience harm-causing double binds. The contradiction, however, is not a logical one. Rather, this contradiction is inherent in social systems characterized by oppression. Furthermore, this is not to say that the double binds faced by whites are just as harmful as the double binds faced by people of color. But I do think that it is important to recognize the ways in which white people are also constrained, constricted, and harmed by the system of race. (Though frequently, white people will behave in racialized ways that directly causes their own harm and suffering.)[9] This is important to acknowledge because it provides a powerful self-interested incentive for white people to be invested in transforming and dismantling this oppressive system.

I have wrestled with a particular manifestation of this double bind throughout the writing of this chapter. This double bind has been experienced in the following way. Over the course of my (ongoing) learning about oppression, race, whiteness, and how these phenomena affect and constitute me personally, I have come to recognize how persistently whiteness re-centers itself. It is typically quite difficult for white people to engage in a discussion about race for long before reasserting ourselves at the dominant and most important pole in the discourse. So I have cultivated a reflexive self-consciousness about my participation in discussions about race. I pay close attention to how I am inserting myself into these discussions (how many times I speak, how forcefully I speak, the degree to which I insist upon uptake of what I say, and so on). To be sure, although I have cultivated a conscious self-reflection, I am doing so against literally a lifetime of socialization and acculturation that shapes my habits.

WHITE ENGAGEMENT

As a white man who sees himself engaged in the struggle against racial oppression and oppression of all forms, I have often felt—quite surprisingly—marginalized among whites engaged in the struggle. I felt this way because their stories didn't resonate with me. The stories that are often told by white people are stories of a particular moment or event that triggered an epiphany in which they suddenly understood the nature of racial oppression and their own implication in this system. I never had such a moment. When I've been asked how I came to my commitment to racial justice, my first reaction is one of discomfort. As a philosopher-academic, I am trained to approach my work in a disembodied, impartial way, and this question cuts across this training. Furthermore, I know enough about whiteness to know that any attention to whiteness risks re-centering white people in the conversation about racial justice. Nonetheless, I also recognize the importance of personal stories of embodied selves to unmasking the operations of the system of race. So I reluctantly begin by saying that it is a rather unremarkable and somewhat boring story, since it is a story not of a triggering event but of a long series of small steps that are not so much on a steady incline toward greater consciousness but are really a series of epicycles in which moments of clarity and insight are repeatedly over run by the continuous tide of white epistemological ignorance. I survived all the way through high school and into my first year of college without developing any hint of a consciousness of broad, societal injustices operating around me. This is not surprising as I grew up in a nearly all white outer suburb of Chicago with parents who were themselves unengaged in social struggles of any sort. Once I transferred to the University of Illinois at Chicago, however, I became exposed to racial and socioeconomic diversity on a daily basis. This raised my awareness of broader injustices, but it wasn't until graduate school that I came to a full understanding that these injustices were systemic and not merely perpetrated by morally bankrupt individuals. In graduate school my first class was with Sandra Bartky from whom (along with several female graduate student peers) I learned just how oppression functions as a system by structuring the sociocultural lifeworld in patterned and regular ways. By the time I finished graduate school I had a solid understanding of the systematicity of oppression, but I had yet to come to understand my role—largely via unconsciously enacted habits (my habitus)—in perpetuating those systems. The next step in the development of my consciousness was when I was living in San Francisco and had just finished up my dissertation. Charles Mills, who had been on my dissertation committee, called me looking for a place to stay while attended a conference on whiteness at UC Berkeley. Since I had the flexibility to do so, I attended the conference with him (which I had not known was even happening prior to his call). This was in 1997. While critical whiteness studies was still in its infancy, all of the major founding theorists seemed to be there. (If only I had known at the time who they were!) I came away from this two-day conference with a novice understanding of the role whiteness plays in sustaining and perpetuating racial oppression, as well as my particular capacity as a white male to engage in the struggle with others to disrupt whiteness. Since that time, of course, my understanding of whiteness and racial oppression has developed considerably, and it continues to develop every day.

Once I had come to realize just how deep and broad the problem of systemic racism is, I realized that I needed to commit in a personal and meaningful way toward working for racial justice. For me, the question was: how can I be most effective? As an academic, I had various options open to me. I could make racial oppression and racial justice the focus of my teaching, I could engage more in social activism, or I could devote my scholarship to solving conceptual problems of social justice. Early in my career, I pursued all of these simultaneously, but I struggled with two issues. First, I worried that I wasn't making enough of a difference. The problem of racial oppression is systemic, I reasoned, so the only effective response to it would need to be systemic as well. It felt that my impact through teaching, scholarship, or activism was simply too constricted and insufficiently systemic to generate change. Now, I think this is partly correct. Despite the efforts of many courageous and dedicated anti-racists, only moderate progress can be said to have been achieved. But this rationale also reflects a degree of white privilege. It shifted the focus from doing something to combat racial oppression to how *I* could make a substantial contribution to deconstructing systemic oppression. There was a presumption that I could make a real, fundamental difference with just the appropriate amount of effort (after all, I was white!). Second, I struggled with the classic and seemingly endemic tension between theory and practice, between developing more adequate explanatory and critical accounts of racial oppression and the effectual work of creating real, substantive structural change. In particular, I worried (and still do) that producing scholarly work in the philosophy of race would reach only a very limited audience and thus produce highly constrained (if any) real change. So how to proceed? I wrestled with these questions especially while I was on a four-year term contract at a small liberal arts college that prides itself on its commitment to social justice. This was my first opportunity to teach at a small liberal arts college, and the environment was perfectly suited to the development of how I saw myself in relation to the struggle for racial justice. First, the college prides itself on its commitment to social justice. Second, the liberal arts environment encouraged extended engagement with and mentoring of students who themselves were deeply committed to social justice. Third, and most importantly, I encountered colleagues who became my mentors by showing me not only how to authentically pursue racial justice as a white person in more effective ways, but also that one way of doing so in the academy was through institutional diversity work. What I mean by diversity work is work directed at creating institutional change that makes the academy more inclusive and equitable for historically excluded and marginalized groups.

I went on to learn the basics of institutional diversity work while at the liberal arts college, and when I moved on to a tenure track job at a public research university, I went in looking to find the opportunities to engage in the same kind of work. Apropos of how being a problem distorts the socio-cultural landscape the way a massive object alters the gravitational field, others' expectations of who I am are often initially distorted. For example, after interviewing at my current institution and accepting their job offer, but before actually arriving on campus to begin my new position, I attended a conference on race and ethnicity in higher education. Since I was determined to continue my engagement in institutional diversity work at the new job, I looked up anyone from there who might be at the conference. And sure enough, the Vice Provost for Diversity, among others, was there. So, I called her up and made arrangements to meet in the lobby the next morning so we could chat over breakfast. The next morning, we both arrived on time in the lobby and proceeded to walk back and forth looking for the other. We ended up walking right past each other multiple times until it became clear that the other might be the person we were looking for. The vice provost, an African American woman, was looking for a person of color, and so as a white guy I didn't fall into the category of possibility. This experience is indicative of how white people are not expected to be interested in diversity and equity. This expectation is grounded in the real, historical lack of interest in diversity and equity on the part of most white people. White people's actual lack of interest and engagement in racial justice has a complex causal origin, but the norming of whiteness plays a central role here. It should also be noted that there is a long history of many white people who committed themselves to the struggle for racial justice, people such as Anne Braden. [10] This history of white antiracism is systematically ignored and marginalized in order that the system of whiteness can remain uninterrogated. As Charles Mills argues, white epistemological ignorance is a key property of the racial contract that establishes whiteness as the dominant norm. [11]

Two years after arriving, I was invited to take on a service assignment of coordinating the diversity programs for the College of Arts and Sciences in the dean's office. In the past eight years, my role has evolved and expanded, with half of my workload in the dean's office as Director of Diversity Programs. In this middle-administrative position, I have been challenged by the question of the legitimacy of a white guy taking on a leadership role in institutional diversity. [12] When white people, and white men especially, are in diversity leadership roles, our privilege becomes relevant in at least four ways. The first way in which having a privileged social identity is relevant concerns the impact upon the structures of power within the institution. The question here is: do white men in such positions support the conventional institutional power relations, or do we (can we) modify those power relations in positive ways? A second way privileged identities are relevant concerns the symbolism involved in such more or less high profile positions. What symbolisms are created, reinforced, or even challenged when white men take on diversity leadership work? Moreover, how will such an appointment be perceived by the community—by both whites and people of color? A third way privileged identities are relevant concerns their relation to the diversity goals of the institution. Do such appointments of, say, white men, to diversity leadership positions further or inhibit the achievement of the diversity-related objectives the institution has set for itself? And fourth, how does possession of a privileged identity contribute to, or militated against, the work of diversity leadership? Does being white and/or male make one more or less effective as a leader in institutional diversity?

Such questions of how having a privileged social identity are relevant to the work and effectiveness of diversity leadership also need to be considered within the specific organizational context. In particular, Bailey Jackson and Rita Hardiman have argued that organizations can be located on a scale that determines their degree of multicultural development.[13] On their model, organizations can occupy one of three stages. In the first stage, the monocultural, organizations are organized around a dominant set of cultural norms and non-conforming groups are either excluded by policy or included but only on the terms of the dominant cultural norms. In the second stage, the nondiscriminating, organizations seek to move away from being monocultural by either increasing numerical diversity or affirmatively focusing on success as well as access. In the third stage, multicultural organizations are actively redefining themselves as multicultural, or they have achieved a genuine degree of multicultural practice and structure.

When is working as an institutional diversity leader who has white privilege problematic? White institutional diversity leaders are most problematic in monocultural organizations since here the power already strongly supports white people in the organizations, and the symbolism of a white person in leadership reinforces the power structure. But when an organization is nondiscriminating, being a white diversity leader is less problematic as being white can actually be an advantage when attempting to engage passively resistant white people in the commitment to, and the work of, diversity. When the organization is at the multicultural stage, then employing white people in positions of diversity leadership is least problematic because the campus communities have a multicultural self-conception and the organization itself—in its demographics, policies, and practices—is multicultural. Two further comments are necessary. First, when a white person works their way into a leadership role by proving their commitment and effectiveness, the problems of power and symbolism are reduced because a degree of trust has been earned. Second, when the white diversity leader ensures that he or she works collaboratively with a team of people of color, problems of white epistemological ignorance, symbolism, and power are again reduced (though not eliminated).

THE WHITENESS OF THE SOCIAL FIELD

Being a problem means being located in a privileged position within a social field that is characterized by oppression. I am a problem because I am racialized as white and gendered as male (among, of course, multiple other intersecting identities). I may or may not be aware of this privileged location that I occupy, and if I am not aware of it, then I don't experience the feeling of being a problem with respect to my whiteness. Finding myself situated in a privileged position in the social fields of race and gender also means that my access to the power and status available in this privileged location generates the responsibility to disrupt the reproduction of that oppressive social system. While a wide range of academic fields have contributed to the growing body of critical whiteness studies scholarship, the very idea of whiteness and the operations of its reproduction remain under-theorized. Whiteness has been the subject of critical analysis since at least Du Bois, but unless we understand the nature of whiteness and how it is reproduced in the social system, we won't develop effective strategies for dismantling it. [14] Fortunately, there are a variety of social-theoretic tools we might draw upon to theorize whiteness. What we should avoid, however, is engaging in disputes about the *most adequate* social theory before we apply that account to whiteness. Such an approach would disconnect the theorizing of whiteness from pragmatic concerns of liberation and racial justice. Instead, the orientation should begin from felt needs for liberation and the utilization of whichever theoretical tools appear at the time to be instrumentally productive of liberation.

A significant obstacle to liberation is the poor understanding both in the dominant discourse and in the scholarship on whiteness of how whiteness structures both the social field and the dispositions and perspectives of the individual, where this structuring occurs within a system in which social fields and dispositions and perspectives of individuals constitute each other within the enacting of practices. Moreover, in addition to a thicker understanding of how whiteness structures both social systems and selves, we especially need an adequate account of how this structuring of the social system is reproduced over time. In other words, we need a historical account of how social systems are maintained via practices, which will in turn provide clarification of where the opportunities are for disrupting that reproduction. I have argued elsewhere that the concept of whiteness should be understood to refer not merely to a racialized identity but also at the same time as a structuring property of the social system. [15] In modernity, whiteness has infected social systems, and it shapes all major sub-systems of those systems, the social (including the economic), the cultural, and the personality system of the individual. But what exactly does it mean that whiteness structures the social structure? How does this relate to the racial identity of whiteness? And how is whiteness in both of these manifestations maintained?

I want to explore the usefulness of Pierre Bourdieu's theory of practice for answering these questions and, in particular, for explaining social reproduction through the mutual constitution of the individual and the social field.[16] The three key terms that form the skeleton of his theory of practice are habitus, field, and capital. The field is simply the social context or, metaphorically, the "social space" in which interactions, transactions, and practices occur.[17] The field is structured very much like a game in which players act strategically to maximize their position within the field. The capacity to improve one's position is promoted by the possession of capital, which comes in a variety of forms: economic, social, cultural, and symbolic, and can be understood essentially as a capacity to achieve one's ends in differentiated fields. The habitus is Bourdieu's term for the embodiment of capital and the location in the social field capital confers on individuals. More precisely, the habitus is the set of embodied dispositions individuals have that are generative of practices. The habitus is how the past becomes embodied and unconsciously shapes practices: it is "embodied history, internalized as a second nature and so forgotten as history."[18] The habitus doesn't merely affect action, however, it also provides the presuppositions and framing for how we see the world and how we see ourselves. We enact our habitus within multiple, intersecting social fields, where those social fields are sites of struggle and where each of us seeks to maximize our relative positions. Social field, habitus, and capital work interactively to reproduce the cultural and social order. The field is the set of structures that shape the broadly general aims of practices; it effectively shapes those practices through the means of the habitus, which in turn is an internalization of the structural norms of the field. The crucial insight (not unique to Bourdieu) is that the structures of the field are reproduced via practices that are generated by the habitus, which is an internalization of the structures of the field. So both the field and the habitus are reproduced in the same practices and at the same time.

Whiteness, then, would be seen as the social field of race where the strategy that is rewarded with economic, symbolic, social, and cultural capital is to act in ways that sustain the normalization of white interests, needs, and values. The capital accumulated translates into privilege and the added-value (according to the logic of the field) capacity to achieve one's aims. And the white habitus would be the ways in which white people internalize the structures of the field that serve the interests, needs, and values of white people.

Applying this framework to thinking about the system of racial oppression and whiteness in particular would allow us to see how systematically whiteness shapes the shared social and cultural space—it functions to essentially set the rules of the game in favor of those racialized as white. Of course, we all, white, black, Latino, and Asian play this game (which is a game only metaphorically, of course). Whiteness rewards those who play the game well by accumulating economic, social, cultural, and symbolic capital, and that capital opens up further opportunities to improve one's position in the system. Whiteness becomes embodied in the habitus by those who play the game well. The embodied dispositions of the habitus in turn shape practices that reproduce the structures of the field, and hence the capital reward system.

A crucial insight of a Bourdieusian account of whiteness (or for any account of whiteness grounded in a theory of practice) is how individuals, who occupy the social space shaped by whiteness, all unavoidably contribute—although to varying degrees—to the reproduction of whiteness. Since the social field is structured to benefit white people, we typically do not see how those structures are functioning or how they are embodied in the white habitus. Anyone can be blinded to the distortions of the field by whiteness, but white people have an interest in not seeing these distortions. Understanding this is crucial for reconstructing the social order in the interests of racial justice. A critical theory of race (and of whiteness) requires vigilant critical reflection about the ways in which my everyday behaviors contribute to systems of oppression. I need to be always asking myself the following questions: How is race shaping this situation? How is whiteness shaping my perceptions of this situation? Is my concern to be a "good white person" shaping my perceptions and actions in way that reproduces whiteness? How is whiteness shaping my dispositions and behavior? How can I disrupt those practices that are reproducing whiteness?

ON WHITE MOTIVATION

"Why do you do this work?" I was asked this question by a black female undergraduate midway through a day-and-a-half long antiracist retreat. The retreat, called the Hamline University Conference on Race and Ethnicity (HU-CORE), consisted of a series of workshops intended to promote understanding and provoke reflection for the multiracial group of undergraduates. I had been asked to serve as one of the co-facilitators of a sub-group because of my teaching on race and my engagement in institutional diversity work. I knew this student moderately well from the various diversity events we had participated in and so I had demonstrated as least *some* commitment to racial justice work. Nonetheless, the relationship of trust between white people and people of color in such contexts is an asymmetrical one. The long history of the supremacy of whiteness[19] has militated against the conditions of mutual cooperation for racial justice by providing people of color with an appallingly long, tragic history of violated promises, good intentions that resulted in painful and deadly consequences, and a typical failure of white people to *act* decidedly for racial justice.[20] When she asked me this question, I felt a twinge of hurt. You know, the kind white people feel when they don't understand the history of racial oppression that has created a justified distrust towards even white people's best intentions. Fortunately, I understood just enough of this history to know from where the question came and why it needed to be asked, and answered, both to her and myself.

"Well," I began tentatively, "I do it because I care about justice." While my answer was honest and sincere, I was unsettled by the question because I had never before seriously thought about my motivations. I had been drawn to matters of social justice for many years though I had never seriously reflected on why I cared about social justice. While sincere, caring about justice can mean simply wanting to care for the unfortunate others without critically examining the unjust system and my own privileged positions within that system. Moreover, an abstract concern for justice can provide only a weak motivation—its abstractness means that the ties that bind me to it are very thin and weak. Because the context of the question was structured by race, and since it was asked of me, a white man, by a black woman, the sense of the question was not so much why do I *care*, but why do *I* care? In other words, why should a white man—whose identity is deeply implicated in whiteness—care about a question of justice that works to his own benefit? This struck me as I later reflected on the question and my answer. Replying that I cared about justice, even when what I meant was *racial* justice, essentially removed how race works from the response. Such a response masks not only my specific interest in racial justice, but also the myriad ways race shapes the context of this conversation. If how race shapes every context isn't consciously examined, then it recedes into the background and the social field will get reproduced with its racialized structure intact.

What I understood only vaguely at the time, and have since come to develop a theoretical explanation for, is the *justified* asymmetry of trust between people of color and white people. For the past four hundred years an astonishingly pervasive system of racial oppression has been developed, justified, elaborated, and defended against challenges. A consequence is that racial oppression has been systematized in the sense that it operates in every domain of collective social life, economics, the labor market, education, politics, culture, the media, and so on.[21] Since most white people have been satisfied not to challenge this system, either at all or in any serious manner, there is no reason to think that most white people seriously care about racial justice. Moreover, the anecdotal evidence is that people of color repeatedly and consistently experience violations of trust in their relationships with white people. These two facts make distrust on the part of people of color towards white people understandable.

The import of the student's question about why I do this work now becomes clear. For while there is a context of asymmetrical trust relations between white people and people of color, there remains a residue of suspicion about why a white guy would act in strategically irrational ways. If the field of race is a competition to occupy the best position possible, and as a white guy I have been conferred a degree of economic, symbolic, cultural, and social capital, then why would I act in ways that would reduce my position, my resources, and my capacities? Bourdieu's theory of practice is not determinist; habitus, the field, and capital combine as generative forces of practices. Bourdieu speaks of the "well-formed habitus" that generates practices in tune with the field. However, there is always room for creative and non-conforming actions within a field. The question for whites who seek to pursue antiracist practices is are we reducing our position, say by forfeiting certain privileges, in order to reduce our guilt, or perhaps to build trust across racial lines? Or, are we doing this as a conscious strategy to disrupt the operations of the field itself, and hence the racial system? The latter should be the primary goal since that will be the only way to decrease (and eliminate) race-based oppression. The former goals (of reducing guilt, building cross-racial trust) have some value, but their value is a short-term value since they do not contribute to the disruption of the system itself. Moreover, the goals of reducing guilt and building trust can function, often unconsciously, as ways to deflect responsibility for the reproduction of the system of race. They can be strategies white people adopt so they can say: "See, my heart is pure and I *am* doing something." This threat of acting out of self-interest can neither be eliminated nor overcome; it is a constant companion for white people who seek to perform authentic antiracist practices. Authentic antiracist practice, then, is essentially linked to the objective of disrupting the reproduction of the racial system. Self-reflective white people who want to practice antiracism authentically should always remember to orient and reorient their actions with this primary goal in mind.

PRACTICING A REFLECTIVE WHITENESS

Being a white problem means being constrained and limited by a set of racial double binds that constitute the social space into which I have been socialized as a white guy. However committed I am to practicing antiracism, I cannot but contribute to the reproduction of whiteness in the social system. Thus, while the racial field is structured to benefit those like me who are racialized as white, I have a direct interest in disrupting that field's reproduction—to dismantle the set of double binds that place constraints and limitations on my behaviors and on who I can be. Unmasking the ways these double binds restrict the potentials of white people to be fully human by not contributing to the race-based harm of others will be an essential step towards a liberated future.

I cannot avoid being a problem. So the very idea of innocence when it comes to being complicit in the reproduction of the racial system needs to be debunked. There is no such thing as an innocent white person when it comes to racial oppression. Nonetheless, the system *is* reproduced by the practices each of us engages in, so what we do is important. I cannot avoid complicity entirely, but I can also be complicit in the disruption of the system by consciously performing antiracist practices. This is not a state to be achieved ("being an antiracist"), rather it is a practice in the sense that I am always trying to be better at it. Just as the best athletes continue to practice to improve their performance, white people who are committed to racial justice must always be practicing to become better at disrupting the system of racial oppression. To this end, whenever possible I should be asking myself these four questions:

1. How has whiteness shaped the formation of this situation?
2. How is whiteness operating right now in this situation?
3. What practices am I engaging in that are reproducing whiteness?
4. What can I do to disrupt the reproduction of whiteness?

An authentic practice aiming at racial justice will be incessantly asking these questions, and directing and redirecting action accordingly.

NOTES

I would like to thank George Yancy, John Gibson, Avery Kolers, and Thomas Maloney for their helpful comments to earlier drafts of this paper.

1. "Whiteness in Du Bois's *The Souls of Black Folk*," *Philosophia Africana* 10:2 (August 2007): 107–26.

2. I use the descriptors "white people" and "black people" instead of the stylistically less awkward "whites" and "blacks" to avoid reducing members of these groups to only their racial identities. Although racial identity is a core aspect of our social identities, we must avoid speaking as if it is the only aspect.

3. W. E. B. Du Bois, *The Souls of Black Folk* (New York: Library of America, 1986).

4. See the essays in B. W. Jackson and C. L. Wijeyesinghe, Eds., *New Perspectives on Racial Identity Development* (New York: New York University Press, 2001).

5. I will use the phrases "system of race," "system of racial oppression," "racial oppression," and "system of white supremacy" as synonyms. The concept of race possesses a reality only through its effects (the system of racial oppression), thus I am always concerned with how race operates in the world—and I think any critical philosophy of race and racism ought to be as well.

6. Marilyn Frye, "Oppression" in *The Politics of Reality* (Freedom, CA: The Crossing Press, 1983).

7. Iris Marian Young, *Justice and the Politics of Difference* (Princeton: Princeton University Press, 1990), p. 38.

8. Sally Haslanger, *Resisting Reality: Social Construction and Social Critique* (Oxford: Oxford University Press, 2012), esp. pp 317–20.

9. I'm appreciative of George Yancy for reminding me of this.

10. See Herbert Aptheker, *Anti-Racism in U.S. History* (Westport, Praeger: 1993). On Anne Braden, see Catherine Fosl, *Subversive Southerner: Anne Braden and the Struggle for Racial Justice in the Cold War South* (New York, Palgrave, 2002).

11. Charles Mills, *The Racial Contract* (Ithaca, Cornell UP, 1997). See also Shannon Sullivan and Nancy Tuana, eds., *Race and Epistemologies of Ignorance* (Albany, SUNY Press, 2007).

12. For a detailed analysis of this question, see Owen, "Privileged Social Identities and Diversity Leadership in Higher Education," *The Review of Higher Education* 32:2 (Winter 2009): 185–207.

13. Bailey W. Jackson and Rita Hardiman, "Multicultural Organizational Development," in *The Promise of Diversity: Over 40 Voices Discuss Strategies for Eliminating Discrimination in Organizations*, E. Cross, et al., eds. (Arlington: NTL Institute, 1994): 231–39.

14. See my arguments in Owen, "Whiteness in Du Bois's *The Souls of Black Folk*," *Philosophia Africana* 10:2 (August 2007): 107–26.

15. Owen, "Towards a Critical Theory of Whiteness," *Philosophy and Social Criticism* 33:2 (2007): 203–22.

16. For the most comprehensive statements of his theory of practice, see especially Pierre Bourdieu, *Outline of a Theory of Practice* (Cambridge: Cambridge University Press, 1977), and Bourdieu, *The Logic of Practice* (Stanford: Stanford University Press, 1990).

17. A useful overview of Bourdieu's conception of field can be found in Patricia Thomson, "Field" in *Pierre Bourdieu: Key Concepts*, edited by Michael Grenfell (Durham, UK: Acumen, 2008), pp. 67–81.

18. Bourdieu 1990, p. 56.

19. I use 'the supremacy of whiteness' to indicate the descriptive meaning of a state of affairs, and not the normative or ideological meaning of 'white supremacy' as a set of ideas concerning the justified superiority of whiteness. I thank my good friend, colleague, and mentor, Francie Kendall for this usage.

20. See, for example, Ronald Takaki, *A Different Mirror: A History of Multicultural America*, rev. ed. (New York: Little, Brown, 2008), and Howard Zinn, *A People's History of the United States* (New York: Harper, 2005).

21. Michael K. Brown, et al., *Whitewashing Race: The Myth of a Color-Blind Society* (Berkeley: University of California Press, 2003), Ian F. Haney López, *White by Law* (New York, NYU Press, 1996), Douglas S. Massey and Nancy A. Denton, *American Apartheid: Segregation and the Making of the Underclass* (Cambridge, MA: Harvard University Press, 1993), and Melvin L. Oliver and Thomas M. Shapiro, *Black Wealth/White Wealth: A New Perspective on Racial Inequality* (New York: Routledge, 1997).

Chapter Twelve

Whiteness, Democracy, and the Hegemonic Mind

Steve Martinot

WHITENESS AND DEMOCRACY

An Introductory Scene

In a documentary made in 1994 about the uprisings (1965 and 1992) in Watts, Los Angeles, an interesting exchange occurs between a young white woman interviewer and a young black man. The documentary's theme was government dereliction in following through on promised reconstruction projects and investment for the area to end its severe impoverishment. The social problems that had led to the uprisings were left to fester and get worse. After 1965, the only businesses that could get funding were liquor stores. And young people who put the zip code of that area on employment applications were routinely not hired. While this interviewer is talking to him, the young black man is busy tagging the side of a low wall on the margins of a small park. She asks him if he votes, and he says no. She asks him why not, and he answers, "what for? Whitey's going have his way either way." She has no response. The scene shifts. [1]

The scene iconizes an intimately antithetical relation between whiteness and democracy with breathtaking starkness. The civil rights movements were pro-democracy movements in their demands for equality and justice—a justice for which all the urban uprisings were an extreme and desperate call. One of the government's responses to those movements and uprisings was to curtail investment and assist the movement of industry out of those areas (or off-shore), imposing a form of economic and cultural famine on black communities and leaving them bereft. In this film dialogue, the interviewer, who

Steve Martinot

speaks from the unabashed standpoint of technological advancement, can still ask about using the electoral process to fix the society's racialized inequalities. The interviewee's response merely mentions the fact that there is a "receiving end" to that political process.

This young black man's assertion proved prophetic for the year 2000 when over 110,000 people of color were disenfranchised arbitrarily and without due process in Florida in order to determine the outcome of a presidential election. The year 2000 also saw the prison population of the United States cross the two million mark, with 75 percent of the inmates being people of color. After a decade of the "war on drugs" and the enhanced subjection to police rule by which it was structured, the disenfranchisement and second-class citizenship imposed on those run through the judicial machine and its prisons had already produced a "New Jim Crow," as Michelle Alexander describes in her book.[2] The act of tagging the wall becomes this black man's only vote, a momentary breech of the law to say he exists as a human being.

The interviewer, on the other hand, embodies the problem of whiteness for white people. We don't know if she actually thinks that the political process works, but she believes in democracy to the extent that she gives those of Watts a brief voice, allowing a few, like this system-deprecating man, to name the problem in a way that includes her as white. The problem is one of democracy and whether, in practice or in theory, whiteness and democracy can co-exist.

Whiteness and its governance are a problem for people of color who find their every attempt to construct community for themselves, or participate in U.S. society, either obstructed or mediated by white people and white institutions. Whiteness is also a problem for white supremacy insofar as it faces ever-renewed rebellion, resistance, or calls for equality (a necessary precondition for democracy) against its hegemony. Insofar as it is supremacist, it expects acquiescence; in confronting non-acquiescence, it feels itself subverted and must engage continually in efforts to reconstruct itself, some of which rely on violence. But whiteness is a most real problem for whites who oppose white supremacy, who wish to build a society based on democracy and justice, but whose skin marks a cultural origin born of that supremacy. If we do not extricate ourselves from the coloniality of whiteness, its racialization and segregation (imprisonment) of others, we remain complicit.

For those of us who favor and foster democracy, the coloniality of the origins of whiteness and the anti-coloniality of democracy create some unusual and exigent necessities. Beyond the issue of coexistence, we face the question of whether whiteness as such stands in contradiction to democracy as such.

Prisons and Electoral Policy

Let's first look at the superficial political aspect of this question. The United States today imprisons more people per capita than any other country. That is, it imprisons more people than the most openly dictatorial or authoritarian regimes in the world. This prison system unfolded as part of a "war on drugs" which, from its onset, was recognized by black political leaders as little more than a war on black people. That is, for them, drugs were not the enemy in the war, but the weapon with which it would be fought. The police and the judicial machine have used this weapon to create a structure of police rule in all urban areas in the United States.[3]

Three significant facts about this massive imprisonment need to be kept in mind. First, if whites roughly outnumber people of color by 3 to 1 in the overall population, and the reverse ratio holds for prisoners, then people of color have a 9 to 1 chance of being imprisoned over whites, though crime rates are roughly the same for both white communities and communities of color. Second, the vast majority of prisoners are there for victimless crimes, meaning that no one is being protected by their arrest and that they themselves are the victims of the judicial machine. And third, the vast majority of these prisoners are there through plea bargaining, which means that there is no trial, no need for evidence, and no proof of guilt. Conviction is gained by confession induced through threats of more severe charges and longer sentences. In other words, the proposition that "two-thirds of all prisoners in the United States are innocent of any crime," cannot be refuted.

The salient fact about the prison industry is that its expansion was never voted on as a question of policy. It was proclaimed by the government, instituted by fiat, and justified by the very policy of mass incarceration it made possible. That self-referential justification then also applies implicitly to all the engines of mass incarceration, namely, police racial profiling, racially biased prosecutions, and the nine-to-one conviction rate. The media has cooperated by faithfully reporting crime as essentially committed by people of color.[4] The increasing severity of imprisonment policies have been welcomed by the white mainstream with equanimity, and police impunity has been seen as a sign of security.

Turning the documentary interviewer's question around, we can ask: where has the white vote been in all of this? White people are the majority. Yet no vote was ever demanded by that majority on either the "war on drugs" or on prison expansion. Three-strikes laws get put on the ballot but only to enhance sentencing. After the fact, politicians ratify such policies by proclaiming themselves to be "hard-on-crime," to the point where not to do so risks putting an end to their political career. Many white people oppose police brutality, the prison industry, mass incarceration policies, and neighborhood segregation, but there are no avenues within the present political culture to contest any of this. In short, the police and prison system, which occupy a critical place in the structure of racialization, remain exempt from democratic procedures.

Though it costs over 50,000 dollars a year to maintain a prisoner in prison in California, which said money could be better expended on the individual's education or for providing a job, few white people have demanded an accounting or expressed concern over whether their tax money is being spent wisely. Instead, cities are forced to close schools, and community colleges are running out of money. Insofar as popular (white) sentiment supports or ignores this, it implies that processes of racialization hold some kind of real benefit, separate from cost dysfunction, for white people, a benefit that expresses itself through a curtailment of democracy.

WHITENESS VS. DEMOCRACY

The Grammar of Race

The modern concept of whiteness and race evolved out of social processes developed in the Virginia colony during the seventeenth century. What was peculiar about Virginia was the corporate structure of the colony, the particular form of human commodification it produced, and the African slavery to which that was applied.[5] Because of the colony's corporate structure, laborers constituted a different form of wealth than they did in the Caribbean or Iberian colonies (Mexico and South America), where enslaved laborers were more casually worked to death, it being cheaper to replace them than to provide for substantial survival. In Virginia, wealth equated to political power, and bond-laborers were preserved as ledger entries. For that reason, a stricter separation of English and African was exacted than elsewhere. A succession of anti-miscegenation laws produced a binary color-coding of both labor and sexuality. If the colony's outward economic form appeared as owner and owned, that represented a profound separation between membership and non-membership in colonial society. (In the Iberian colonies, there was group mixing and a complex spectrum of social levels whose social membership was also hierarchically arranged.) Whiteness, which emerged in Virginia as a social identity after the codification of slavery (1682), included a juridical insistence on a purity of descent (matrilinearity) to prevent there being brown children who might lay claim to political rights through their fathers.[6] It became a cultural identity in the 1700s through a system of violence (the patrols) against the enslaved Africans, a system of terrorism to instill obedience.[7]

As a cultural identity, whiteness depended on that purity concept, which codified the social separation between the colonists and those hyper-commodified as bond-laborers. As such, it constitutes the defining moment in the invention of the modern concept of race. The concept of race was then developed by European naturalists in the 1720s. But whiteness came first, with the modern concept of race generated out of it. It was a purely political operation, given that a purity concept is an ideological and political notion (nature knows no purity concepts).[8]

Based on that purity concept, race emerged from that binary division of white and other that it defined. The concept of race then became the organizing principle for the entire system of of socio-political practices producing human commodification and the ritualization of terrorism and oppression toward the commodified laborers. These practices are the actions of one group of people (whites) toward others through whom they define themselves as white. "Race" is something that white people do to others in that self-defining process. It is wholly a relational concept, as a system of social and cultural activities (which vary from epoch to epoch).

This means that the term "race" is more properly understood as a verb rather than a noun. The verb is "to racialize," and it is something that white people do to others in the process of constructing themselves as white. The social institutions that manifest the processes of racialization, to which white people belong as white, place them in the subject position of the verb, with those who are racialized as other by whites placed in the object position of the verb and objectified. The term "racism" may superficially describe those practices, but it does not begin to name the cultural forces that drive them. What the structures of racialization produce, by organizing enactment and performance by whites (the verb's subject position) is a sense of membership in a white socius (a group characterized simply by a sense of belonging, without necessarily having community cohesion or political expression as a party). The relation between the way white people think of themselves and the structures of racialization constitutes the culture of whiteness—understanding the notion of culture as what is taken for granted or what goes without saying in one's relations with others. In that sense, "racism" is a relation between whites for which people of color are the means.[9]

As an identity, whiteness forms part of a symbolic relation to the social structures of racialization. The symbolic character of whiteness refers to socius membership, providing an assumption of entitlement and unquestionability, often with the expectation of deference. One sees this character of whiteness often in U.S. labor history, where the culture of whiteness supersedes the ideals of class solidarity. For example, in 1899, in a mine strike in Illinois, black and white union miners (UMW) acted in concert, side by side. The company brought in black strikebreakers from out of state. Though the strike was won, the white miners afterwards expressed hostility toward the black union members as if, through their white eyes, blackness rendered the others strikebreakers rather than union members.[10]

The Vietnam anti-war movement provided a more recent example of this. In its early stages in New York City, many black churches, black and Latino neighborhood associations, and Puerto Rican independence organizations got involved in opposition to the war, contributing their resources to anti-war events. They had a concrete understanding of the colonialism implicit in U.S. aggression against Vietnam from their own experience as colonized, while that character of the war confused many white activists insofar as it contradicted the mythology of the United States as a democracy. Black and Latino people tried to explain what colonialism was about as a structure and offered leadership in the struggle against it, but most white activists couldn't hear them and even marginalized them. The result was that the anti-war movement at home (though not in Vietnam among the troops themselves) ended up a white movement.

U.S. labor and protest movement history is replete with examples in which white identity trumps class solidarity, negating class experience. To see this simply as racism or racial prejudice engendered by employers to divide and rule (which it also is) is to ignore its underlying cultural force (what makes it work so well). White identity, as a cultural identity, has greater solidarist immediacy for white workers than worker identity insofar as its symbolism provides a sense of belonging more powerful than ideology. Insofar as whites occupy the subject position of the verb, they relate to each other through it. Even in social justice movements such as the early abolitionists, or trade unions, or current anti-racist movements, white identity constitutes a sense of symbolic sanctity, a sense of unquestionability and entitlement.

The sense of unquestionability that emerges from the entitlement whiteness assumes for itself is in effect a license to predetermine for oneself who others are. This is different from prejudice, insofar as it produces a need for a greater degree of inequality than mere prejudice. Equality instills fear in most white people. It is what has brought them historically to act against their own economic interests and to coalesce behind institutional violence. It is a fear that one's identity and one's sense of belonging would be lost if the exclusionism that generates that identity and membership were discarded. Justice and democracy, because they depend on equality, intuitively spell a dismantling of that identity and its hegemony.[11] Violence often appears to be more legitimate, especially when committed by institutions.

Among mainstream whites, the fear of equality often leads to a real acceptance of institutional racism. The unequal funding of educational facilities, the impoverishment of communities of color, bank redlining, traditional racialized redistricting procedures and the attendant minoritization of people of color, police racial profiling and the prison industry, and the general criminalization of people of color are all forms of institutional violence.[12] All constitute different dimensions of the structure of racialization, and all are accepted practices as norms of the social order insofar as they extend the subject-object relation that white racialized identity establishes with others. The very pretension to innocence concerning inequality or racial violence (the person who says "what's the matter with being white?") is an expression of that normativity. The norm is also designed to dodge the relationality of race (those who say, "I'm proud of being white").

But the ability to embrace institutional inequality and racism emerges from a more essential extension of the white subject-object relation, namely, a tacit or open demand for obedience. Obedience is the logical extension of the presumption to determine who the other is as an object of one's own identity construction. Today, we see this requirement for obedience expressed in the escalation of police violence toward people of color, accompanied by a general white equanimity toward the criminalization of the victims and the inflation of the prison system. Indeed, in many of the recent police killings, the only possible rationale was an arbitrary police-administered punishment for disobedience (discounting the police explanations of threats and guns for the killings, which generally fall apart under further investigation).

Oscar Grant was shot in the back while on the ground with three cops sitting on him. Alan Blueford was shot while lying on his back for having run from an arbitrary police challenge. Kenneth Harding was shot in the back for jumping a two-dollar bus fare. Gary King was shot in the back for walking away from an officer. Ramarley Graham, a teenager in the Bronx, was spotted by police going into his tenement and shot in his own apartment when they followed and broke down the door. Kenneth Chamberlain was shot in his own apartment for having refused to open the door to police answering an accidental and false medical assistance alert. [13] In the aggregate, the notion that these are rogue cops falls apart. In reality, each killing was the immediate response to disobedience to a command. Each killing represents a demand for obedience.

The mind that can subjectively accept this racializing violence with its lethal ethos of institutional obedience is a mind that has already centered itself in the hegemony expressed by these actions. It is what can be called a "hegemonic mind." It becomes a signifier for an inherent anti-democratic dimension for whiteness in its subject-object relation to those it racializes.

And this brings into focus the structural problem of whiteness for pro-democratic whites. Under the aegis of the hegemonic mind and its demand for obedience, one can't be white identified and anti-racist at the same time. That is, one cannot accept a racializing subjectivity and be anti-racist. Theoretically, white people have the choice to accept the racializing aspect of the white identity given them by this society or not. But practically, that identity brings with it the dependence on racialization that produced it. White identity is always a racialized and racializing identity. [14] The problem for pro-democracy white people is not only how to end racism and inequality but how to stop functioning or participating in the subject position of that verb.

Some Political Implications of This "Grammar"

The most direct implication of this racializing grammar is that white people are the only ones with a real interest in "race" itself. They are the only ones with a cultural interest in racializing others and with an overriding interest in a racial hierarchy. It is this that drives racism. As a mode of oppression and domination, racism is white racism. Black or indigenous or Latino or Asian people in the United States, as an element of their resistance, are often thrust into a position of recuperating their subjectivities and communities in racial terms against that objectification by the white socius (black race consciousness and black power, for instance, or La Raza in Aztlán). As a form of resistance to their racialization, it represents a form of oppositional coopting of the concept of race for themselves.

A second implication is that white identity presents a vulnerability (in its need to racialize) to the threat of deprivation that its dependence on the other (those defined as other, as black or brown) produces, as a constant insecurity. It is against that insecurity that the hegemonic mind is developed as a shield. And that shielding obstructs the ability to know how to stop fulfilling the subject position of that verb.

Thirdly, though some anti-racist and pro-democratic whites may seek to abandon their whiteness, that is an idle endeavor because whiteness is a cultural structure. The hegemonic mind is not simply an attitude toward those it acts to racialize; it is a relation to other white people as well. The hegemonic mind must be dismantled socially.

There are those who say that white people must own the fact that they are white. And that is true. A white person cannot be anything but white in this racialized society. But the core of the problem is acting white, fulfilling the subject position of the verb "to racialize." Acting white is a performance that is taught to each white person, beyond feelings of prejudice or superiority, though rationalized by them. Acting white may take the form of adopting an objectifying manner, or being patronizing, expressing gratuitous hostility or obsequious concern, and so on, toward the racialized, not to mention the broad spectrum of social violence. To refuse to accept the subject position of the verb "to racialize" means to stop acting white. To stop acting white means to stop fostering the cultural institutionality of whiteness as a social relation. And that means to stand in opposition to one's whiteness as a cultural identity. Not to stand in opposition to that identity is to accept the violence of its culture toward others.

The Anti-democratic Nature of Whiteness

Equality is one of the indispensable foundations for democracy. Democracy means that the people who will be affected by a policy not only get to decide for or against the policy but also how the issue to be decided is defined and how the policy is articulated to resolve the issue. That is, before there is a vote on a policy, there must be discussion and dialogue among those who will be affected by it. The many times in U.S. history that white people have debated whether black people should have a vote, the issue has been decided by white people and not through discussions of the issues of voting and democracy that included those to be affected. To have entered such a dialogic relation would have meant a white recognition of an equal subjectivity for black people, obliterating the subject-object relation. More usual is an instance in the 1820s when a petition to Congress by black people led to a debate on how to curtail the right of black people to petition Congress.[15] Today, it is the proclamation of "illegal" status for immigrants that represents the same paradigm.[16] The culture of whiteness is one that grounds itself in exclusionism and inequality. Even the recent populist refusals of universal health care (led by the Tea Party) or educational opportunity are ongoing representations of this.[17]

The passage of civil rights legislations during the 1960s occurred only because of the massive protests by black people against having little or no voice in making policy that affected them. Protest movements in general exist because people are given no voice in specific policy issues, such as war, the prison industry, foreign policy, social asset privatization, the legitimization of racial profiling and the enhancement of search and obedience powers for the police, corporate personhood, and so on. Each protest demonstration is a demand that a policy decision made without the people participating be rescinded and decided again democratically. The existence of protest movements does not simply represent a flaw in the political system but a structural absence of democratic inclusion. It presents an opposition to traditional presumptions of hegemony. The cultural form that arbitrary political hegemony takes differs from country to country. For the United States, its paradigmatic form is the corporate elite and white supremacy. The first conditions the stratification of U.S. society and the latter its structure of exclusion and social inequality (see note 5).

Many white people struggle against the legacy and continuity of prejudice and institutional racism. But racism is a symptom of the culture of whiteness and white racialized identity. Racism remains an expression of the real interest that white racialized identity has in race and in racializing others. Racism is the cultural technology for producing a racialized hierarchy (and here I'm not referring to the forms of ethnic hierarchy that one finds elsewhere—for instance, in Japan—but the specific culture of whiteness as it has developed in the United States).

The problem of whiteness obstructs the struggle for democracy for all people. Whites cannot work for democracy while thinking of themselves as naturally white, that is, as existentially white in and of themselves, because that ignores the relationality of race, and the cultural constructedness of white subjectivity. To look for a pro-democratic whiteness means to misrecognize the power of the exclusionism and inequality contained in the subject-object relation that white identity depends on. It carries a supremacism into the struggle for equality. We saw this with respect to the issues of "multiculturalism" and "diversity." The notion of the United States being multicultural was initially advanced by those cultures and peoples marginalized by white hegemony (black, Latino, indigenous, Asian, etc.) against the uniformity of the dominant white voice and as a demand that their second-class status be ended. It was a form of rebellion. Liberal white people picked up the idea and then included, themselves, and through themselves, all white people in the domain of the multi-cultural (rather than embrace the autonomy and sovereignty that those in rebellion were proclaiming for themselves as separate from whiteness). Thus, they reintroduced their hegemonic voice into what stood against it. It transformed the act of rebellion by those subjected to exclusion into a horizontal region of diversity in which white majoritarian interests could co-opt the concept of diversity, sweeping the rebellion and what it was against under the rug.

One still observes this kind of seizure of hegemony, even in the Occupy movement. In Oakland, black and Latino participation was extensive during the first (encampment) stage. Police repression of the encampment forced the movement to decentralize into other forms of organizing. Too often, meetings became white led and white planned. People of color in both New York City and Oakland raised the issue of white dominance critically, but an awareness of how to incorporate that into the movement's thinking remained sparse. A group formed to propose incorporating the concept of "decolonization" into what the movement was about—a decolonization of the movement and a decolonization of the white hegemonic mind—but it was refused, and they were thrust into the margins as simply a special committee. Meanwhile, activities planned to involve communities that were predominantly black were organized and carried out by groups that were predominantly white. These activists could see the effects of white hegemony but could not immediately reflect on what they had been doing to bring that about.[18]

Ultimately, for white people, a social justice movement is the only way one can function in a democratic manner in the United States Movements provide the arena in which white people can confront their own whiteness while struggling against the injustices of it as a cultural structure. But it only presents an opportunity. They must take seriously what the arena of social justice movements provides and face the real necessity of overcoming the white hegemonic mind.

THE WHITE HEGEMONIC MIND

Entitlement

What essentially characterizes the hegemonic mind is its feeling of entitlement. Entitlement involves the assumption that one is to be respected as a source of knowledge or an arbiter of proper comportment and activity. The hegemonic mind presumes its contributions to events or planning have greater weight than that of others, which leads to assumptions of control. When not granted deference, white people often feel themselves belittled or reduced to menial status, losing a sense of acting in concert with others, shoulder to shoulder. I actually heard a white activist blurt out in a meeting that was part of Occupy Oakland, "So it's left to a white man to do all that drudge work." It reflects a sense of self-importance on a cultural rather than egotistical level, which appropriates the attempts at autonomy and sovereignty by others to the point of speaking for them and instructing them. But the act of "instruction" itself contradicts the anti-hegemonic motif of autonomy. Even the liberal attitude of "helping" those victimized by racism presumes them to be unentitled. The alternative would be to stand in solidarity with those seeking to construct their own sovereign identity, which would mean expunging all entitlement and its hierarchical impositions.[19] Though the hegemonic mind may psychologically think its actions are for the purpose of social cohesion or even unity of purpose, its implicit effects are quite at odds with that.

In a secret sense, the entitled fear those they treat as unentitled, envisioning resentment or hostility. They seek protection in social and emotional distance, which only heightens their sense of entitlement.[20] In other words, there is an unavoidable sense of paranoia attached to it. Addressing that dimension of paranoia in social justice movements is one of the most difficult tasks for white people.

As an anti-democratic attitude, entitlement reflects a sense of social permission rather than pre-judgment. It is not the same as prejudice because it pertains to social membership and self-inclusion in the social source of authority rather than an individual act of derogatory exclusion. It is a permission that is structural, an *a priori* moment in the construction of a cultural identity.

The unfolding of the white hegemonic mind and its essentially undemocratic nature was clearly revealed in the way civil rights gains were rescinded. After the 1954 Supreme Court school desegregation decision, the Voting Rights Act of 1965, and affirmative action legislation, it appeared for a brief period that the nation had accepted its democratization, and a fundamental cultural structure of the United States seemed to be crumbling of its own weight. [21] Everyone knew that none of that would have been possible without massive demonstrations, the spread of autonomous organization to other people (the movements of black people were soon joined by women, Latinos, Native Americans, Asian, an anti-war upheaval, communities of alternate sexualities, a counter-culture, and environmental defense against corporate despoliation), and the occurrence of community uprisings in Harlem, Detroit, Watts, and other cities/neighborhoods. Insofar as the civil rights movements were powerful pro-democracy movements that actually brought more people into participation and decision-making in the United States, the process of lessening its effects amounted implicitly to an anti-democratic process and to a reconstruction of white hegemony.

The first stage of response by the white governing establishment was the repeal of affirmative action, followed by the defunding of employment opportunity offices, the subsidizing of runaway shops, and legal norms that made racial discrimination almost impossible to contest or prosecute. [22] Many white people accepted the political inversion of terms like "discrimination" (affirmative action as reverse discrimination). It reflected the hegemonic mind's sense that if it were not in control, it was suffering victimization. A more concrete inversion has occurred in the realm of education. Higher education was opened up by affirmative action but reduced funding of urban grade schools on a discriminatory basis, leading to proposals for a voucher system and the privatization of education, has eviscerated equality of educational opportunity in many parts of the country.

The second stage has involved urban police power, a prison industry and mass incarceration. The story of militarized policing of grade schools and the creation of a school-to-jail pipeline for students of color is too complex for the space available here. [23] But the act of declaring immigrants to be "illegal persons," with massive ICE (Immigration and Customs Enforcement) raids and deportations that break up families, leaving children deprived of parents, clarifies the punitive character of establishing an "otherness" for those who are to be dominated. [24]

The role of the runaway shop movement in all this is important. During the first half of the twentieth century, a vast number of black people migrated from the south to northern industrial centers. When the industrial union movement gained a footing in the 1920s and '30s, it was in terms of organizing a heavily integrated work force. The economic stability this bestowed on black and brown communities was critical to the later political resistance they were able to raise to segregation. The industrial unions were the ones primarily affected by the runaway shops. The startling aspect of the entire deindustrialization process, however, was that not a single union, city council, or county council raised any objection to the removal of industrial facilities, nor to the vast unemployment that it would bring about. (Only in Youngstown, Ohio, was an attempt made by rank and file workers to keep the steel mills there from closing. It failed.) Both the union leaders and the city councils knew that the employment opportunities provided by new investment that would flow into the economic space left by industry would go to white people first. Thus, it was expected to roll back the integration of the labor force and reduce the economic strength that black and brown communities had gained. That was not a disappointed expectation. For white employment, it provided only a temporary disruption. The absence of resistance to the loss of industry made clear that the strength of white cultural coherence comes not from economic interests but from an identity structure, a commonality of belonging, with class interests only riding along in its wake.

Hierarchy in U.S. society is a lamination of strata according to income and occupation (on a corporate model). To be white in this stratified structure is to see class hierarchy as social and to see class as sociological. European descriptions of class, of class history, and conflict are too binary to be applicable. They do not include the gradations of stratified status. What is binary in the United States is its racialization (white defined through black, and other people of color defined under its aegis). Class in the United States is racialized. Black people or brown people who have the same income levels as white people do not have the same social standing. Many whites have welcomed the fact that some black and brown people could fight their way up into the middle class social strata, the professions, and so on, because it implicitly affirmed a class-based society while disguising the fact that society's stratification was racialized. At the same time, few white people thought to impede the repeal of affirmative action programs that made that rise in status possible. This then defined an essentially white view of hierarchy. When white people say, "But I'm also oppressed," they are assuming a white sense of hierarchy. It is a different system of oppression than that of racialization. If class discourses hide social racialization, and class discourses don't work to describe corporate stratification, then the social hierarchies by which the white hegemonic mind dominates remain unarticulable.

This dichotomy of systems of oppression is important for understanding the meaning of enhanced police obedience statutes, which have transformed the police into a new color line. In essence, these statutes give the police the power to criminalize anyone they wish at will. The police are given a high degree of autonomy through the system of victimless crime laws, which allow them to dispense with a complainant in approaching individuals. Police commands that will be humiliating to a person, insofar as the person refuses them in defense of dignity or self-respect, opens the person to charges of disobeying an officer and resisting arrest. The nine-to-one imprisonment ratio clearly indicates that racial profiling informs such police procedures. Police actions then represent a selection process between those whose humanity will be respected (the non-profiled) and those whose humanity will be discounted and disrespected (the profiled). A color line is thus drawn, which hides the activity of racialization under the stratified social problem of criminality.

The confluence of black and brown criminalization and the paranoia inherent in whiteness create a complicated paradox for pro-democratic whites. Opposition to police impunity and violence in the name of humanity and democracy gets translated into a disregard of the crime problem (or even support for criminality). To stand in opposition to crime means to affirm the police and their segregationist and anti-democratic color line. To speak for democracy from behind the color line is to deny democracy by affirming it as white. To cross the color line and stand in opposition to the police is to lose political focus through opposition to fighting crime. That is, "democracy" resides on the same side of the color line as segregation, while anti-segregation stands for anti-democratic chaos and lawlessness. Pro-democratic white people find themselves reduced to calling for "due process" and Constitutional rights (civil liberties), while daily police practices increasingly dispense with both. White pro-democracy finds itself with nowhere to stand.

Ultimately, for pro-democratic white people, the construction of alternate political structures, many of which are pointed to by social justice movements, become necessary for stepping outside the crime-democracy paradox that the police and the political system have created.

Why White Skin Privilege Is a Misguided Notion

Many white people attempt to dispel the anti-democratic nature of whiteness by seeking to abandon their own white skin privilege. White skin privilege consists of a long list of things that white people don't have to think about, don't think twice about doing, things they take for granted without worrying about the structures of power ambushing them or catching them unawares.[25] When the police stop a black motorist, it looks like an ordinary traffic stop when seen in its singularity. But it becomes a violation of fairness and justice when seen in the aggregate. White skin privilege is the privilege of seeing each instance in its singularity. Many whites who seek to abandon it gain the ability to see such things in the aggregate.

But the idea of giving up white skin privilege is a dodge. Giving something up, as white, is itself a privileged idea. And it sees only half of what is contained in white hegemony. Professor john powell has allegorized white skin privilege with an image of two escalators, one going up and the other going down.[26] Those on the up-escalator will all eventually get to the top. Those condemned to enter the down-escalator will have to run up those moving stairs to reach the top. Some will get there, but most will get tired or be unable to overcome the machine's velocity and end up at the bottom again. In powell's analogy, the ability to use the up-escalator at will is the sign of white skin privilege.

But the difference constitutes a structure of subjection and subjugation because imposed by force. In powell's analogy, there are two activities at work, and white skin privilege looks at only one of them. The first is that there are two escalators, one going up and the other down. The second is that there are people, white people, at the bottom, forcing people of color over to the down-escalator while allowing white people to proceed to the up-escalator (the institutionality of racialization). Running up the down-escalator is not chosen voluntarily. In other words, "white skin privilege" is actually a system of selection deployed by power through an institutionality that involves the actions of the entire white socius. It appears normal to white people because it manifests a process of selection to which they are already members. For them, the notion of crime prevention, security, and social peace is only the operation and preservation of that selection process. But the force of selection stands at the core of the structure of racialization.

Force is indeed the issue, especially for privilege. Privilege is something that is given by those who have the power to do so. And if given, then it can be taken away. It reflects a power relation. Those who are de-privileged are the victims of the power to de-privilege. Because the concept of white skin privilege looks at privilege rather than at the acts of de-privileging, it blinds itself to the imposition of that deprivation. To see the up-escalator as privilege means to look only at the escalator and not the acts forcing others to use the down-escalator. In effect, the power to give up white skin privilege means that its abandonment is not an abandonment of power.

If race is something that white people do to others, then whiteness represents something taken from others through those social actions of deprivation and derogation. "Taking" is a very different relation to others than "being given," in the sense that white skin privilege is given. Whiteness is not a structure of privilege but a structure of deprivation of others. The problem is the system that deprives others in order to control them. It is a systematic divestment of others' humanity through their objectification and commodification (which is what is meant by "coloniality"). In essence, white skin privilege continues the coloniality of racialization. All white people are enlisted in this process through acceptance of the symbolic meaning of their whiteness as both natural (simply human) and hegemonic. The problem is not "white skin privilege" but "white skin coloniality." Privilege is a benign designation. Coloniality on the other hand assumes intention.

Now, suppose a white person on the up-escalator discerns that something is wrong, turns around and attempts to walk back down. If all this person discerns is the unfairness of sending others over to the down escalator, then being on the up-escalator might look like a privilege. However, it would only be the concept of privilege that such a white person would confront. Having been selected for upward motion, she or he would already be beyond the selection process itself, which is the core of the problem. To try to abandon white privilege, the person would have to work almost as hard, going down the up-escalator, as others work to go up the down-escalator. And should the attempt to "abandon" white privilege stop to rest, the escalator will carry the person to the top. Rather than an abandonment of privilege, it is the cessation of all racializing activity, a brake put on the escalators themselves, with the selection process at the bottom brought to an end. Or, to put that in terms of this chapter's argument, it is an end to the subject-object relation of coloniality and its structural foundation that is needed.

The white problem for white people is how to put a stop to the coloniality that whiteness carries with it as a cultural identity as well as a legacy. That will mean two things: a cessation of the operations of racialization and the opening of social space to the self-rehumanization of those who have been subjected to racial coloniality, and to endless dehumanization and derogation at the hands of white racializing subjectivity. It will not mean granting others privilege or subjectivity. The pretension to grant anything in this social sense (though not in an ontological sense) is still within a subject-object relation. It will mean stopping the machinery of whiteness, dismantling the structures of racialization, and getting out of the way of the efforts of those formerly subjected to reconstruct themselves as they see fit.

A DU BOISIAN ALTERNATIVE

Pro-democracy whites face multiple problems with whiteness. The first is how to bring about a democratization of the United States against it. Second, there is a tendency that their efforts will be marginalized by mainstream white society in its attempt to preserve white hegemony. Third, their natural allies, those subjected to white coloniality, often marginalize them because they are white. Communities of color know that anti-racist whites can leave and return to the white socius when the struggle gets too hot. That is not a fault of race but a cultural condition expressive of a structure of force, terror, and oppression, the system of social activities by which white identity generates itself and its concept of "race." In the United States, pro-democratic white people have no solid political ground upon which to stand. I say this blatantly not to be discouraging but to enable us to face reality. We have to understand fully the thrust of the white hegemonic mind, both in us and against us. If for no other reason, that understanding alone should guide us toward the development of alternate political structures and away from the given.

Du Bois raised the question of what it was like to be a "problem" as a black person (in the first paragraph of *The Souls of Black Folk*) three decades after the Reconstruction experiments in democratic processes had been overthrown by white paramilitary gangs. Du Bois articulated the dual consciousness experienced by black people under the force of white reconstruction at that time—to have to see oneself through others' eyes, to strive to be "black Americans" while prevented from being "Americans" because black. The problem that black people posed for white racialized identity at that moment was precisely the fact of their having seized some level of equality and having stepped onto the political stage. White racialized identity depends on a subordinated black population as the source of its self-definition.

A similar process is in progress today, a process of white reconstruction. The present process of white reconstruction uses a different technology of racialization than it did after Reconstruction. It is a technology based on police rule (a blue color line), the largest prison system in the world (judicial rather than legislative segregation), and a two-party system whose willingness and ability to disenfranchise in the interest of policy is extant.[27] The purpose of this political technology is the same as the populist forms of segregation and disenfranchisement deployed by Jim Crow, namely, the reconstitution of white subject-object relations to others. Black and brown people can rebel against this, but white people can't. The problem for whites is that a cultural structure cannot be reformed or overthrown; it can only be transformed. For white identity to attempt to free itself by rebellion from white supremacy would only reassert a white identity in rebellion and reconstitute the supremacy assumed by its self-definition.

To live in equality with others, it is the white hegemonic mind that would have to be dismantled. To dismantle the hegemonic mind is the same as decolonizing white identity. The hegemonic mind and the white racialized identity in which it resides are both practical and symbolic aspects of an ongoing coloniality.

And by "dismantle," I do not mean either revolutionary overthrow or reform. I am speaking of a cultural structure, not a power structure. A cultural structure can neither be overthrown, since it is not a power structure, nor can it be reformed for that would mean joining it and attempting change it from within, having accepted all its basic assumptions. An example of dismantling a cultural structure would be the consciousness raising groups that emerged in the women's movements. They neither overthrew patriarchy nor did they attempt to reform the structure of male hegemony in all social or personal relations. Instead, they rejected that hegemony, concerned themselves with redeveloping women's identity such that women could step out from under patriarchal power and at the same time speak with the collective voice of a movement that provided an alternate mode of survival, breaking men's monopoly on that domain. To construct an alternative, be it an ethic or a political structure, does not reform; it existentially separates hegemonic structures from their foundation in the acceptance by those subjected to them.

One possible step toward beginning to dismantle the cultural coloniality of whiteness would be a white form of the Du Boisian double consciousness. A white double consciousness would be one that would see itself as those whom whites racialize see it. Inverting the subject and object positions of the verb "to racialize" would mean seeing oneself as one is seen by those on the receiving end of the structures of racialization. That does not mean granting subjectivity to people of color, because they are already subjects in their own lives. It means to see oneself as an object for that subjectivity, as an object in the racialized other's look, in the consciousness of those who have had to defend themselves against white supremacy every day of their lives. This would hopefully provide some understanding of how one's own actions (as a white person) racialize others, and how one is complicit in the structures of racialization that produce one's white racialized identity—and thus bring about a consciousness of what it is that has to stop.

NOTES

1. *The Fire This Time*, a documentary film about South Central Los Angeles, directed by Randy Holland, and produced by Randy Holland and Mark Mori, 1994.

2. Michelle Alexander, *The New Jim Crow* (New York: New Press, 2010).

3. Steve Martinot, *The Machinery of Whiteness* (Philadelphia: Temple Univ. Press, 2009). Chapter 4 gives a brief description of how this happened.

4. An Asian man who was studying at Oikos University in Oakland went to the college on April 2, 2012, with a gun and killed six white people. The media immediately started spending a lot of time on the lives of these six victims. Who were they? What were they doing? What were their families like? What have other people lost by their deaths? Of the shooter, the only question the media asked was his motive. How could he be so hostile to these nice (white) people? The next week, April 8, 2012, two white men in Tulsa, Oklahoma, took some guns, drove into a black neighborhood, and began shooting people on the street at random. They killed three and wounded two. And the media? About the victims' lives, or their families there was not a word. The media focused on the shooters. Who were they? What were their families like? Where did they come from? Thus the media grants humanity and personhood to white people, and withholds it from people who are not white.

5. There is an intimate connection between corporate development and the enslavement and segregation of black people, or between corporate personhood and the refusal of full humanity and citizenship for black people by white supremacy. One discovers this in two judicial decisions by Chief Justice Roger Taney in the decades before the Civil War. In the Letson case of 1844, he granted corporations personhood because, though chartered in states, they had to have standing in federal court in order to respond to interstate suits. In the Dred Scott case (1856), he refused personhood to black people using an inversion of the same argument. Cf. Allen Austin, *The Origins of the Dred Scott Case* (Athens, Ga.: University of Georgia Press, 2006).

6. Steve Martinot, *The Rule of Racialization* (Philadelphia: Temple University Press, 2003), p. 49–59.

7. Ibid, p. 67–69.

8. Color is produced in the human (like most human traits) on a continuous spectrum. Between any two people of different color, it is possible to find someone whose color lies between them. If color lies on a continuum, then there are no natural breaks in the spectrum of human color by which to divide humanity (which also holds for other traits). If race is based on color, as the modern concept of race would have it, then divisions had to be invented in that

continuum. The first invented break was that between the whiteness of Europeans and the color of all others. Hence, the importance of miscegenation laws. In order for a person to be white, all one's foreparents must be white. Cf. Martinot, *Rule*, p. 21–23.

9. White people define or enact their relation to whiteness differently, across a spectrum of attitudes ranging from white supremacist and white liberal to whites in resistance (in alliance with anti-oppression and anti-colonialist struggles). For white supremacists, the present racial hierarchy is natural, whiteness is given sanctity, and the need for police rule and prisons is unquestionable. For white liberals, the violence of racism is wrong, so there is a dual desire as whites to alleviate the injuries suffered while educating the prejudiced to the error of their ways. For them, institutional racism would be alleviated by making democracy work better. For radical anti-racist whites, insofar as they seek alliance with people of color, whiteness becomes a dual hindrance, first as a legacy (the hegemonic mind) to overcome, and second as a constant source of distrust by people of color. White liberals stand in alleged opposition to racism, attempting to reason with racist individuals, to show them that their prejudice has no basis in reality, and that they are acting against their own real interests. But they generally oppose movements for the sovereignty of the oppressed, such as black power, or native self-govern-ance, and seek solutions to racial oppression in law, legislation, and government action. The liberal ethic will counsel people of color to be more obedient and law abiding, in order not to give white supremacy an excuse for further travesties. But the implication is that the victims are in some sense instigators of those attacks, and thus of the oppression they face, while assuming that the police and prison systems are basically legitimate and necessary.

10. Herbert Hill, "Myth-making as Labor History." In *Politics, Culture, and Society*, vol.2(2), Winter 1988, p.165.

11. Social movements, which focus on political and economic issues, fail against cultural structures. Class rebellion in Europe, for instance, was defeated by the cultural structures of nationalism. In the U.S., class rebellion, abolitionism, and civil rights have all been defeated by the cultural structures of whiteness. It was white supremacy that transformed aspects of civil rights into threats (reverse discrimination, a quota system, crime), demanding general social identification with itself against the "travesty" of these threats. Once whites accept the need to defend against the threat, the threat becomes real.

12. As an unrequited example of institutional racism, the Supreme Court legitimized racial profiling by ruling that a person's color can be considered suspicious behavior by the police. Cf. Alexander, *New Jim Crow*, p. 62-63, 128–36.

13. It is a growing list of people murdered by police for no other reason than disobedience. Every week a new case emerges of a black or brown person shot or beaten to death by police or white civilians. On Sept. 2, 2012, the most recent killing in the San Francisco Bay Area (as I am writing this chapter) was Mario Romero, shot thirty-one times while sitting in his car by two officers in Vallejo. The arbitrary murder of Amadou Diallo (1999) marked a turning point in this, not in terms of massive reactions against the killing itself but rather the awareness of the extent to which the police had been militarized. The four cops who shot him were part of a special unit that had been patrolling the streets, looking for just such an incident for themselves. They were so fixated on shooting him that the last two bullets to hit him went through the bottoms of his feet. This militarization is not just in terms of weapons and tactics, but in prioritizing weapons of war for common deployment as a first option rather than a last resort. It doesn't happen overtly in the name of whiteness, but rather in the name of "law and order." But the legitimization of racial profiling (by the Supreme Court) effectively racializes the concept of "law and order," placing it at the core of the structure of racialization (see note 12).

14. I discuss the internal structure of white racialized identity, elsewhere, in *The Rule of Racialization* (p. 68–70; see also Chapter 4). Essentially, as a cultural structure, it has a number of components that generate each other, namely, a sense of white solidarity, a paranoia toward people of color, and a need for violence. The paranoia emerges from a recognition of white exclusion and derogation of people of color, who are imagined to be threatening (not without reason, but not as imagined). That paranoia creates a need for white solidarity against the imagined threat. And social violence is welcomed insofar as it represents a defense that mani-fests solidarity against the threat while making the imagined threat seem real. All oppressive structures do face a threat of rebellion against themselves. But they have the choice to cease

being oppressive to alleviate that threat. Not to do so is to embrace the paranoia and make it an essential part of one's identity and sense of being. But today, if what whites get out of the oppression of racialization is their identity as white, then to cease imagining the threat would be to cease being white. Indeed, paranoia is so deeply ingrained in U.S. culture that it has become a necessary component of social coherence, inventing threats to preserve a sense of self-recognition. Since World War II, the threats have included communism, cold war hysteria, a war on drugs, a war on terrorism, black and brown criminality, Islam, Middle Eastern people, and "illegal" (Latino) immigrants.

15. Leon Litwack, *North of Slavery* (Chicago: Univ. of Chicago Press, 1961), p. 33–34.

16. Pennsylvania is an example. Before 1830, free black people voted. After the elections of 1832, they were first disenfranchised by the state courts, and then their disenfranchisement was written into the Pennsylvania Constitution of 1836.

17. When Obama fostered a health care reform, there were proposals for it which constituted an interesting spectrum of possibilities, from single-payer (universal) to public option to major overhaul of the medical insurance industry. He allowed Republican opposition to force him to consider a lowest common denominator, minor insurance reform, without insisting on debate on the real issues of responsibility to citizens. Ultimately, it was the universality of health care, and the sense of equality that it would foster, that was defeated.

18. For instance, a BBQ was being planned for a neighborhood of Oakland that is predominantly black (the fourth in a series of such BBQs in Oakland). The majority of the committee planning it was white, while a number of black people attended the meeting. The topic of discussion was leafletting the neighborhood about the BBQ. The black participants generally stood in the background, were not given space in planning, and hesitated to volunteer for things. When they made suggestions of things to do, they were told, "we have already taken care of that."

19. Sovereignty is the radical content of identity politics, while integration is its liberal content. Sovereignty and integration are not opposites. The opposition that appears is the priority given to them, to integrate as sovereign, or to integrate into another's sovereignty. Liberal activists complain that identity politics stands in the way of unity and solidarity. Radical activists recognize that people must find their way to self-organization and leadership on their own terms in order to enter into solidarity with others. Not to guarantee the sovereignty of the racialized is to assume the continuation of white hegemony.

20. The feeling of guilt is often a response to one's recognition of implicit complicity in the existence of hegemonic domination. To feel guilt is to lack the strength to abandon one's role. Personal defensiveness is substituted for opposition to social oppression. It is a refusal to contest the structures of racialization, or the hegemonic mind. One feels guilty in order to preserve one's white identity and membership in the white socius.

21. In 1975, Samuel Huntington called it a "Crisis of Democracy." He argued before the Trilateral Commission that the movements had brought too much democracy to the nation, and that measures had to be taken, which he spelled out, to insure that this should never happen again. In general, the measures he advocated have been put in place. Cf. Samuel Huntington, *the Crisis of Democracy: Report on the Governability of Democracies to the Trilateral Commission* (New York: New York University Press, 1975).

22. Alexander, *New Jim Crow*, p. 106–9.

23. Victor Rios, *Punished: Policing the Lives of Black and Latino Boys* (New York: New York University Press, 2011); Annette Fuentes, *Lockdown High: When the Schoolhouse Becomes a Jailhouse* (New York: Verso, 2011).

24. The progression seen here follows a pattern that has appeared twice before in U.S. history, the first time against the abolitionist movement in the wake of the revolution, and the second time in the wake of Reconstruction. Both revealed the same three stages, the first being legislative, the second being a phase of massive police or populist action (in the era of Jim Crow), and the third being a stage of racial violence designed to inculcate absolute obedience in subjected communities.

25. The reader should note that there are many scholars who write about white privilege who don't believe that white privilege can be simply abandoned through an act of fiat (for example, Peggy McIntosh, George Yancy, John T. Warren, Barbara Applebaum, et al.).

26. john powell, "Regionalism and Race," in *Race, Poverty, and the Environment,* Vol. 17 (1), Spring 2010, p. 45–48.

27. Though the Republican Party benefited directly from the disenfranchisement of the over 100,000 people in Florida in 2000, the Democratic Party colluded in it. They prevented a court suit by the NAACP, which had collected over 10,000 affidavits claiming illegitimate prevention from voting. And they refused to challenge the legitimacy of the Florida delegation to the electoral college, though there was an opportunity to do so.

Chapter Thirteen

Am I the Small Axe or the Big Tree?

Steve Garner

I am driving. Bob Marley is on the MP3. I am singing along, with gusto, that "we" are the small axe. Marley's voice convinces me that we are both ready and sharpened to cut down the big tree. [1]

The pleasure you get out of this derives from imagining you are part of the "we" proclaiming itself as the small axe. Whichever part of the big tree your focus is on, it feels good to define yourself in opposition. I expect most white scholars engaged in writing and researching and teaching about racism like to think of themselves as progressive allies of people of color, whose experience has led them to understand the concept of white privilege. Why would you do something as perverse as propel your caboose backward up the rail track of dominant culture if you didn't believe that you were acting ethically, that your tiny contribution to the struggle for equality and justice *for everyone* was not important? You'd have to be crazy, right? But you have to recognise that you're on a journey that hasn't finished; that whatever you do, you're still white, still privileged. You have the option to not bother—without any cost to yourself—and that's part of what confers privilege. So wait. What if you are also sometimes the big tree, or worse, *only ever* the big tree, after all?

What would a journey to a place where the question can be answered look like? This chapter is a trip through a small section of the baggage of being a white scholar engaged in researching the racialization of white identities, in which I try to problematize instead of sanitize the whiteness inherent in my positions. As Vice argues, I must place myself among the group of people racialized as white who realizes that the self that I am is "constituted by habits of white privilege" [2] and is thus an ongoing problem that is not fully resoluble in the context of an unequal society. I have broken the journey down into a number of illustrative vignettes with reflections.

I have peered across the Atlantic, both literally and figuratively, on a number of occasions in my professional and private life. Literally, from the coast of Cornwall, England; the Southwestern tip of County Kerry, Ireland; the coast of Portugal and Western France. I looked toward Europe from the broad sweeping northern shoulder of South America, where the ocean turns brown. I have spent years reading the work of American scholars and novelists to whom I turn for insights on the "white problem" of racism and tried to make sense of what using the scholarly paradigm of whiteness could add to our European-derived knowledge.[3] When I come to write up findings of the fieldwork I do in provincial English cities, the voices of my American colleagues are never far from mine, providing contexts, comparable experiences, ways of knowing, speaking, and thinking. I hope that they can get something useful from this text, which, on re-reading, I find very European.

THE BROADWAY, SOUTHALL, THE EARLY 1970S

I grew up in Norwich (pronounced with a silent "w"), which is a small city by North American standards, in the east of England. It was in an area that had been left virtually untouched by the post-war waves of immigration as it was not a manufacturing base and was surrounded by a largely agricultural hinterland. We moved there when I was four. The rest of our family lived in Outer London, to the West and the South, and we traveled frequently between Norwich and London until I went to university.

I don't remember how often I was taken shopping by my grandmother before I was secondary school age. She lived on an estate (a project) near Heathrow Airport, and the closest reasonable shopping spots for items more sophisticated than could be found in the main street of the place she lived in were Southall and Uxbridge. The former was one of the earliest places in Britain to become a synonym of Commonwealth immigration and settlement, and therefore "otherness," within British urban space. Not a port with long-standing communities of color, Southall was a chunk of West London, about ten miles from the center, which had been full of factory and railway employment. South Asian immigrants were established in Southall by the '70s, and the main retail area, The Broadway, was full of shops catering to these diasporic communities. Later, Southall would be the site of confrontations between locals, police, skinheads, and anti-racist demonstrators,[4] but the afternoon I remember was just brimming full of traffic, people, the multicolored saris and materials displayed in the windows of the shops we walked past, and the smell of lunch from the numerous Indian restaurants. It was almost a sensory overload of richness. I was a little white kid in one of the few busy shopping spaces in England where white people were in the minority. At some point, either during or after one of these trips, it became fixed in my mind that Norwich was not the center of the universe: that other places existed and were not the same. Other people existed, and they seemed to be doing more or less the same stuff here as the people where I lived, but that it looked, smelled, and sounded a bit different. This is the most mundane insight imaginable, but as I was growing up in a part of England where many people did not travel far or imagine their lives encompassing much mobility, where the local was everything, and the local was virtually all white, this mooring point of Southall Broadway became more and more significant to me. This, plus the various other routine mixing of the West London street and public spaces that I did, enabled me to speak from experience of the ultimate banality and normality of multicultural Britain.

Of course, this assessment evacuated the power relations and structural parameters that I now recognize as a sociologist. Saying I wasn't scared of difference is implicitly a statement that there was something to be scared of in the first place, which would not occur to you unless the weight of the discourse suggested this to be the case. Unfortunately, this type of topic (difference is not scary/difference is scary) represented the low levels of discussion throughout secondary school (and, sadly, into university in many cases). The talk of the Other in white spaces is often not very sophisticated, and in that context I often appeared more sophisticated than the level of discussion.

AT SCHOOL, 1977

In the mid-1970s, the nationalist far right (especially the National Front party) mobilized successfully in Britain. It organized large rallies, and marches through city centers, had local councilors elected, and infiltrated football (soccer) to the point where many well-supported clubs had sizeable cells of NF sympathizers, fellow travelers, and/or people who enjoyed fighting, and especially enjoyed fighting black and Asian people, and especially when they outnumbered the latter. At this stage, the National Front published a magazine, which I think was called *The Patriot*. It circulated among skinheads. Someone had brought one to school, and it was doing the rounds. The storylines of the articles were predictable, and I summarize here: all the crime is committed by black people and Asians (I translate the racist terminology); they are backward, dirty, stupid and neither part of, nor ever could be part of, Britain. Solution? All non-white immigrants should be deported; there should be no more non-white immigration.

I read it on the school bus with my best friend at the time, and we agreed it was a really crap magazine. The thing that we found hilarious, however, was the constant assertion that white people were superior in everything.

Now we weren't active anti-racists or anything like it, but we did know a bit about sport and music.

The summer before, for example, we had both witnessed the test match (international cricket fixture) at The Oval, in London, where West Indies had utterly thumped England. Some of the individual performances were so breathtaking that we frequently talked about them. I still have vivid memories to this day. We sat virtually side-on to the wicket on one of the days we went to that game, and I remember the great Jamaican bowler, Michael Holding, running in, his arms swaying ever so slightly, his balletic take-off stride, and the dust explosion every time he bowled. Viv Richards (now Sir Vivian Richards) had battered 200 runs in a day, a display so muscular and imperious that I spent the next few years trying to match the spirit, if not the execution, of his batting. The very partisan crowd where we were sitting made that day special. In those days people were allowed into sports events carrying machetes! These were used to slice watermelons, which were then passed round to everyone. The drumming, singing, and slicing seemed endless. It was a bad day to be a watermelon. It should have been a bad day to be an England cricket fan, but it wasn't. It was not a surprise to discover that the West Indian supporters were far from the sly, smelly, criminal figures of the pages of *The Patriot*, but people who knew how to have fun, who were friendly, engaged in banter, sang, demonstrated unswerving loyalty to their team: and that, in the version of English masculinity I grew up in, counted for a lot.

This was also the period in which black soccer players were beginning to become more numerous in the English leagues. At the time, people like Laurie Cunningham, Cyrille Regis and Brendan Batson were coming under increasing media focus. Viv Anderson, the first to be selected for a senior England team, made his debut for the country in 1978. Our home team, Norwich City, had had an Indian goalkeeper, Kevin Keelan, for as long as either of myself and my friend could remember. He had visited our school and was occasionally seen in the city center: the most famous person of color in Norwich.

As for music, the radio stations in Britain were not as specialized as the American ones and usually played a mixture of genres. Although this was the era of the emergence of punk and New Wave, if you listened to commercial radio stations you were just as likely to hear Motown, reggae, and a vernacular British sub-category of reggae called lovers' rock.

For my friend and I, if the authors of *The Patriot*'s departure point was that white people were superior (try telling that to the all-white English national cricket team, 0-5 in the series!), they were clearly illiterate in relation to sport and music. We reasoned that if the NF had got that pivotal element of its argument so profoundly and incomprehensibly wrong, why should we believe anything else they said?

The purpose of this recollection is to point out that even though we resisted the narrative of naturalized white hegemony, our resistance was itself based on a racist script: black people are good at music and sport (implication—but nothing much else), so even in our eschewal of the white master frame, we utilized a lesser strand of it, backed up by our thin personal knowledge. Richard Dyer argues that the "good" versions of whiteness portray themselves as progressive and supportive, usually in relation to the "bad" extreme nationalist versions.[5] The problem is that this "good" positioning merely adopts the opposite of the bad conclusion but is generated entirely within the same frame. Both viewpoints see "race" as real and as difference, but the bad version sees this as disruptive and dangerous, while the good version sees it as interesting and unthreatening. I have come to understand this as ultimately missing the point: they are actually two bad versions. In evacuating the material elements, the power relations, and the complexities of various black subjectivities from the equation, the "good" white position[6] demonstrates its occupants' capacity to not listen, to disregard, to center themselves in the narrative as the adjudicators.

AU PARC DES PRINCES, PARIS, 1994

I lived in Paris from 1990 to 1997. In April 1994, I went to watch the soccer match between Paris St.Germain (PSG) and Olympique Marseilles (OM) at the Parc des Princes in Paris. At that time, the French norm was to police matches by frisking everyone on the way in, but then waiting outside the ground. At the end of this game, a group of around 20 OM supporters ran round to the PSG end and went hunting for black faces. I say "hunting" because that was exactly the word they chanted: "*Chassez les nègres, tuez-les! On les aura!*" ("Hunt the niggers, kill them! Let's get them!") One man in his thirties or forties got surrounded and fell. He went into the foetus position to protect himself. Despite all the shouting, you could hear the rubbery thud of Doc Martens boots on his skull. Fights were breaking out, with individual black men being chased through the crowds. The police watched them from outside through the mesh fencing.

I got involved briefly in one that had broken out near me, where a very tall kid, maybe nineteen, had been backed into a corner by three or four of them. He could really fight, and I remember he had a very long reach and managed to land a decent punch on the cheek of one of his assailants, knocking him sideways. The way he handled himself made me think this was not a new experience for him. There was a lot of swearing. People were filling up this small area. At one point, the balance seemed to be tipping toward the attackers. I managed to get one of them on the floor, and a couple of other younger men were also swinging fists and feet on the tall kid's side. The balance of power shifted. Suddenly, it all stopped, and the attackers ran off looking for easier meat elsewhere. The tall kid briefly touched hands with the two other guys. We nodded at each other.

The man on the floor was still there when the crowd dispersed, and someone was down on their knees next to him shouting at the police to get medical help. They weren't interested—although they did find time to stop me and those two young French lads who had waded into the same fight as myself. They told us they were watching, and if there was any more trouble, blah, blah, blah, as if that was our fault.

I don't know what happened to the people who started that episode and by then I didn't care. For a very brief moment, when there were feet and fists flying around and that rubber thudding noise was in my head, and the row of police, wearing weapons, were just looking at us from about twenty meters away, collectively opting not to bother to intervene—it became clear to me that in certain conditions, not acting is just as much an exercise of power as acting, and that who the police protect properly becomes crystal clear at particular moments. This is obviously not news to anyone who has grown up where the police are more feared than trusted, but it became spectacularly embodied for me on this occasion.

The following weekend in the restaurant after a seminar at the university where I was doing my PhD, one of the lecturers was adamant that what you had in France was "just" (his phrasing) cultural racism. This led to a discussion, to which my contribution was a brief summary of the above incident. I ended by saying I was sure the man who had his head kicked in was by now relieved that he had been the victim only of cultural racism, as the alternative would have been far more painful. I don't think the comment was well received or as sardonic as I imagined it: things lose a little in translation, but it drew me further into recognizing my implication in structural racism and its reproduction.

This relatively minor scuffle forced me to think about white supremacy and the way it decimates people's lives (white people's too, dehumanizing them in different ways), and how learned white people's discussions about different categories of racism is an effect of this supremacy. These discussions lie at one end of the spectrum. At the other end of the continuum, to paraphrase George Orwell, is the sound of boots stomping on a man's head as he lays on the ground, with the people whose job it is to protect him choosing not to do so.

WHITE STEVE IN THE JUNGLE, 1996

When I carried out fieldwork in Guyana in the 1990s, I was hailed racially in a number of ways. One day a full minibus (the main public transport) stopped next to me at a traffic light while I was on the pavement. A man put his head out of the window and called "*Ey White boy! Wha' you doin' 'ere?*"[7] Although unexpected, this question was posed without malice, it seemed to me, as a genuine query, and I called back, "working" and waved. He raised his hand as the bus sped away. On other occasions, to attract my attention, people hailed me mainly as "big man" (preceded by a short hissing sound) or occasionally "red man," "yellow man," and twice (both by elderly women), "blue eyes."

The racialized white bodies of Europeans who live in Europe, North America, or Australasia frequently pass unmarked unless some specific incident or observation draws attention to them. In Guyana, people read different things onto pale skin and European features; questioning why such a body is here, in this space, where most people are brown-skinned, imagining that I am: American, Canadian, an aid worker, interested in buying drugs, an easy mark for begging, and/or a repository of British values—of which several of my older interlocutors demonstrated profound knowledge. People chatted to me about Britain (although I was living in France at the time): people they knew there . . . "Do you know this family/that person? They live in Manchester." In no way however did I ever feel that this racialization of my identity was based on: a) the idea that the speakers considered themselves better than me; or b) that it was malevolent.

Or, even more oddly, in Linden, a small bauxite mining town in the interior of the country, I was walking with my local gatekeeper to meet some people I was going to interview when an African-Caribbean man came round a corner ahead. I thought to myself that he was walking as if he were in an urban area of Britain, rather than alongside a South American river, next to a jungle. As we approached he said 'All right?' in a London accent. I laughed and said I knew he was British from the way he walked, and he said exactly the same thing about me. I cannot explain how it was that we recognized each other. I bumped into him again, in Georgetown, the day before I left. We were still apparently walking like British people, whatever that means.

All this underscores firstly, that in that context, being racialized as white by people of color is not the equivalent of being racialized as black or Asian by white people (when a and b, two paragraphs above, are often the opposite). Second, it made visible or embodied a difference in experiences that is hidden when white researchers research other white people. In Guyana, I was interpellated as a racialized and gendered body, but in England, doing fieldwork about the racialization of white identities across provincial cities in the first decade of the twenty-first century, the most important distinction between me and my respondents has been class or at least our mutual construction of class differences.

SOCIAL CLASS

It is summer 2012. I am in another meeting about research on white working-class communities. This one takes place in the offices of a large research organization. As the participants join the discussion, the majority of them weave into their opening remarks the fact that they themselves are from a working-class background. After a while, this becomes a mantra. The two people around the table who are explicitly representing such communities don't do this. Nor do the two British Asian people (although one of them actually also grew up in mainly white working-class neighborhoods) as the rhetorical strategy is in part a way to validate one's authenticity and thus the right to intervene at all in this discussion. I note that nobody owns up to being white (obvious, right?), only to having working-class origins, which in this context is positive.

I want to go on a brief diversion, if you'll bear with me, because the thrust of this argument is about the intersection of social class and racialized identities, not just one of them. Of course, I am selecting elements to depict myself in what I consider to be a positive light, which demonstrates the power inherent in controlling the narrative yourself. Indeed, as a researcher I think this is the most important part of the research process: telling the story of others that is accredited as authoritative and legitimate is about as powerful as you get in this line of work. It's all about frames: the act of telling a story is about choices of what is significant but most importantly involves suppositions about the right way to tell a story in the first place. Being the invisible "I," "we," or universal point of reason from which deviance is measured has always been core to white privilege,[8] as it has to class and gender privilege. So at this point, I need to state where I am in this narrative.

Here is my positioning. I admit to being motivated by what people in privileged social locations call "the politics of envy," i.e., thinking that rich people have too much power and opportunity and me wishing it was more evenly distributed. I realize that I should think that the acquisition of goods and more capitals (social, economic, and cultural) is a model, but the sticking point is that frankly, my family has not been middle class long enough to master any of the modes of reproduction and hence my continual ambivalence and the comedy of non-recognition. I seldom feel that the term "middle class" applies to me. Just like Scooby Doo, when someone refers to him as a dog, he looks around, puzzled: "A rog? Where?"

That's how I feel: I'm not a "rog," not really. Even the good job (after a decade of one and two-year temporary contracts), the nice house (after living in shared houses, renting then buying on housing estates), studying as a mature student, and being the first person in my family ever to go to university don't make me middle class. Or if they do, they're not the right criteria. These aren't classic middle-class biographical details, yet I'm here now, a student of behaviors, waiting to be unmasked as an impostor at any moment, like Datchet does to Pip in *Great Expectations*. Hang on. Which way does the port get passed again? Why should I be so interested in school league tables and period dramas on television? How come this person got promotion and I didn't because I am not very "visible" within the faculty? How can I learn to behave with the confidence that says I always know exactly what I am doing and am demonstrating dazzling leadership, when objectively speaking, I am a pompous, incompetent boor? Why, oh why do I hate golf so much? End of diversion.

THREE CLASSROOM EXPERIENCES

These all involve teaching undergraduate classes, either "The Sociology of Racism" or "Racism, Class and Gender," and all at my previous university, where I never taught a class where less than a third of the students were people of color. Often more than half fell into that category.

I. In a seminar session dealing with anti-racist practice in the UK in the 1970s and 80s, the point emerges from the selected reading that the term "black" was used at this time as a political rallying point and included people of Asian descent. This revelation is met with disbelief by students not even born until the late 1980s and early 1990s. Two-thirds of the students are of color. I asked them: if they had to describe their identities what would they say? A litany of distinctions emerge: British Pakistani; Black Londoner; British Muslim; White Brummie, and so on. [9] There were as many versions of identity as there were students. In fact, in the discussion evolving out of this kaleidoscope, it turns out that I am the only person in the room who thinks using "black" as a strategic starting point is a good idea. To me this indicates three things. The first is that this is a beautifully eloquent reflection of the centripetal forces acting upon social identities in the UK since the 1980s. This is especially true of the fallout from 9/11 and 7/7 on the category "British Asian," which I now hear less and less frequently in students' mouths. It used to subsume religious difference into geographical origins, and for American readers, "Asian" in Britain means "South Asian." Second, it is a warning that I might be a man out of time, who should listen more closely to minority students when they articulate struggles and identities. Whatever way round they are looking at it, the strategic use of an umbrella term is not on their agenda. Third, on the theme of individuals vs. the collective, it is a reminder to work even harder on encouraging students to think sociologically about their individual relationship to wider patterns and struggles in society. The essays submitted at the end of this second-level class often read as though I had made no input to do with the structural or systemic dimension of racism, and that the social world is *only* about individuals overcoming or not overcoming obstacles.

II. In my final-year class on racism, class, and gender, we do two two-hour sessions on whiteness: one in relation to the United States, then one in relation to the UK. In the UK-based one, I ask people to think about ways in which their racialized identities might have impacted on their lives and talk about them in small groups. There are obviously reasons why some students might want to not tell traumatic stories, so I don't usually expect anything deep. This activity is aimed at instigating a dialogue. Some students are always brave enough to reveal something that can be used to escalate the conversation past the "I had a conversation with a racist, whose views I do not share" type of report, which is the story I get from many white students. It's really to make the latter consider the possibility that they have managed to avoid having to go through something on account of being white, by listening to other people's stories. I should add that this final hour of the four on this topic comes after three previous hour-long sessions over two weeks, all making white privilege explicit and giving examples of it. However, I'm not prepared for the question one student asks me. She is of Indian origin, very well-spoken, and has previously told me she comes from rural Surrey (an area to the southeast of London with very, very high house prices). "I'm confused," she says. "What possible advantage could a white person have over me?"

It's great to be so confident, but her response demonstrates that she hasn't taken on board any of the contents of the previous three hours' classroom time. I give her some suggestions but start thinking while I am doing so. Am I always doing people a favor in trying to open them up to ideas of structural disadvantage, or am I potentially using my position of authority to instill anxieties that did not previously have a home? This student seems to have class advantage, and I am sure this is why she does not see whiteness as a privileged identity in relation to hers. Although I have tried very hard to emphasize the uneven privilege that whiteness bestows upon white people by class and gender, that message does not seem to be getting through to the majority. Am I completely mucking up some people's heads by planting in them the idea that whiteness is powerful?

III. In the same class as above, we do a session on "race" and science, followed by a seminar on cosmetic surgery and skin lightening as examples. In some ways, I love this session, because it is so clearly engaging with popular culture that people always have a lot to say. They talk so much that they forget they are learning, which is always a good outcome. However, one emerging theme from these discussions is the establishment of an equivalence between skin lightening and tanning as social practices. White people use fake tan, have tanning sessions, and have their lips plumped, goes the argument, and darker-skinned people lighten their skin and straighten their hair, so everyone is trying to be like everyone else. For me, this is wildly out of balance, not comparing like with like—just think here of the notion of "reverse racism." If whiteness is a "deranged" space, as William Ackah[10] maintains, it seems as if this discussion about who changes their bodies both re-orders whiteness, and makes its effects appear less insane: everybody's doing it, racism works both ways, and so on, so the logic returns to its safe fulcrum, wherein nobody is really doing anything remarkable, and the power relations recede from view. I have not resolved this: my structuring of the class allows the students to develop the momentum, and again I might be the only one dissatisfied. So when students leave the module and go on to other things, have the elements I thought were clear and important sunk in, so at least they have to perform the intellectual task of dismissing them? Or have I produced a parody of my central ideas? I feel responsible for having an unintended opposite effect and am extremely relieved when people email me years later with an insight they say started developing in their minds within the context of one of my modules.

I AM THE STATE (2003–2011): COULD THERE BE A BIGGER TREE?

In order to understand this crucial leg of the story, my American readers will have to know a number of things:

1. The European Union (which I shall refer to as the EU from now on) is a federation of European states, pooling some of their resources and having developed a set of institutions that have a relationship with the individual member states' own institutions—similar to the United States (state and federal levels), only with different countries taking the role of the individual American states. In some areas, policy is de facto agreed upon at the EU level as well as at the national level. Immigration rules is one of these areas.
2. There are two parallel sets of immigration rules: the EU one, developed through jurisprudence and agreed upon by justice ministers at EU summits; and the national ones decided on by member states' parliaments. The EU-level set of rules is most important because it frames the others. The most significant element of this is that EU member state nationals do not require visas for travel, residence or work within any other EU member state. As this effectively means that other EU nationals are no longer counted as immigrants, and the flows are impossible to regulate, individual nations have to focus elsewhere to carry out what Wayne Cornelius, et al.[11] refer to as "symbolic instruments" that create the "appearance of control," that is, establishing that it is in control of the borders of the nation. Only those

bodies originating from *outside* the EU can legitimately be targets of the state's policies. This has been true for some nations from the late 1980s, although the story differs for each individual nation as it signs up to the relevant parts of European agreements and implements its own specific and frequently vindictive regulations. [12]

DEFINITELY THE BIG TREE

When we first came to the UK from France in 1997, I was not married to the woman who is now my wife, Anne, a Guyanese national. We swapped houses with a Canadian colleague who had a place in County Waterford, Ireland, while she and her family lived in the flat I had in Paris. It was impossible for us to stay legally in the UK for more than six months without getting married, so Ireland provided breathing space. Anne was pregnant with our eldest daughter at the time, and she was born in Cork, just before Christmas 1997. We married the month afterward, and my wife was thus covered by a regulation entitling spouses of EU nationals to some of the resources enjoyed by the latter. My status was as that of an "EU national worker" in the Republic of Ireland, and Anne's status was dependent on mine. We can see the outline of what is to come in this administrative relationship. Regardless of whether you want it to be this way, the EU national's body is the intermediary of rights. The "non-EU national" receives rights only through the EU national's body. The distinction between EU national and non-EU national is the most significant administrative binary in the tale. So the EU rules produce two tiers of people, one dependent on the other. At the time I did not view it like this. Relief was the major emotion. We could get on with planning to stay. The previous months had been full of anxiety about what our next step would be.

We stayed six more years. All three of our kids were born in the same hospital, the last two of them in the same delivery room. I lost my job at the university on Easter 2003, and found another one, in England. When I added it up, I realized I had been working on temporary contracts (usually one year) for a total of twelve years (1992–2003) and was sick of it. I took a tenured job in England with pleasure, not realizing what impact this would have for the family. It is also worth noting that we had both already applied for Irish nationality in 2002, having lived there for the required five-year period. However, the processing of the forms took so long (a year) that by the time the Department of Justice got back to us, we were no longer residents in the Republic of Ireland and were thus disqualified from naturalization.

Now, in our early days in Ireland (1997–1998) we had sought a visa for Anne to study. She had to leave Ireland to get a student visa and then return. We went to London for this. During our time at the embassy in Dublin before leaving, we had spoken to an official who was knowledgeable, sympathetic, took time to listen to our story and find alternative routes. He even turned the microphone off at one point and suggested we might, as a last resort, just go and overstay the visa until we were married and had a child. As it turned out, we didn't need to go down that path, but realizing some embassy officials were also ethical human beings was important.

By the time we were preparing to settle in England, six years later, however, a lot had changed. The Dublin embassy had been audited and many practices considered "wasteful" had been eliminated. One of these wasteful practices was officials from the consulate having more than minimal face-to-face interaction with those applying for visas. The type of conversation we had had in Dublin in 1997 was by this time no longer possible. Even the function of handling inquiries had been outsourced to a company that was only contactable through a call center on a premium-rate line. This organization led to the experience which, more than any other, convinced me that I was always, whatever else I could be, and however unwilling I was, part of the "big tree" that Bob Marley refers to in his lyrics.

According to the visas-'R'-us employee I spoke to, two visas were available: one was free (EU) and the other (British immigration rules) cost £70 (about 90 dollars). There was no difference in the entitlements they gave rise to.

Yet this was absolutely not accurate information. I should have checked and double-checked the implications rather than take the word of the embassy hotline cowboys. When we got to Britain and began attempting to change the entry visa into a residence visa, it became apparent that something was wrong. Somehow, the information I sent in had been misconstrued. The visa was for a spouse of an EU national, not for the spouse of a UK national (even though I am a UK national). Confused yet? Remember the distinction between EU rules and national rules? We were now in the EU regulations stream and not the UK immigration rules stream.

What's the difference? In the UK stream, you can apply for citizenship through being married to a UK national after two years' residence. In the former, you could apply only after five years' residence, if you are married to an EU national. However, you are not in danger of being deported, which is why the refugee and immigration advice bodies I contacted were not the slightest bit interested in our predicament. We did not even register on their scale of urgency.

I then engaged on an ultimately fruitless path of querying why I was being dealt with as an EU national rather than a UK national in my own country. As each line of inquiry got closed down I had to explain to Anne how I couldn't make any headway: and as there was no rational explanation, I was ultimately upholding the discipline of the state. I began to realize that basically the state can do what it wants, that the British state was co-opting me to be my wife's tormentor. I was the tar baby she was stuck on.

What was actually at stake for us in this? Why should we care? If deportation was not on the table, why worry? The answer is the right and freedom to travel without hassle. On a passport from a developing world nation, like Guyana, you had to go to the consulate of the destination country so that they could scrutinize and interrogate you. We had to prove we had somewhere to go and sufficient funds (copies of bank statements, letters of invitation) every time we traveled out of the country. This costs money, time for travel, and pride. We do not live in London, and the trip there and back is expensive and takes up most of a day.

At the French consulate they make people stand outside in the sun for hours and treat them like cattle. After standing in the sun and being treated like cattle in July 2005, Anne vowed never to do it again, although she later softened, it proved a waste of time, but I am getting to that bit. The point is that if you got a British passport (or any other EU passport) you would never have to go through this ordeal again. Never have to queue up in the "All Other Passports" line at the airport while the people in front of you get grilled, filtered out of the line, and set aside for questioning. All in all, it made my wife feel like she was a criminal, constantly under surveillance, having to prove she had resources before traveling and was not going to overstay her visa and scrounge off the French/Spanish/German state. Everything depended on *my* status, which, for someone as independent as she happens to be, is a blow in itself. Considering the things that she had come through,[13] this situation was pathetic: much less potentially damaging, but so impossible to control.

In 2008, we hired a very experienced immigration lawyer to appeal against my wife's status and apply for citizenship through marriage to a British national. It cost us more than £1,100 ($1,800) to pursue. We had to send our passports and an application to the Home Office. He said he'd never seen anything like my re-categorization as an EU national before and always talked to me as if my wife wasn't there in the room with me. So I'm now supporting patriarchy as well as institutional racism.

During this process, my mother-in-law, Mary, died in Guyana. When we called the Home Office, they said, yes, you can have your passport back . . . but then you must return to the back of the queue and have to pay all the fees again (hundreds of pounds/dollars). Given this event, she didn't travel in order to get the status we had been seeking for years. And finally, our appeal was rejected anyway and marked "no appeal possible." In the letter the Home Office sent us, I am referred to as a person "having the status of an EU national," which is true but only if you leave out the bit in my passport where I am also a British national. We were invited, without irony, to start the process again from the beginning, with me being reclassified as British. We calculated that this would delay access to British citizenship even further, so it was not worth doing.

The resentment and frustration both of us felt by now is compounded by the mismatch between Britain's historical and postcolonial legacy, and its current membership of the European Union. People in my wife's family, along with many other Guyanese, fought for the Allies in the Second World War. The British went to her country (in fact, created the country's current borders) in the nineteenth century and made considerable profits from the sugar industry (Bookers PLC, for example). So, within the framework of her logic, Guyanese should be compensated with preferential treatment vis-á-vis people from EU countries, who by dint of their EU member-state passports can come and go unhindered, unharassed, and unhumiliated. The white privilege attaching to this freedom of movement is extremely visible at this point.

Eventually, UK nationality law changed again, so that the qualification period is not just five years, but five followed by an application for Indefinite Leave to Remain (ILR), which must be held for twelve months as the necessary pre-requisite to application for citizenship (making six years in total). For us, this turned into seven years, because the semi-governmental agency now charged with dealing with immigration (then called the Borders Agency) held Anne's passport for thirteen months before returning it with her ILR stamp. I am convinced that it would still be languishing in their intray if I had not lobbied our member of Parliament (congressperson) to telephone their offices twice to enquire on the application's progress.

During this inordinate "qualification period" (2003–2010), the rules on how long you had to live in the UK before you could apply to be British changed more than once. There was also perhaps the most spiteful EU directive ever. It was August 2010: we were planning to go to rural France on a week-long family holiday. Anne had agreed to return to the hated embassy and apply for a visa so that we could all travel to the house my parents had renovated. However, in April 2010 an EU directive had come into effect preventing the bearers of passports that were ten or more years old from the right to a tourist visa.[14]

Now, only nationals of developing world countries that cut costs by not replacing passports but instead *renewing or extending* them with official stamps would be affected. Guyana is one of these countries. Anne's passport was issued in the 1990s but is renewed with a stamp every five years. So we spent the usual couple of hours on the application form, booked an interview online, and she spent all day traveling to and from London. At the interview she was told that even though her passport was fully valid, the French consulate would not put a visa in it because it was "too old." At this point, the weight of attempting to dis-identify with the state became appallingly oppressive for me, and I am still trying to deal with this period's psychological legacy. Dis-identifying from whiteness–of which this was one painful step on the journey—is a long, uneven, frustrating, and tiring process. If you're a white person who wants to go there, you'd better surround yourself with people who get it and who don't need it spelled out, or it will be a lot more tiring and frustrating. This particular experience made clear the limits of dis-identification. Through the process, shrouded in its administrative logics and aporia, I could see the impacts of racism on the person I most care about, and felt unable to disentangle myself from the postcolonial British state.

The reason why there was an issue in the first place is because the status of a "non-EU national" is so precarious. The set of white European postcolonial states that constitute the European Union (and its smaller "European Economic Area" satellites) now develop policy on the basis of a dividing line between unproblematic European-origin migration, and problematic immigration from outside the EU. In practice, the countries whose nationals experience the most difficulty obtaining visas (believe me, we have had a lot of trouble and some refusals trying to get Guyanese relatives to come to the UK) are a subset of these.[15] So because status depends on me, the EU national, I am and unwilling but irretrievably part of the power relationship whose impact on my family's intimate life has been years of concern, guilt, frustration, and resentment.

How did this end? The rules changed again. In January 2011, Anne now had to take the UK citizenship test online. This type of test is now a prerequisite for obtaining citizenship (not only in the UK). It requires the purchase of a guide book (*Life in the UK*) and studying its 140 pages of material. She passed the online multiple choice test (you need a score of 75 percent), which you must pay to take. I use questions from this test in the classroom. My British students are frequently appalled at how difficult some of them are, and our suspicion is that if the whole British public were to take the test, there would be a high fail rate among the group of people who never have to pass through this route to be British nationals.

The expensive grail was getting closer. We then filled in the citizenship application form (after another ambiguous conversation with officials at the Border Agency, who could not stipulate exactly which parts of the form the applicant had to fill in). Having gone through an advice service in a nearby city hall (mayor's office), the final application was submitted in February. In April, Anne received notice that her application had been approved and that she was now required to attend a citizenship ceremony (another change in the rules since we arrived in England). This ceremony was attended: no citizenship document can be obtained without attending it, and you have to pay for it. After this, she had to fill in another form for the Passport Agency, which required her to have an interview before issuing her first UK passport. The first question she was asked in this final, final interview (which focused on details of our lives) was if she could spell her name. We supposed this was an anti-fraud device to make sure she was who she said, but after all these years of frustration and resentment, it was an anti-climactic way to finish.

In May 2011, Anne finally held her British passport, and we have traveled successfully within Europe since then. Throughout and after this nerve-shredding and exhausting process, I have resented the elements of the British state that were structuring my family life. And now that I have time to sit and reflect on it, I know that part of the reason for this resentment is because it drew my attention to the very simple relationship that white people have to power. Whether I like it or not, I—or my racialized body at least—was an instrumental actor in this story. The privilege I enjoy through being white and British in this context functions exactly in relation to the dis-privilege not enjoyed one little bit by my wife, the brown-skinned national of a former British colony. Privilege is relational. In this respect, I always have privilege, and even if somehow the British government "forgot" I was British, the safety net was "EU national," which although not technically exclusively a category for white people, it may as well be, because in turn, its "Other" is the majority world beyond the European Union's expanding borders.

As I sit writing this chapter, I am reminded again of Charles Mills's concision and elegance of phrase. In relation to the racial contract (underpinning white supremacy), he states that: "all whites are beneficiaries to the contract, though some whites are not signatories to it."[16] What I have experienced is a traumatic realization of my benefit and the bitterness that my resistance to signing it usually means nothing concrete that would benefit anyone else. I have acknowledged my whiteness being embodied as property.[17] As Skeggs[18] argues, in relation to middle-class (as opposed to working-class) subjectivities in Britain: "property is determined as a set of entitlements, which are exclusive to an owner, or to the holder of the proprietary interest. Exclusion from, and access to, objects, people and practices to propertize, are central to both the formation of middle-class subjectivity (in its various new configurations) and the exclusion of others from recognizable worth, that is, proper personhood."

The core of this statement also applies to whiteness: I hold a proprietary interest in whiteness, and one of the ways in which I know I have privilege is because other bodies, not racialized as white, are excluded from proper personhood—and in the case of "non-EU nationals," have to constantly prove themselves worthy of the privilege of cross-border travel. They have to provide proof of income, trustworthiness, and guarantees that they would be unlikely to abscond and ruin everyone else's life by breathing European air, living in European space, defrauding European taxpayers through welfare scams, and so on. In short, they must open themselves up to levels of scrutiny that would be considered intolerable in other areas of life, in a one-sided struggle. Finally, for most people, this process is also accompanied by large payments, totalling hundreds of pounds sterling (just as is the case with U.S.

visas by the way). For most people, the border is not at the airport, but in
some bureaucrat's head at a consulate in your country of origin. I swear if I
hear another unbearably smug postmodern conclusion that the world is now
"borderless" as an assumption on which a theory is constructed, I will
scream. This white fiction of a world where borders "don't matter" is elaborated on the real and massive, dangerous jagged-edged borders of bureau-
cracy, the geo-administrative incivility that constitutes the immigration regimes of most wealthy states. Based on figures from the French NGO,
OWNI,[19] *at least* fifty-three people every month died trying to get into the
European Union without papers between 1988 and 2010. And based on our
experience, it's not hard to see why you wouldn't bother trying the "legal"
route in.

For me, the experience of my wife's painful and protracted crawl through
barbed wire toward British citizenship, like the images of African and Asian
people crammed into flimsy boats in the Atlantic and Mediterranean attempting to sneak undetected onto Europe's underbelly, reminds me that although
I will never sign the racial contract, I am *categorically* a beneficiary of it, and
that white supremacy in its postcolonial form is a potent, degrading force that
does its best to shrivel the life chances, material and emotional lives of those
that are constituted as its racial Others.

CONCLUSION

In the film *Shrek* (2001), the eponymous character explains to Donkey that
Ogres are complex, that they have layers, like onions. At the risk of being
ridiculed by Donkey as "Onion boy," this metaphor also serves the uneven
and complicated journey illustrated above. The various layers I have outlined
are of course not the only incidents or thoughts that propelled me on this
journey, but they are indicative that as you become increasingly aware of the
content and extent of white privilege, you constantly re-assess your thoughts
and actions through more powerful and subtle lenses. The layer in which I
became aware that people were different culturally from me but that I liked it
rather than being afraid of it (Southall Broadway in the early 1970s) seemed
a big deal to me until my early twenties, because in the mainly white spaces I
inhabited, this simple observation already acted as a resistance to full whiteness and marked you out as deviant.

Now the professional has become entwined with the personal to the extent where I cannot go a day without reassessing what ethical path I ought to
take. I feel as though I am making better choices and have passed through to
a relatively advanced layer, and am practicing to put my hands on that small
axe. Then something occurs, like the immigration status fiasco described
above, which descended upon me like a form of hubris, reminding me of

structural parameters that encroach even within the intimacy of a relationship.

When I stated that the problem of being white was not fully resoluble, I did not mean that the resolution project should be a priori abandoned or submerged in something else, such as "I only see class. I don't see 'race'— it's all false consciousness"; or, "I only see gender: patriarchy is the enemy"; or even, "I only see sexuality: homophobia is the enemy." The latter part of all these claims are, of course, partially true, but in their eradication of the possibility that any of the three subaltern positions to which they give voice might be lived *differently* by people not racialised as white, they are essentially "whitely scripts"[20] : i.e., exactly what I am trying to avoid engaging *in*, although engaging *with* them is my work. And my work is also often my private life. There are certainly many more layers ahead. It's just as well that I like onions.

Where do we go from here? The silence of whiteness in these class, gender, and sexuality scripts, inter alia, is precisely what must be shattered. While the legitimate guilt and shame that Vice analyses[21] seem from my reading of her to require silent private redemptive labor, my understanding is that such work is not its own end but instead part of the preparation for the necessarily noisy, public, painful, and often unpleasant engagement with whitely norms and the support for the emancipatory projects of other racialised groups that must evolve from the recognition of one's whiteness. So while the temptation is to identify with the small axe, what you see in the mirror is actually Bob Marley's "big tree": a profoundly rooted edifice of privilege and control with centuries of growth behind it. I am not certain how Marley envisaged the tree, and maybe the point is not to visualize its specifics: the power of this image is that it allows you to view whatever you are fighting against when you hear the lyrics. For me, the tree is a force that has to be chipped away at, by small axes: it's not coming down in one go. Maybe the fruit on the tree is what accrues to people racialized as white, and you can, theoretically, redistribute that. However, the deep roots are just as important. They are already grown, already strong—ideas, practices, ways of being, ways of thinking, ways of not knowing—and these are harder to sever, because in essence, in my way of framing it, I am excising what makes me white: which is simultaneously necessary, painful and liberating. The parts that make me a white problem hurt to chop off. Everyone hurts after being seriously cut, but this is more like a life-saving, no—a life-restoring operation, and as Toni Morrison writes in *Beloved*, in the words of the white character, Amy, "Anything dead coming back to life hurts."[22]

If, as a white scholar engaged in what you hope is anti-racist scholarship, you work hard enough to see who you really are and what you could make of yourself, you might get to put a hand on the small axe now and then. Yet this is an aspiration. The difficulty is to always remember to view this not as the outcome of an individual project (despite the intensely personal journey described here) but as one where the individual learns a range of liberation songs from the people who are doing the act of liberating, songs to which you must listen extremely carefully, and to which you may then sing very gentle backing vocals. All this, in order to sever, as far as it's physically and psychologically possible, what makes you part of the big tree.

It is summer 2014. I am driving. Bob Marley is on the MP3. The idea that I am really part of the "we" who constitute the small axe is now aspirational, and the humble path is to acknowledge this. I am sticking to backing vocals.

NOTES

1. See http://www.azlyrics.com/lyrics/bobmarley/smallaxe.html

2. S. Vice, "How Do I Live in This Strange Place?" *Journal of Social Philosophy* 41(3), 2010: 323–42; quote on p. 327.

3. Steve Garner, *Whiteness: an introduction* London: Routledge, 2007; "The Uses of whiteness: what researchers working on Europe can draw from US work on US work on Whiteness" *Sociology* 40(2), 2006: 257–75.

4. A young Sikh man, Gurdip Singh Chaggar, had been the victim of a racist murder in 1976, and his killers were never arrested. On April 23, 1979, there was a riot in Southall sparked by a National Front rally. It ended with a confrontation between the protestors and mounted police and police in riot gear (http://www.youtube.com/watch?v=7Kc7d5T175Q) in which several people were badly beaten. Anti-racist activist Blair Peach died after being hit on the head by a Special Patrol Group (riot police) officer, and Clarence Baker, the manager of the reggae band Misty in Roots, went into a coma after being struck with a baton.

5. Richard Dyer, *White*. New York: Routledge, 1997.

6. See Janine Jones, "The Impairment of Empathy in Goodwill Whites for African-Americans" in G. Yancy (ed) *What White Looks Like*: *African-American Philosophers on the Whiteness Question* New York: Routledge, 2004, 65–86.

7. I can't convey the musicality of his accent, and I don't want to standardize the spelling to give the impression he was speaking a flat, standard, British English like I do.

8. bell hooks, "Representing Whiteness in the Black Imagination" in *Black Looks: Race and Representation* Boston: South End Press, 1992, 165–79; Dyer, 1997; L. T. Smith, *Decolonizing Methodologies: Research and Indigenous Peoples* London: Sage, 2000.

9. A native of Birmingham (silent 'h'): the city in which my former university is based.

10. William Ackah, "The Experience of my Experience: reflections on working in deranged white academic space," in M. Christian (ed) *Integrated but Unequal: Black Faculty in Predominately White Space* Trenton, NJ: Africa World Press, 2012.

11. Wayne Cornelius et al (eds) *Controlling Immigration: A Global Perspective* Stanford, CA: Stanford University Press (2nd edition), 2004.

12. See L. Lund Pedersen, "Intimacy with the Danish Nation-State: My Partner, the Danish State and I—A Case Study of Family Reunification Policy in Denmark" in K. Loftsdóttir and L. Jensen (eds) *Whiteness and Postcolonialism in the Nordic Region: Exceptionalism, Migrant Others and National Identities* Farnham: Ashgate, 2012: 141–58, for an account of Denmark's rules.

13. A. Lyken-Garner, *Sunday's Child* Cary, NC: Pulse Press, 2012.

14. Article 12(c) of Regulation (EC) No 810/2009: http://eur-lex.europa.eu/LexUriServ/LexUriServ.do?uri=OJ:L:2009:243:0001:0058:EN:PDF

15. D. Bigo and E. Guild, *Controlling Frontiers: Free Movement Into and Within Europe* Farnham: Ashgate, 2005.

16. Charles W. Mills, *The Racial Contract* Ithaca, NY: Cornell University Press, 1997, 11.

17. C. Harris, "Whiteness as Property" *Harvard Law Review* 106(8), 1993: 1707–93.

18. B. Skeggs, "The making of class and gender through visualizing moral subject formation" *Sociology* 39(5), 2005: 965–82; quote on 997.

19. OWNI's map of deaths at the borders can be accessed at: http://owni.fr/2011/02/18/app-la-carte-des-morts-aux-frontieres-de-leurope/

20. Allison Bailey, "Locating Traitorous Identities: Toward a View of Privilege-Cognizant White Character" *Hypatia* 13(3), 1998: 27–42

21. Vice, op.cit.

22. Toni Morrison, *Beloved* New York: Alfred Knopf, 1987.

Chapter Fourteen

Contort Yourself

Music, Whiteness, and the Politics of Disorientation

Robin James

White people want to have it both ways: we want the benefits of whiteness, but we want them to come without a cost. For example, whiteness imparts mastery over the body, but this same mastery overrides one's ability to experience the body in and on its own terms. White bodies are oriented by a disorientation from corporeality.[1] White privilege allows whites to feel intellectually and culturally fluent (because intellectual and cultural norms are white), but this intellectual and cultural fluency comes at the expense of white corporeal fluency and fluidity. Whites, especially white men, are taught to experience their bodies as sites of control—whites can master and repress bodily desire and sensation, but whiteness does not provide any direction as to how to experience the body as a site of "free play" (i.e., of aesthetic pleasure, let alone sexual pleasure).[2]

So, whiteness has a body problem. Whiteness disorients people from bodily pleasure, sensuousness, and other non-instrumental attitudes to the body. In performing whiteness, white people experience their bodies as awkward, clumsy, and disoriented. Many scholars have written on this.[3] In this chapter, I analyze musical expressions and descriptions of white bodily disorientation. I distinguish between two different ways white pop musicians have addressed whites' feelings of alienation from their bodies: one which reinforces white hegemony, and one which can (possibly, under the right conditions) be an opening for a critique and de-centering of white supremacy and normative structures of whiteness. More simply: White people can feel like their whiteness is a problem, but this is not necessarily anti-racist in intention, sentiment, or effect. It matters how and why white people problematize their whiteness.

I've chosen to examine the collection's theme—"How does it feel to be a white problem?"—from the perspective of these musical styles because they open up analyses of both the problem part of the question, and, more importantly, the feeling part of the question. What happens when we find our feelings, or aesthetic tastes, likes and dislikes, politically distasteful? How can and should white people respond to their discomfort with and distaste for their own whiteness? The response to this question hinges on why white people think their whiteness is a problem.

To address these questions of how and why, I examine the use of musical irregularity and distortion in New Wave, as represented by Devo, and No Wave, as represented by James Chance.[4] Devo and Chance use similar musical practices to depict the white body problem and to problematize whiteness. Outgrowths of punk, New Wave and No Wave repudiate rock's norms for musical excellence. They use awkward and disorienting musical techniques—repetition, abrasive and/or dystopian themes and timbres, abrupt and jerky affects, halting and awkward covers of rock and pop songs, and so on—to evoke whites' discomfort with their white bodies.[5] I take this aesthetic similarity and use it as a means to distinguish between two distinct political approaches to whiteness.

Though New Wave, at least in its more avant-garde incarnations, might have more aesthetically in common with No Wave, its approach to whiteness has more politically in common with classic rock. Classic rock aesthetics are informed by white hipness. White hipness proposes to solve the white body problem by having whites appropriate stereotypical black musical and corporeal styles.[6] Many scholars have written on this "love and theft" dynamic in American popular culture; its roots date at least to the nineteenth century.[7] In the 1970s, New Wave musicians tried to distinguish themselves from previous generations of white rockers by rejecting the love and theft solution.[8] Refusing the detour through (what white people thought was) black culture, artists like Devo instead hyperbolized and exaggerated white bodily anxieties. Like the classic rockers from which they tried to distinguish themselves, Devo thought whiteness was a problem for white people. Chance's No Wave, however, suggests that whiteness, specifically the white body problem, is a problem for white people *because* whites have made whiteness a problem for people of color. His songs contort, disorient, and destabilize rock music aesthetics by pointing out the racism of the love and theft solution to white bodily discomfort.

The Chance songs I analyze in this chapter are concrete examples of what Sara Ahmed calls "a politics of disorienation." If whiteness is hegemonic, it can be said to orient our epistemic, political, and cultural discourses. White supremacy means that the world is orientated with reference to whiteness; it is a sort of centripetal force that organizes everything around and with reference to it. A racialized politics of disorientation would seek to de-center whiteness, to undo, limit, or undermine its orientating force. I argue that some of Chance's songs portray white bodily disorientation. Can this white bodily disorientation be, if not an instance of, at least a model for the disorientation of whiteness more generally and systemically? Can Chance's music be a way to help whites acclimate themselves to such disorientation?

In the next section, I follow Theo Cateforis's analysis of whiteness in Devo's songs and performances to explain how whites can problematize their whiteness in ways that *reinforce* white hegemony. Then I show how the musical noise in some of Chance's songs can introduce epistemic noise into whites' understanding of their bodies and their racial identity. Finally, I consider these musical and epistemic disorientations as instances of what Sara Ahmed calls "a politics of disorientation."

THE (D)EVOLUTION OF WHITENESS?

In this section, I use Cateforis's analysis of Devo's cover of the Rolling Stones's "(I Can't Get No) Satisfaction" to show that what he identifies as "the whiteness of the New Wave" is actually continuous with the approach to whiteness that characterizes mainstream rock music from the 1950s through the 1970s.[9] The Stones and Devo adopt opposite approaches to the same underlying assessment of whiteness.

According to this underlying view, whites are "enslaved . . . to a stringent mechanized work ethic"[10] that prioritizes "self-denial and self-control."[11] Whiteness is so rigid, rule-bound, and immersed in intellectual-technological pursuits that it is an impediment to aesthetic, sensory, and sexual pleasure. Alienating, inhibiting, and all-around no fun, whiteness is treated as a problem for white people. Classic rock bands address this problem by dis-identifying with whiteness: they reject white cultural norms and appropriate (what they understand to be) black musical and corporeal styles instead. In the mid-twentieth century, it was a common stereotype that black men were not alienated from but in fact too strongly connected to their bodies, bodily pleasure, as well as aesthetic virtuosity and aesthetic pleasure. So, many whites adopted this stereotypical blackness, hoping it would "cure" their problematic whiteness.[12] This is the approach the Stones took, and it was common among both British Invasion and U.S. rock bands in the 1960s and '70s.[13]

Instead of dis-identification, Devo critiques white squareness with exaggerated identification and parody. Devo hyperbolizes whiteness. Performing "a white male [body] too controlled and too disciplined to appear natural," Devo critiques "white middle-class emotional sensibility, where abstinence and repression are designed to regulate the white body, to conquer its fleshy imperfections and elevate the spirit over the troubled torso."[14] This is what is "new" about them: they don't attempt to reject white "squareness," to escape from it in black music; rather, via a musical argument ad absurdum they explicitly adopt white "squareness" in order to point out its flaws.[15] Crucially, this critique overlooks racism and white privilege as causes or components of the problem with whiteness—it is treated as a body problem, not a political or moral problem. White people may have problems, but, at least for Devo, racism doesn't appear to be one of them.

HOW DO THEY DO THIS?

In their Stones cover, Devo use various compositional and performance tactics to create "discomforting" affects[16] : (1) rhythmic irregularity (an obscured, asynchronous downbeat), and (2) sabotaging the standard "tension-release" structure of a rock song (only tension, no release). I will review each of these techniques very briefly, so that I can later discuss Devo's aesthetic similarity (and political dissimilarity) to Chance.

(1) Rhythmic irregularity: Cateforis argues that Devo's "use of rhythms could act directly on the body, encouraging a rigid, robotic, and discomforting reaction in their audiences."[17] For example, Devo obscured the downbeat in their cover of "Satisfaction." This cover uses a modified reggae convention for "dropping" or "skipping" the downbeat—so, the reggae convention won't sound right to rock audiences, and Devo's modification "seems to bear little relation to a reggae beat."[18] The instrumentals do not establish a recognizably rock or a recognizably reggae downbeat. The difficulty in locating the downbeat is exacerbated by the fact that the vocals put the emphasis on different beats—the vocals follow the rock convention of emphasizing 1 and 3, while the instrumentals emphasize 2 and 4. The song thus feels "out of synch."[19] This "serve[s] to jolt the listener, making one acutely aware of the skewed relation between the voice, body, and music."[20] In this way, Devo uses odd, awkward musical structures to prevent listeners from relying on implicit understanding. They force listeners to respond with "self-conscious control." This "self-control [is] required to avert the physicality of other dancing"—i.e., regular dancing to classic blues-based rock.[21] So, Devo used musical awkwardness to turn listeners' attention to the nerdiness and squareness of white bodies.

(2) All tension, no release: Devo used formal structures to intensify the affective anxiety and discomfort generated by the rhythmic irregularity. More specifically, they excised and/or reworked the tension-release structures the Stones used in their original version of "Satisfaction," so that the song built tension but did not release or resolve it. "The original," Cateforis argues,

is a classic model of what musicologist Richard Middleton has referred to as the "tension/release" popular song form. The Rolling Stones set the "tense" tone immediately with the timbre of the opening distorted guitar hook . . . the release comes during the chorus. [22]

Devo pushes against audience knowledge of the original Stones version of the song, delaying or deleting the release points (i.e., harmonic development, cadences) that the audience anticipates. [23] So, instead of building to a "climactic point of tension" [24] as the Stones do, Devo uses repetition to interrupt the buildup. It's a different kind of tension that they build: they're not developing teleologically toward a climax and dénouement; they're repeating "monomanical[ly]," [25] exponentializing discomfort. Devo builds tension by intensifying rhythmic, vocal, and formal irregularities. As Cateforis explains, "Mothersbaugh's use of these quirky, nervous vocal patterns helps to intensify the images of awkward, twitching human bodies . . . the quirky vocal exaggerations and the frantic bodily motions all came to be trademarks of new wave's particular white-tinged style." [26] White audiences experience these musical irregularities as intensifications of their own "awkward, twitching human bodies." [27] The perceived musical "problems" express or augment the white body problem.

MEET THE NEW BOSS, SAME AS THE OLD BOSS

Devo's awkward, twitchy approach to the white body does not begin from a new political approach to whiteness or the white body problem. In their cover of "Satisfaction," whiteness is a problem for white people because it causes and/or contributes to the white body problem. Devo does not develop a new response to this problem. Instead of dis-identifying with white cultural practices and aesthetic norms, as the Stones did with their appropriation of the Delta blues, "what new wave did reject, at least from a musical standpoint, was the expressive history of the blues and other African American forms as any kind of unequivocal authenticity." [28] So, as Cateforis argues, Devo's awkward, disoriented, herky-jerky aesthetic is an attempt to dis-identify with the previous generation of white musicians' solution to the problem of white alienation. [29] Devo, like the Stones, thinks whiteness is repressive for white people. So, their refusal to appropriate blues, rock, and R&B styles has the effect of more intensely focusing on white people and their/our issues. [30] Though Devo and Chance both rejected the classic rock response to whiteness, they disagree as to what is, exactly, the problem with whiteness. Chance can be interpreted as critiquing the racism that underwrites white aesthetic pleasure.

DO STOP, YOU'VE GOTTEN ENOUGH

In Devo's work, whiteness has the effect of regimenting and quantizing both the music and the listening/performing body; bodily disorientation is the effect of too much organization and control. In James Chance's No Wave aesthetic, whiteness has the effect of disorganizing *both* the music *and* the body. In my reading, the musical irregularity in some of Chance's songs can interrupt whites' experiences of white privilege—bodily disorientation results from Chance's critique of normative whiteness. These songs suggest that whiteness ought to be discomforting for whites because it is oppressive for black people.[31] While these songs continue to engage with African American musical styles and practices, what they reject is the idea that this interaction will somehow remedy whites' uneasiness with their white bodies. Rather, the appropriation of African-American musical traditions makes white people feel more uneasy with their white bodies, not just because they are white but *because they are implicated in white supremacy*. The problem isn't that white people have difficulty feeling aesthetic and/or bodily satisfaction. Rather, the problem is that whites' "satisfaction" is (historically, contextually) predicated on racism. The musical irregularity and distortion in these songs can subvert and stunt what we white people have learned to experience as musical and physical satisfaction. The musical noise can be epistemically noisy.[32]

MUSICAL NOISE AS EPISTEMIC NOISE

In her fabulous article on No Wave band The Bush Tetras, Caroline O'Meara argues that the Tetras use musical noise to express or represent "epistemologically noisy"[33] phenomena. A type of cognitive dissonance, epistemic noise is what happens when one's "concept" of something "may not be reconciled" with "the lived" phenomenological experience of it.[34] Chance's music generates epistemic noise from musical noise: interruptions and malfunctions in pop conventions translate into interruptions and malfunctions in racialized implicit understanding (the habits and pre-reflective learned responses that manifest in and through the body).[35] In this section, I argue that Chance's work often appropriates black music in a way that exacerbates, rather than domesticates, its foreignness to white hipster ears; (mis)perceived blackness can no longer function to ameliorate whites' anxieties about their bodies. His dance music appropriates black styles but in ways that make dancing harder, not easier, for whites. Musical noise interrupts our habitual bodily responses, like dancing, thus giving rise to corporeal dissonance, i.e., to noisy implicit understanding.[36]

To facilitate comparisons to Devo's music, I focus my discussion of musical noise in Chance on the same two elements, plus one extra: rhythmic and formal irregularity and lyrics.

(a) Rhythmic Irregularity: As music critic Simon Reynolds explains, the "Contortions' music was riddled with tics and jerks, a prickly, irritable sound, like a speed freak scratching at hallucinatory bugs under the skin . . . Soul, denied an outlet, becomes cystlike . . . a painful pleasure that was almost dehumanizing."[37] Chance's music refuses to settle into a groove, generally opting for either asymmetrical metric patterns or hyper-fast tempos. His songs are difficult and exhausting to follow, due to overly complex patterns or excessively fast paces. For example, his cover of Michael Jackson's disco classic "Don't Stop 'Til You Get Enough" revs up the original's very moderate tempo of about 110 beats per minute (120 beats per minute is standard for dance music) to a breakneck 155bpm (or thereabouts). While the tempo is relatively consistent, it is irregularly fast for a dance track—it's easy to fall behind, get out of breath, and so on. With a non-metric bridge, a tendency to shift emphasis among beats, and a not-entirely-consistent shifting between meters (3/4 and 4/4), Chance's "Contort Yourself" is rife with rhythmic irregularity. However, because this rhythmic irregularity is tied to its formal irregularity, I will discuss it in the following section.

(b) Formal Irregularity: "Contort Yourself" has a contorted formal structure. Its basic structure can be represented as:

Intro (4 measures in 4/4)
A (4 measures in 4/4)
A
B (3 measures in 4/4)
C (20 measures in 3/4)—emphasis shifts between 2 and 3 throughout
Intro
A
A (last line of lyrics continue into . . .)
B
C^1 (17 measures in 3/4)
X (one extra beat)
$Intro^1$
X^1 (one extra measure in 4/4)
A
A
X^1
D (unmetered bridge)
C^2 (25 measures in 3/4)

While there are some regular sections—Intro, A, and B—I want to focus on the irregular sections: C, X, and D. Section D is entirely unmetered. C is in

3/4, a different meter than the rest of the song; this contributes to rhythmic irregularity, as does the shifting emphasis in this section between beats 2 and 3. As in Devo, it's difficult to get a firm sense of the downbeat. Formally, what is most notable about C is its inconsistent length: it appears in 20-, 17-, and 25-meter versions. X is also inconsistent in length. At times, anywhere from one beat to a full 4/4 measure is added to the end of an otherwise (relatively) consistent formal element (like an A section). So, section "X" interrupts the regular ABCD flow with "extra" beats or measures.[38] This interruption throws off listeners' attempts to keep track of the beat: for example, the extra beat in X throws dancers off-kilter, for example, putting you on the wrong foot. Both rhythmically and formally, this song is very hard to follow, even for someone with a fair degree of musical expertise. Any attempt to get into a groove, to go with the flow of the beat and the meter, is continually thwarted by small-scale rhythmic irregularities and large-scale formal irregularities. The rhythm and musical form are constantly contorted.

(c) Lyrical Content: In "Contort Yourself," contortion is the effect of unlearning common sense; to contort oneself is to "Try being stupid, instead of smart/Once you take out the garbage that's in your brain." In a context of hegemonic whiteness, critiquing and subverting white privilege will require whites to contort themselves.[39] Because whiteness's hegemonic (and thus centering and orienting) force is grounded in its invisibility, naming whiteness as such is a necessary, but not sufficient, step in de-centering it; the mere awareness of one's whiteness can be dis-orienting for whites. Chance does this in many places in his oeuvre, most obviously in the name of his post-Contortions band, James White and the Blacks. Here he lays bare the racial dynamics of "love-and-theft" style cultural appropriation, pointing out that whites tend to get all the fame and fortune, while black musicians are relegated to anonymous supporting roles. The lyrics of "Almost Black, part 1" similarly problematize love-and-theft conventions. I have analyzed this song extensively in another article, so I will keep my remarks here very brief.[40] The song's sarcastic premise is this: Chance, a white guy, plays music so well he seems "almost black." According to this logic, musical success requires the performance, by whites, of unflattering and racist stereotypes about blacks (hypersexuality, primitiveness, etc.)—for example, having "moves" or "sass," as the lyrics claim. Drawing attention to the racism that is otherwise invisible and implicit in love-and-theft style musical appropriation, Chance's lyrics distort the logic of white hegemony (which is predicated on its own invisibility) and force white listeners to acknowledge, and even feel bad about, their complicity in it.

Because this does not reflect particularly well on whites, it is not just politically uncomfortable for them/us, but also intimately, corporeally uncomfortable. With its rhythmic and formal irregularity, Chance's music expresses or represents this bodily discomfort: it is irregular, we don't know how to dance or move to it, and so on. While the use of musical noise is quite common in post-punk, the specific types of noise Chance uses lead to specific types of epistemic noise. Many post-punk acts incorporate noisy elements like dissonance, mistuned pitches, grating timbres, and amateurish performance. Chance definitely uses the first three types, but these are surface-level musical features—they don't necessarily impact a song's underlying structure. Sure, they sound "ugly," but they don't impact our bodily and affective experience of music in the same way that rhythmic and formal irregularities do. Rhythmic irregularities (like obscured downbeats) and formal irregularities upset the patterns listeners follow, often with their bodies (in clapping or dancing, for example), to make sense of a song. This musical noise generates epistemic noise at the level of implicit, corporeal knowledge: listeners don't know what to do with their bodies.

Bodily awkwardness is symptomatic of stereotypical whiteness but also precisely what black musical styles are supposed to cure. Chance's use of black music does the opposite: if racist stereotypes about blacks are what allow whites' experiences of their bodies and of music feel seamless and smooth, Chance's music complicates this pleasure. Even avant-garde rock critics who championed No Wave thought music had to feel black in order to be immediately, unrestrictedly "fun" for white audiences.[41] Chance's music makes explicit the self-deception whites have to practice in order to experience racism and cultural theft as "fun." So, while music critics thought No Wave could break the mainstream only by (re)turning to black music, to disco—that is, to dancing, to experiences of corporeal enjoyment, facility, and virility—Chance shows that whites' understanding of "fun" is actually really brutal for non-whites. With this knowledge, it might not be so fun for white people anymore, either.

In this way, then, Chance practices what Sara Ahmed calls a politics of disorientation. If white supremacy orients the world around and for the benefit of whiteness, then making whiteness noisy can both disorient the white world and contort its inhabitants.

WHITE CONTORTIONS AND THE POLITICS OF DISORIENTATION

Orientation as a Theory of Sociopolitical Inequality

Sara Ahmed treats power, hegemony, and privilege as "orientations." Orientations are the background conditions that give form to our perceptions: they're the "lenses" that allow some things to come into focus (at the expense of others), or the program behind the interface, making some things easy to do and others nearly impossible. In each cultural or subcultural context, there are systems of practices, conventions, and habits that allow us (especially our bodies) to "fee[l] at home" and "fin[d] our way."[42] We are oriented when we can unreflectively navigate a situation. So, when you don't have to think about riding a bike but just hop on and pedal, or when you don't have to think about comporting yourself in a gender-appropriate way, that's being orientated.

Ahmed argues that whiteness is a form of orientation: it's one of the programs through which we interface with the world and with others. "The world of whiteness," she argues, is "the familiar world . . . a world we know implicitly."[43] Because "colonialism makes the world 'white,'"[44] this "we" includes more than just white/Western subjects—everyone has to be familiar with whiteness. Whiteness directs global flows of resources, labor, and so on. If whiteness orients the world, those with legibly white bodies and comportments will have an easier time navigating this world than people with insufficiently white bodies and comportments. White supremacy means that disorientation disproportionately affects non-whites—they don't get the "invisible knapsack" with the map, compass, and so on.[45] In fact, when non-whites feel like their very existence is a "problem" (as Du Bois famously put it), these feelings of dis-orientation are further evidence that the world is oriented by white supremacy. In such a context, disorientation is an impediment for non-whites. As my discussion of Devo shows, in a generally white-oriented world, disorientation is not necessarily an impediment for whites—it can be an excuse to focus more resources and attention on white people. Here, I use Ahmed's work on the politics of disorientation to clarify what is potentially critical and counter-hegemonic in the type of white racial disorientation I locate in Chance's work.

A Politics of Disorientation

If white hegemony is a type of orientation, then how can disorientation be the corresponding anti-racist strategy for white people? The disorientation non-whites experience vis-à-vis white supremacy is qualitatively, phenomenologically, and politically distinct from critical anti-racist white disorientation. Non-whites are already dis- or mis-oriented by whiteness, and non-whites often hyberbolize their disorientation to build alternative communities and counternarratives within white supremacist societies (e.g., in Afrofuturism). According to Ahmed, white supremacy disorients blacks in two ways. First, it reduces them to objects. If "racism 'stops' black bodies,"[46] disorientation takes the form of blocked orientation. This blocking is the effect of a very specific cause: blacks are not granted full subject status as moral/political persons, citizens, and so on. "Reduced as they are to things among things,"[47] blacks can participate in white-oriented worlds but only as objects. Second, white supremacy negatively mediates blacks' process of critical self-reflection. As both Du Bois's and Fanon's discussions of multiple consciousness reveal, "racism ensures that the black gaze returns to the black body, which is not a loving return but rather follows the line of the hostile white gaze."[48] So, when blacks take their own bodies as the objects of critical self-reflection, their self-regard is mediated by normatively white ideals of subjectivity, gender, beauty, humanity, citizenship, and so on. They see themselves through the eyes of another, in third person (as a "he" or "she," not an "I" or "me").[49]

When anti-racist whites subject themselves to critical self-reflection, they may be disgusted or ashamed at their implicit and explicit racism, but this gaze is not necessarily hostile, as in the case with non-whites. This gaze does not require whites to adopt a form of subjectivity that necessarily denies their status as a (potential) subject. Whites may be taking their own bodies as the object of their critical reflection, but they are not necessarily reducing themselves to things, at least insofar as they are white.[50] White supremacy shapes the world in a way that allows whites to be both subjects and objects: even when they objectify themselves, they are never just objects. If there's any hostility in this critical self-reflection, it comes from anger and disappointment in one's self: it is an emotional and affective relation of the individual to him or herself; it is not, as in the case of anti-black racism, a structural hostility resulting from systematic oppression. Moreover, critical self-reflection is different than social and political change. Whites can problematize their own personal attributes and beliefs while simultaneously participating in white-oriented institutions, social structures, and so on. So, whites can feel bad (guilt, shame, etc.) without thereby "diminish[ing] their capacities for action."[51] As I have argued extensively in my writing on hipness, whites often use dis-identification with whiteness as a source of aesthetic and social capital.[52] Further, Ahmed argues that the disorientation can be the source of feelings and actions that are politically critical or politically reactionary.[53] So, for example, working-class whites are feeling increasingly disoriented by structural changes in the economy, by the increased prominence of Spanish-language media, and so on, and this disorientation leads to retrenchment (e.g., in the Tea party).

The white disorientation I'm interested in is a question of aesthetic, corporeal (dis)pleasure, the intersection among musical noise, epistemic noise, and bodily "noise." White privilege, within a white-oriented world, means that whites don't have to live with much, if any, such noise. As Monique Roelofs has argued, one manifestation of privilege is the "racialized aesthetic nationalism that expects to be able to organize the environment in accordance with its own taste and preferences."[54] White privilege means that white people get to live in worlds they like and which make sense to them—they get to lead noiseless lives. However, in worlds less centrally organized by whiteness, white people won't necessarily feel as easily orientated; they'll run up against more noise. So, if privilege includes aesthetic orientation, white aesthetic disorientation can be both (a) one avenue by which to make inroads in white privilege, and (b) evidence of whiteness' diminished capacity to orient the/a world. With respect to (b), disorientation can follow from the critical awareness of one's privileges as white. White hegemony hinges on the invisibility of whiteness and white self-deception: whites believe themselves and the world to be non-racist. Insofar as whites are encouraged to be ignorant of white hegemony, white disorientation can occur when anti-racist whites realize that things they previously thought were not oriented by whiteness are in fact saturated with it.

With respect to (a), disorienting, epistemically noisy music can be one way to acclimate whites to the disorientation that they will experience in worlds less centrally orientated by white supremacy. Chance's music forces whites to consider the conditions of our aesthetic preferences, and thus complicates the pleasure we take in music. It makes whites explicitly aware of the biases implicit in their musical tastes and affective, bodily responses to music. By "disturbing the very technologies through which we make sense"[55] of music, like love-and-theft style cultural appropriation, Chance "converts good feelings into bad."[56] It's important that a white man is behind this conversion from good to bad feelings, because, as Ahmed argues, "it is the agency of the white man that converts unhappy racism to multicultural happiness."[57] Or, it's the agency of white audiences that converts cultural theft into supposed admiration, that mistakes abuse for love. Chance's work prevents, or at least troubles, this conversion. And if this conversion is something whites are responsible for, whites will need to learn to stop doing it, to stop obscuring the harms of racism, if these harms are ever going to be lessened.

Individual whites' subjective experience of racial disorientation can often be compatible, if not actively complicit, with the general orientation of the world around whiteness. In order for white aesthetic and corporeal disorientation to affect this world orientation, white disorientation has to go beyond individual affective and emotional experience, and attack the structures that organize and orient collective phenomena. Chance's music, because it addresses the love-and-theft discourse in white pop music, does target its attack beyond individual experience; it aims at the underlying discourses of aesthetic pleasure.

CONCLUSION

There are better and worse ways for white people to problematize their bodies. Some ways, like the love-and-theft solution, or Devo's approach, reaffirm white hegemony. Other ways, like the one I develop in my analysis of Chance and Ahmed, can erode it (though not necessarily so). While whites often use their awareness of their racism to prove their elite status among whites, Chance's music provides us with a resource for thinking about a critical, anti-racist white disorientation. His work can express what it might feel like to know that your whiteness is a problem for you because it is a problem for non-white people. It familiarizes us with the experiential, affective, and even emotional crises that are a necessary first step in addressing one's complicity in (often implicitly) racist projects.

These awkward and disorienting musical techniques are, to me and to many other fans, the source of aesthetic pleasure in music; in dancing to this music, it can be a source of bodily pleasure, even specifically white bodily pleasure. But if, as whites groomed by a white supremacist culture, our aesthetic taste, our possibilities for pleasure in art, for pleasure in our dancing bodies, are grounded in racist norms and practices, do we white people (and I say "we" because I'm white) have to give up pleasure tout court? Or can we experience complicated and conflicted pleasures? We have models of complicated and conflicted pleasures from aesthetics—for example, Kant's sublime is a pleasure in the overcoming of a threat.[58] In Kant, the pleasure derives not from the threatening object, but from our success in conquering it. So the pleasure itself isn't complex and contradictory, even though the aesthetic experience as a whole is. Chance's work can be a model of pleasure that doesn't overcome threats to our satisfaction because it tolerates and even welcomes problematization. This pleasure is indirect in several ways: not only is it combined with some degree of displeasure (in the form of disorientation, awkwardness, or discomfort), but, more importantly, (1) it is mediated by knowledge of one's whiteness, and (2) the progressive versions are mediated by an awareness of one's political complicity in racism and white privilege.

I personally find these styles of musical irregularity and distortion really pleasurable: I, a white girl from the Midwest, like this music. I find it pleasurable not only because I hear anti-racist and often feminist and queer politics in it but primarily because I like the way it sounds. I like its awkwardness, its herky-jerky, jaggedy, irregular, contorted aesthetic. Maybe it reflects my own dis-orientation, the epistemic and affective noise I feel in my complex inhabitance of whiteness and contradictory relationship to white hegemony. If being white means participating in and benefiting from white privilege, then I am, in some ways, on the one hand, condemned to be and do things that disgust me. On the other, less flattering hand, I may appreciate, at some level, privileges that I intellectually know are immoral and unjust. But, it's also possible that I aesthetically approve and identify with music that I find politically disgusting and whose politics I cannot identify with. Further, I may enjoy this music because I approve of and identify with its politics, even if these politics complicate and problematize my aesthetic tastes.

Whites need to learn that we can't have it both ways. This aesthetic and corporeal disorientation may be one way to acclimate us to the kinds of disorientation from which privilege otherwise insulates us.

NOTES

1. Whiteness is of the mind—it is, as Richard Dyer puts it, "in" the body but not "of" it. Dyer, Richard. *White*. London: Routledge, 1997.

2. White women have a more complicated experience of their bodies. As Iris Young suggests, insofar as white women experience their bodies as feminine, they feel subject to their bodies; however, insofar as they experience their bodies as white, white women may feel some sense of control or mastery over their bodies. For example, ideals of female sexual purity or body size often require white women to exercise strict control over bodily appetites. For more information, see: Young, Iris. *On Female Body Experience: "Throwing Like a Girl" and Other Essays*. New York: Oxford University Press, 2005. Given the binary black/white logic that has historically governed race discourse in the United States, the disassociation of whiteness and embodiment implies, logically, the association of blackness and embodiment. This plays no small role in the literal and metaphorical objectification of black bodies and the social, economic, and political devaluation of blackness. My thanks to George Yancy for pushing me on this point.

3. See, for example: Gooding-Williams, Robert. *Look! A Negro*. New York: Routledge, 2005. James, Robin. "In But Not Of/Of But Not In: On Taste, Hipness, and White Embodiment." Spec. issue of Contemporary Aesthetics. Vol. 2 (2009). http://www.contempaesthetics.org/newvolume/pages/article.php?articleID=549. Last accessed 5 Sep. 2012.

4. New Wave and No Wave are both late '70s post-punk genres. No Wave was a short-lived movement localized to the New York Downtown scene. New Wave was both longer-lasting and wider-reaching, including both commercial and avant-garde artists in the United States and the UK. See Gnendron, Bernard. Between Montmartre and the Mudd Club. Chicago: University of Chicago Press, 2002. Simon Reynolds's *Rip It Up & Start Again* is a really good introductory overview of both scenes, their histories, their intermingling, and their divergences. See footnote 37.

5. For more on this point see Yancy, George. *Black Bodies, White Gazes*. Lanham: Rowman & Littlefield, 2008.

6. These philosophical/political approaches to whiteness are not universal to the subgenres with which I identify them; rather, I take two "representative" artists—Devo and James Chance—to tease out two different political approaches to generally similar musical and aesthetic material. So, this is not a historical thesis about what bands did or thought, but a philosophical analysis of concepts, discourses, and judgments. I'm taking works by Devo and Chance as examples of the philosophical approaches to whiteness that 21st century audiences hear and feel in listening and dancing to them.

7. For more on white hipness, see Monson, Ingrid. "The Problem of White Hipness: Race Gender and Cultural Conceptions in Jazz Historical Discourse." *Journal of the American Musicological Society*. 85.3 (1995): 65–101. Print. For further discussion on white hipness, see: James, Robin. "In But Not Of/Of But Not In: On Taste, Hipness, and White Embodiment." Spec. issue of *Contemporary Aesthetics*. Vol. 2 (2009): n. pag. Web. 5 Sep. 2012.

8. See Lott, Eric. *Love and Theft: Blackface Minstrelsy and the American Working Class*. New York: Oxford University Press 1995.

9. It is likely that this shift is due to generational tension among whites (thus keeping whiteness at the center, non-white people and identities persist in their instrumentality and marginality). One of the ways white artists in the late 1970s could distinguish themselves from the previous generation of white rock avant-garde, which was their present-day rock mainstream, was by adopting different attitudes toward and techniques of cultural appropriation.

10. Cateforis, Theo. "Performing the Avant-Garde Groove: Devo and the Whiteness of the New Wave." *American Music*. 22.4 (2004): 564–88. Print.

11. Ibid. 565.

12. Ibid. 568.

13. Ingrid Monson's article on white hipness (see footnote 6) is excellent on this topic.

14. As Susan McClary explains, "English fans" lacked "a particularly clear sense of black culture in America; they used their musical allegiances to meet their own needs. Yet it was significant that it was the music of black males they idolized, for African Americans were thought to have access to real (i.e., preindustrialized) feelings and community". Mclary, Susan. *Conventional Wisdom: The Content of Musical Form*. Berkeley: University of California Press, 2000. 55.

15. Cateforis, 581.

16. "Moving their bodies in a series of sharp, jerky motions, they proceeded to reduce one of rock's most sacred cows, the Rolling Stones '(I Can't Get No) Satisfaction,' to an absurd procession of minimalist, stunted riffs and nervous vocals. To many, the band's performance was a bewildering, antagonizing intrusion into their weekend entertainment" (emphasis mine). Cateforis, 564–65.

17. Cateforis, 567.

18. Ibid. 567.

19. Ibid. 572.

20. Ibid. 574.

21. Ibid. 574.

22. Ibid. 568.

23. Ibid. 574-5.

24. "The tension here," in Devo's version, "arises from . . . incessant repetition played against our knowledge and expectations of the original's form." Ibid. 576.

25. Ibid. 576.

26. Ibid. 576.

27. Ibid. 580–82.

28. It's worth noting that these twitching bodies are noticeably awkward only because their habitual musical experiences are disrupted. Anyone who has played an instrument knows that it involves a lot of awkward, "twitchy" movement: crooking one's neck to play violin or viola; rapid, stylized, difficult movements of the fingers over strings or keys; odd facial expressions; etc. We, both as instrumentalists and listeners, have just become habituated to the movements and postures involved in playing a musical instrument. We don't read regularly musical bodies as awkward and twitchy. So, musical irregularity can point out the bodily irregularity required to perform music.

29. Cateforis, 583.

30. "Devo's stiff bodily movements ultimately defuses and mocks the emotive, sexualized gestures typical of the late-seventies male 'cock rocker,' the aggressive masculine performer stereotype." Cateforis, 579.

31. Cateforis argues that New Wave's rejection of mainstream musical and political norms "could only ever be a revolt against the self." Ibid. 583.

32. I limit my claim here to blacks because Chance's work is narrowly focused on black-white relations. In a more general context, however, it is certainly true that all of racism's effects are cause for concern, and that white disorientation is a problem not just for blacks, but all people of color.

33. I want to clarify that I'm doing a reading of songs and performances from the perspective of a contemporary audience. I'm not making claims about the original context, about the musicians' intended meanings, their personal and/or professional politics, etc. These artworks, regardless of authorial intent or original meaning, allow for—if not encourage—certain readings/interpretations today. I'm using Chance to think through some philosophical issues related to the politics of whiteness and white embodiment. O'Mera, Caroline Polk. "The Bush Tetras, 'Too Many Creeps' and New York City." *American Music*. 25.2 (2007):193–215. Print. 209.

34. Ibid. 209.

35. See Shotwell, Alexis. *Knowing Otherwise: Race, Gender and Implicit Understanding.* University Park: Pennsylvania State University Press, 2011.

36. For more on corporeal dissonance and the role of music in inducing this phenomenon, see my article "These.Are.The Breaks: Rethinking Disagreement Through Hip Hop." *Transformations.* No. 19 (2011): Web. 5 Sept. 2012.

37. Reynolds, Simon. *Rip It Up and Start Again: Postpunk 1978*-1984. New York: Penguin Books, 2006. 150.

38. I also called this section X because their irregularity, their lack of clear "fit" with any one section, leaves their placement and function up to interpretation. My schematization is the most justifiable account I can come up with, but this was after significant deliberation. It is also possible, for example, to interpret C prime as 16 measure in 3/4 followed by one measure of 4/4.

39. Rock critics thought this punk-funk was No Wave's only chance to break with the mainstream, because the mainstream discourses of white aesthetic pleasure required a detour through blackness. "With this 'sinister murky brew' of 'jazz, R&B, and soul,' the Contortions were anointed the no wave band with the 'most potential for commercial success.'" Gendron, Bernard. *Between Mountains and the Mudd Club: Popular Music and the Avant-Guarde.* Chicago: University of Chicago Press, 2002. 285.

40. Ahmed, Sara. *Queer Phenomenology: Orientations, Objects, Others.* Durham: Duke University Press, 2006. 9.

41. Ibid. 111.

42. Ibid. 111.

43. Ibid. 111.

44. Ibid. 111.

45. The "invisible knapsack" concept comes from Peggy McIntosh's essay "White Privlege and Male Privilege" in McIntosh, Peggy. "White Privilege and Male Privilege: A Personal Account of Coming to See Correspondences Through Work in Women's Studies." 1988. Print.

46. Ahmed, Sara. *Queer Phenomenology*, 111.

47. Ibid. 111

48. Ibid. 111.

49. For more on this point see Yancy, George. *Black Bodies, White Gazes.* Lanham: Rowman & Littlefield, 2008.

50. As Iris Young has pointed out, white women are encouraged to regard their female and feminine bodies as impediments. In Young, gender (and sex), not race, is the cause of this objectification. In fact, white women's hostile regard of their bodies can appear to be only gender-based because their whiteness positively orients them to/in white hegemony. Non-white women are complexly disoriented. See footnote 2.

51. Ahmed, Sara. *Queer Phenomenology*, 111.

52. Or, in Ahmed's terms "disorientation" can sometimes function as "a way of experiencing the pleasure of deviation." In order for deviation to be experienced as pleasurable, even in part, requires a certain level of privilege—the deviation isn't making your life unlivable, isn't putting your very health and survival in question (at least if you're legibly straight, able-bodied, and cis (what is this word, "cis"?) male, as is Chance). Ahmed, Sara. *Queer Phenomenology: Orientations, Objects, Others.* Durham: Duke University Press, 2006. 177.

53. "It is not that disorientation is always radical. Bodies that experience disorientation can be defensive, as they reach out for support or as they search for a place to reground and reorientate their relation to the world. So, too, the forms of politics that proceed from disorientation can be conservative, depending on the 'aims' of their gestures, depending on how they seek to (re)ground themselves. And, for sure, bodies that experience being out of place might need to be orientated, to find a place where they feel comfortable and safe in the world". Ibid. 158.

54. Roelofs, Monique. "Sensation as Civilization: Reading/Riding the Taxicab." Spec. issue of *Contemporary Aesthetics.* Vol. 7 (2009): n. pag. Web. 5 Sept. 2012.

55. Ahmed, Sara. *The Promise of Happiness.* Durham: Duke University Press, 2010. 80.

56. Ibid. 49.

57. Ibid. 255, note 20.

58. For more on this, see Battersby, Christine. *The Sublime, Terror, and Human Difference.* London: Routledge, 2007.

Bibliography

Aanerud, Rebecca. "The Legacy of White Supremacy and the Challenge of Antiracist White Mothering." *Hypatia*, 22.2 (2007): 20–38.

———. "Thinking Again: *This Bridge Called My Back* and the Challenge to Whiteness," In *This Bridge We Call Home: Radical Visions for Transformation*, edited by Gloria E. Anzaldúa and AnaLouise Keating, 69–77. New York & London: Routledge, 2002.

Ackah, W. "The Experience of my Experience: reflections on working in deranged white academic space." In *Integrated but Unequal: Black Faculty in Predominately White Space*, edited by M. Christian. Trenton. NJ: Africa World Press, 2012.

Ahmed, Sara. "Declarations of Whiteness: The Non-Performativity of Anti-Racism." *borderlands* 'e-journal 3, no. 2 (2004). http://www.borderlands.net.au/vol3no2_2004/ahmed_declarations.htm (accessed June 19, 2012).

———. "The Affective Politics of Fear." In *The Cultural Politics of Emotion*. New York: Routledge, 2004.

———. *Queer Phenomenology: Orientations, Objects, Others*. Durham: Duke University Press, 2006.

———. *The Promise of Happiness*. Durham: Duke University Press, 2010.

Alexander, Michelle. *The New Jim Crow*. New York: New Press, 2010.

Allen, David G. "Whiteness and Difference in Nursing." *Nursing Philosophy*, 7 (2006): 65–78.

Allen, Theodore. W. *The Invention of the White Race Vol. 1: Racial Oppression and Social Control*. London & New York: Verso, 1994.

Anzaldúa, Gloría E., and Cherríe L. Moraga, eds. *This Bridge Called My Back: Writings by Radical Women of Color*. Berkeley, CA: Third Woman Press, 2002.

Applebaum, Barbara. *Being White, Being Good: White Complicity, White Moral Responsibility, and Social Justice Pedagogy*. Lanham, MD: Lexington Books, 2010.

———. "White Ignorance and Denials of Complicity." *The Center Must Not Hold: White Women Philosophers on the Whiteness of Philosophy*, edited by George Yancy. Lanham, MD: Lexington Books, 2011.

Aptheker, Herbert. *Anti-Racism in U.S. History*. Westport: Praeger, 1993.

Austin, Allen. *The Origins of the Dred Scott Case*. Athens, GA: University of Georgia Press, 2006.

Austin, John Langshaw. *How to Do Things with Words*, 2nd edition. Cambridge, MA: Harvard University Press, 1975.

Avyazian, Andrea. "Interrupting the Cycle of Oppression: The Role of Allies as Agents of Change." In *Race, Class, and Gender in the United States: An Integrated Study*, 5th edition, edited by Paula Rothenberg. Worth Publishers, 2000. 609–15.

Bailey, A. "Locating Traitorous Identities: Toward a View of Privilege-Cognizant White Character" *Hypatia* 13, no. 3 (1998): 27–42

Bailey, Alison. "Despising an Identity They Taught Me to Claim." In *Whiteness: Feminist Political* Reflections, edited by Chris Cuomo and Kim T. Hall. Lanham, MD: Roman & Littlefield, 1999. 85–104.

———. "Privilege: Expanding on Marilyn Frye's 'Oppression.'" In *Oppression, Privilege, and Resistance: Theoretical Perspectives on Racism, Sexism, and Heterosexism*, edited by Lisa Heldke and Peg O'Connor. Boston: McGraw Hill, 2004. 301–16.

Baldwin, James. Quoted in "Take this Hammer," produced by KQED-TV for National Educational Television, 1964. https://diva.sfsu.edu/collections/sfbatv/bundles/187041.

———. Speaking at National Press Club. December 10, 1986. http://www.youtube.com/watch?v=SYka_Tq_mTI&feature=related.

———. "White Man's Guilt," *Ebony* 20 (1964): 47–48.

———. "White Man's Guilt." In *The Price of the Ticket: Collected Nonfiction 1948–1985*. New York: St. Martin's Press, 1985.

———. *Collected Essays*. New York: Library of America, 1998.

———. *The Fire Next Time*. New York: The Modern Library, 1995.

———. *The Price of the Ticket: Collected Nonfiction 1948–1985*. New York: St. Martin's, 1985.

Bartky, Sandra Lee. "Race, Complicity, and Culpable Ignorance." In *"Sympathy and Solidarity" and Other Essays*. Lanham, MD: Rowman & Littlefield, 2002. 151–67.

Battersby, Christine. *The Sublime, Terror, and Human Difference*. London: Routledge, 2007.

Bay, Mia. *The White Image in the Black Mind: African American Ideas about White People, 1830–1925*. Oxford: Oxford University Press, 2000.

Bennett, Lerone. "The White Problem in America." *Ebony*. Chicago, Johnson Publishing Co. (1965): 29–36.

Bergoffen, Debra. February 22, 2001: "Toward a Politics of the Vulnerable Body." *Hypatia* 18, no. 1 (2003): 116–34.

Berlak, Ann. "Teaching and Testimony: Witnessing and Bearing Witness to Racisms in Culturally Diverse Classrooms," *Curriculum Inquiry* 29, no. 1 (1999): 99–127.

Bertrand, Marianne, and Sendhil Mullainathan. "Are Emily and Greg More Employable than Lakisha and Jamal? A Field Experiment on Labor Market Discrimination," *American Economic Review* 94, no. 4 (2004): 991–1013.

Bigo, D., and E. Guild. *Controlling Frontiers: Free Movement into and within Europe*. Farnham: Ashgate, 2005.

Bonilla-Silva, Eduardo. *Racism without Racists: Color-Blind Racism and the Persistence of Racial Inequality in the United States*. Lanham, MD: Rowman & Littlefield, 2003.

Bourdieu, Pierre. *Outline of a Theory of Practice*. Cambridge: Cambridge University Press, 1977.

———. *The Logic of Practice*. Stanford: Stanford University Press, 1990.

Britzman, Deborah. *Lost Subjects, Contested Objects: Toward a Psychoanalytic Inquiry of Learning*. Albany: State University of New York Press, 1998.

Brown, Michael K., et al. *Whitewashing Race: The Myth of a Color-Blind Society*. Berkeley: University of California Press, 2003.

Butler, Judith. *Giving an Account of Oneself*. New York: Fordham University Press, 2005.

———. *Precarious Life: The Power of Mourning and Violence*. New York: Verso, 2006.

———. *Undoing Gender*. New York: Routledge, 2004.

——— "What Is Critique? An Essay on Foucault's Virtue." In *The Political*, edited by David Ingram. Boston: Blackwell, 2002. 212.

Butler, Judith, and William Connolly. "Interview." *Theory & Event* 4, no. 2 (2000): http://muse.jhu.edu/journals/theory_and_event/toc/archive.html

Case, Kim, and Annette Hemmings. "Distancing: White Women Preservice Teachers and Antiracist Curriculum." *Urban Education* 40, no. 6 (2005): 606–26.

Cateforis, Theo. "Performing the Avant-Garde Groove: Devo and the Whiteness of the New Wave." *American Music* 22, no. 4 (2004): 564–88.

Center for Constitutional Right. "Racial Disparity in NYPD Stops-and-Frisks." http:// ccrjustice.org/stopandfrisk.

Chavez Chavez, Rudolfo, and James O'Donnell. *Speaking the Unpleasant: The Politics of (non)Engagement in the Multicultural Education Terrain.* Albany: State University Press, 1998.

Chizhik, Estella Williams, and Alexander Williams Chizhik. "Are you Privileged or Oppressed? Students' Conceptions of Themselves and Others," *Urban Education* 40, no. 2 (2005): 116–43

Chödrön, Pema. *The Places That Scare You: A Guide to Fearlessness in Difficult Times.* Boston: Shambala Press, 2001.

Clark, Christine, and James O'Donnell. "Rearticulating a Racial Identity: Creating Oppositions Space to Fight for Equality and Social Justice." In *Becoming and Unbecoming White: Owning and Disowning a Racial Identity*, edited by C. Clark and J. O'Donnell. Westport, CT: Bergin & Garvey, 1999. 1–9.

Cone, James H. "Theology's Great Sin: Silence in the Face of White Supremacy." *Union Seminary Quarterly Review* 55, no. 3–4 (2001): 1–14.

Copeland, M. Shawn. "Racism and the Vocation of the Christian Theologian." *Spiritus* 2 (2002): 15–29.

Cornelius, W. et al, eds. *Controlling Immigration: A Global Perspective, 2nd edition.* Stanford, CA: Stanford University Press, 2004.

Daly, Mary. *Gyn/ecology: The Metaethics of Radical Feminism.* Boston: Beacon Press, 1990.

Davis, F. James. *Who Is Black: One Nation's Definition.* University Park, PA: Pennsylvania State University Press, 1991.

DK 22B101 Kahn, C. *The Art and Thought of Heraclitus.* Cambridge University Press, 1979.

Du Bois, W. E. B. *The Souls of Black Folk.* New York: Penguin, 1996.

Dunbar-Ortiz, Roxanne. "The Opposite of Truth Is Forgetting: An Interview with Roxanne Dunbar-Ortiz by Chris Dixon." *Upping the Anti* 6 (2008): 47–58.

Dyer, Richard. "White." *Screen* 29 (1988): 44–64.

———. *White.* London: Routledge, 1997.

Dyson, Michael Eric. *I May Not Get There with You: The True Martin Luther King, Jr.* New York: Free Press, 2000.

Evans, Fred. *The Multivoiced Body: Society and Communication in the Age of Diversity.* New York: Columbia University Press, 2008.

Fernandes, Leela. *Transforming Feminist Practice; Non-Violence, Social Justice, and the Possibilities of a Spiritualized Feminism.* San Francisco: Aunt Lute Books, 2003.

Fineman, Martha A. "The Vulnerable Subject: Anchoring Equality in the Human Condition." *Yale Journal of Law and Feminism* 20, no. 1 (2008.): 1–23.

Fosl, Catherine. *Subversive Southerner: Anne Braden and the Struggle for Racial Justice in the Cold War South.* New York: Palgrave, 2002.

Frankenberg, Ruth. "When We Are Capable of Stopping, We Begin to See: Being White, Seeing Whiteness," In *Names We Call Home: Autobiography of Racial Identity*, edited by Becky Thompson and Sangeeta Tyagi. New York & London: Routledge, 1996. 3–17.

———. *White Women, Race Matters: The Social Construction of Whiteness.* Minneapolis: University of Minnesota Press, 1993.

Freire, Paulo. *Pedagogy of the Oppressed, New Revised 20th-Anniversary Edition.* Translated by Myra Bergman Ramos. New York: Continuum, 1996.

Frye, Marilyn. "Oppression." In *The Politics of Reality.* Freedom, CA: The Crossing Press, 1983.

———. "On Being White." *The Politics of Reality: Essays in Feminist Theory.* Freedom, CA: The Crossing Press, 1983.

———. "White Woman Feminist." *Willful Virgin: Essays in Feminism.* Freedom, CA: The Crossing Press, 1992. 147–69.

———. *The Politics of Reality: Essays in Feminist Theory.* Trumansburg, NY: Crossing Press, 1983.

———. *Willful Virgin: Essays in Feminism, 1976–1992.* Freedom, CA: Crossing Press, 1992.

Fuentes, Annette. *Lockdown High: When the Schoolhouse Becomes a Jailhouse*. New York: Verso, 2011.

Garner, S. "The Uses of whiteness: what researchers working on Europe can draw from US work on US work on Whiteness" *Sociology* 40, no. 2 (2006): 257–75.

———. *Whiteness: an introduction*. London: Routledge, 2007.

Gendron, Bernard. *Between Montmartre and the Mudd Club*. Chicago: University of Chicago Press, 2002.

Gilson, Erinn. *Vulnerability, Ignorance, and Oppression. Hypatia* 26, no. 2 (2011.): 308–32.

Gooding-Williams, Robert. *Look! A Negro*. New York: Routledge, 2005.

Gwaltney, John Langston, ed. *Drylongso: A Self Portrait of Black America*, 1st New Press edition. New York: New Press, 1993.

Haney López, Ian F. *White by Law*. New York: NYU Press, 1996.

Harris, C. "Whiteness as Property." *Harvard Law Review* 106, no. 8 (1993): 1707–93.

Haslanger, Sally. *Resisting Reality: Social Construction and Social Critique*. Oxford: Oxford University Press, 2012.

Hill Collins, Patricia. *Black Feminist Thought: Knowledge, Consciousness, and the Politics of Empowerment*, revised 10th anniversary edition. New York: Routledge, 2000.

Hill, Herbert. "Myth-making as Labor History." In *Politics, Culture, and Society* 2, no. 2 (Winter 1988).

Hinson-Hasty, Elizabeth. "Revisiting Feminist Discussions of Sin and Genuine Humility." *Journal of Feminist Studies in Religion*, 28, no. 1 (2012): 108–14.

Holland, Nancy J. *Ontological Humility: Lorde Voldemort and the Philosophers*. Albany: SUNY Press, 2013.

Holland, Randy. *The Fire This Time*, a documentary film about South Central Los Angeles. Produced by Randy Holland and Mark Mori, 1994.

hooks, bell. "Representing Whiteness in the Black Imagination." In *Black Looks: Race and Representation*. Boston: South End Press, 1992. 165–79.

Huntington, Samuel. *The Crisis of Democracy: Report on the Governability of Democracies to the Trilateral Commission*. New York: New York University Press, 1975.

Hurley. *Concise Introduction to Logic, 10th edition*. Belmont, CA: Thomson, 2008.

Hytten, Kathy, and John Warren. "Engaging Whiteness: How Racial Power Gets Reified in Education." *Qualitative Studies in Education* 16, no. 1 (2003): 66.

Jackson, Bailey W., and C. L. Wijeyesinghe, eds. *New Perspectives on Racial Identity Development*. New York: New York University Press, 2001.

Jacobson, Matthew Frye. *Whiteness of a Different Color: European Immigrants and the Alchemy of Race*. Cambridge: Harvard University Press, 1998.

James, Robin. "In But Not Of/Of But Not In: On Taste, Hipness, and White Embodiment." Special issue of *Contemporary Aesthetics* 2 (2009). http://www.contempaesthetics.org/newvolume/pages/article.php?articleID=549.

———. "These.Are.The Breaks: Rethinking Disagreement Through Hip Hop." *Transformations* no. 2 (2011).

Jenkins, Fiona. "Judith Butler: Disturbance, Provocation and the Ethics of Non-Violence." *Humanities Research* XVI, no. 2 (October 2010).

Jensen, Robert. "Beyond Race, Gender, and Class: Reclaiming the Radical Roots of Social Justice Movements." *Global Dialogue* 12, no. 2 (Summer/Autumn 2010): http://www.worlddialogue.org/content.php?id=487.

———. *The Heart of Whiteness: Confronting Race, Racism and White Privilege*. San Francisco, CA: City Lights Books, 2005.

Jones, Alison. "The Limits of Cross-Cultural Dialogue: Pedagogy, Desire, and Absolution in the Classroom." *Educational Theory* 49, no. 3 (1999): 299–316.

Jones, J. "The Impairment of Empathy in Goodwill Whites for African-Americans." In *What White Looks Like: African-American Philosophers on the Whiteness Question*, edited by George Yancy. New York: Routledge, 2004. 65–86.

Kaufman, Cynthia. "A User's Guide to White Privilege," *Radical Philosophy Review* 4, no. 1–2 (2002): 30–38.

Keating, AnaLouise. *Teaching Transformation: Transcultural Classroom Dialogues.* New York: Palgrave MacMillian, 2007.

King, Martin Luther Jr. *A Testament of Hope: The Essential Writings and Speeches of Martin Luther King, Jr.* James M. Washington, ed. New York: HarperCollins, 1991.

———. "I Have a Dream." Speech at the March on Washington, August 28, 1963. In *I Have a Dream: Letters and Speeches That Changed the World*, edited by James Melvin Washington with a foreword by Coretta Scott King. New York: HarperCollins, 1986. 101–6.

Kinsman, Gary William, and Patrizia Gentile. *The Canadian War on Queers: National Security as Sexual Regulation.* UBC Press, 2010.

Krysan, Maria, Reynolds Farley, and Mick P. Couper. "In the Eye of the Beholder: Racial Beliefs and Residential Segregation." *Du Bois Review* 5, no. 1 (2008): 5–26.

Lee, Mun Wah. *The Art of Mindful Facilitation.* Berkeley: StirFry Seminars and Counseling, 2004.

———. *The Color of Fear.* DVD. Berkeley, CA: StirFry Productions, 1994.

Leonardo, Zeus. "The Color of Supremacy: Beyond the Discourse of 'White Privilege.'" *Educational Philosophy and Theory* 36, no. 2 (2004): 137–52.

Lester, Julius. "James Baldwin—Reflections of a Maverick." *New York Times* (May 27, 1984): http://www.nytimes.com/books/98/03/29/specials/baldwin-reflections.html

Levine-Rasky, Cynthia. "Framing Whiteness: Working through the Tensions of Introducing Whiteness to Educators." *Race, Ethnicity and Education* 3, no. 3 (2000): 271–92.

Lewis, David Levering. *W. E. B. Du Bois, 1868–1919: Biography of a Race.* New York: Holt Press, 1994.

Litwack, Leon. *North of Slavery.* Chicago: University of Chicago Press, 1961.

Lorde, Audre. *Sister Outsider: Essays and Speeches by Audre Lorde.* Berkeley: The Crossing Press, 1984.

Lott, Eric. *Love and Theft: Blackface Minstrelsy and the American Working Class.* New York: Oxford University Press, 1995.

Lugones, Maria C. "On The Logic of Pluralist Feminism." In *Feminist Ethics*, edited by Claudia Card. Lawrence: University of Kansas Press, 1991.

Lund Pedersen, L. "Intimacy with the Danish Nation-State: My Partner, the Danish State and I—A Case Study of Family Reunification Policy in Denmark." In *Whiteness and Postcolonialism in the Nordic Region: Exceptionalism, Migrant Others and National Identities*, edited by K. Loftsdóttir and L. Jensen. Farnham: Ashgate, 2012. 141–58.

Lyken-Garner. A. *Sunday's Child.* Cary, NC: Pulse Press, 2012.

Malcolm X. *Malcolm X Speaks: Selected Speeches and Statements.* George Breitman, ed. London: Secker and Warburg, 1965.

Mani, Lata. *Sacred/Secular: Contemporary Cultural Critique.* London & New York: Routledge, 2009.

———. *The Integral Nature of Things: Critical Reflections on the Present.* London & New York: Routledge, 2013.

Manning, Marable. *Malcolm X: A Life of Reinvention.* New York: Viking, 2011.

Martinot, Steve. *The Machinery of Whiteness.* Philadelphia: Temple University Press, 2009.

———. *The Rule of Racialization.* Philadelphia: Temple University Press, 2003.

Massey, Douglas S., and Nancy A. Denton. *American Apartheid: Segregation and the Making of the Underclass.* Cambridge, MA: Harvard University Press, 1993.

McClary, Susan. *Conventional Wisdom: The Content of Musical Form.* Berkeley: University of California Press, 2000.

McHugh, Nancy. "Telling Her Own Truth: June Jordan, Standard English and the Epistemology of Ignorance." In *Still Seeking an Attitude*, edited by Kinloch, V. and M. Grebowicz. Lanham, MD: Lexington Books, 2004.

McIntosh, Peggy. "White Privilege and Male Privilege: A Personal Account of Coming to See Correspondences through Work in Women's Studies." Working Paper #189. Wellesley College Center for Research on Women (now Wellesley Centers for Women), 1990.

———. "Interactive Phases of Curricular and Personal Re-Vision with Regard to Race." Working Paper #219. Wellesley College Center for Research on Women (now Wellesley Centers for Women), 1990.

―――. "White Privilege: Unpacking the Invisible Knapsack." In *White Privilege: Essential Readings on the Other Side of Racism*, edited by Paula S. Rothenberg. New York: Worth, 97–101.

McIntyre, Alice. *Making Meaning of Whiteness: Exploring Racial Identities with White Teachers*. Albany, NY: SUNY Press, 1997.

McNamee, Stephen, and Robert Miller Jr. *The Meritocracy Myth*. Lanham, MD: Rowman & Littlefield, 2004.

McRobbie, Angela. "Vulnerability, Violence and (Cosmopolitan) Ethics: Butler's *Precarious Life*." *British Journal of Sociology* 57, no.1 (2006): 78.

McWhorter, Ladelle. "Where Do White People Come From?: A Foucaultian Critique of Whiteness Studies." *Philosophy & Social Criticism 31* (2005): 533–56.

Mills, Charles. *The Racial Contract*. Ithaca: Cornell University Press, 1999.

Mills, C. W. "White Ignorance." *Race and Epistemologies of Ignorance* (2007): 11–38.

Monahan, Michael J. *The Creolizing Subject: Race, Reason, and the Politics of Purity*. New York: Fordham University Press, 2011.

Monson, Ingrid. "The Problem of White Hipness: Race Gender and Cultural Conceptions in Jazz Historical Discourse." *Journal of the American Musicological Society* 85 no. 3 (1995): 65–101.

Moore, Richard O. *Take This Hammer*. TV Broadcast. R. O. Moore, producer. KQED: San Francisco, 1963.

Moraga, Cherrie. *This Bridge Called My Back: Writings By Radical Women of Color, 3rd edition*. San Antonio, TX: Third Woman Press, 2002.

Morrison, T. *Beloved*. New York: Alfred Knopf, 1987.

O'Connell, Maureen H. "After White Supremacy? The Visibility of Virtue Ethics for Racial Justice." *Journal of Moral Theology* 3, no. 1 (2014): 96.

―――. "Confessing Complicity: Catholic Moral Theology and White Claims to Moral Goodness in Racial Injustice." Paper presented at the meeting of the Catholic Theological Society of America. St. Louis, MO, 2012.

O'Mera, Caroline Polk. "The Bush Tetras, 'Too Many Creeps' and New York City." *American Music* 25, no. 2 (2007):193–215.

Oliver, Melvin L., and Thomas M. Shapiro. *Black Wealth/White Wealth: A New Perspective on Racial Inequality*. New York: Routledge, 1997.

Ortega, Mariana. "Being Lovingly, Knowingly Ignorant: White Feminism and Women of Color." *Hypatia* 21, no. 3 (2006): 56–74. doi:10.1353/hyp.2006.0034.

Owen, David S. "Privileged Social Identities and Diversity Leadership in Higher Education." *The Review of Higher Education* 32, no. 2 (2009): 185–207.

―――. "Towards a Critical Theory of Whiteness." *Philosophy and Social Criticism* 33, no. 2 (2007): 203–22.

―――. "Whiteness in Du Bois's *The Souls of Black Folk*." *Philosophia Africana* 10, no. 2 (2007): 107–26.

Pager, Devah. *Marked: Race, Crime, and Finding Work in an Era of Mass Incarceration*. Chicago: University of Chicago Press, 2007.

Parker, Pat. *An Expanded Edition of Movement in Black*, expanded edition. Ithaca, NY: Firebrand Books, 1999.

Plato. *The Apology*. Benjamin Jowett, translation http://classics.mit.edu/Plato/apology.html.

powell, john. "Regionalism and Race." *Race, Poverty, and the Environment* 17, no. 1 (Spring 2010).

Pratt, Minnie Bruce. "Identity: Skin, Blood, Heart." In *Yours in Struggle; Three Feminist Perspectives on Anti-Semitism and Racism*, edited by Elly Bulkin, Minnie Bruce Pratt, and Barbara Smith. Ithaca: Firebrand Books, 1984.

Probyn, Fiona. "Playing Chicken at the Intersection: The White Critic in/of Critical Whiteness Studies." *Borderlands* 13, no.2 (2004): http://www.borderlandsejournal.adelaide.edu.au/vol3no2_2004/probyn_playing.htm.

Regan, Paulette. *Unsettling the Settler Within: Indian Residential Schools, Truth Telling, and Reconciliation in Canada*. UBC Press, 2010.

Reynolds, Simon. *Rip It Up and Start Again: Postpunk 1978–1984.* New York: Penguin Books, 2006.

Rich, Andrienne. "Towards a Politics of Location." In *Feminist Theory Reader: Local and Global Perspectives*, edited by Carol R. McCann and Seung-Kyung Kim. New York: Routledge, 2003.

Riggs, Damien. "Benevolence and the Management of Stake: On Being 'Good White People.'" *Philament* 4 (2004): http://www.arts.usyd.edu.au/publications/philament/issue4_Critique_Riggs.htm.

Rios, Víctor. *Punished: Policing the Lives of Black and Latino Boys.* New York: New York University Press, 2011.

Roberts, Michelle Voss. *Feminist Theology: The Journal of the Britain & Ireland School of Feminist Theology* 18, no. 1 (2009): 50–73.

Roediger, David R. *The Wages of Whiteness: Race and the Making of the American Working Class.* London & New York: Verso, 1991.

Roelofs, Monique. "Sensation as Civilization: Reading/Riding the Taxicab." Special issue of *Contemporary Aesthetics* 7 (2009).

Roman, Leslie. "White is a Color! White Defensiveness, Postmodernism and Anti-racist Pedagogy." In *Race, Identity and Representation in Education*, edited by Cameron McCarthy and Warren Crinchlow. New York: Routledge, 1993. 71–88.

Rushing, Sara. "Preparing for Politics: Judith Butler's Ethical Dispositions." *Contemporary Political Theory* 9, no. 3, 284–303.

Shotwell, Alexis. *Knowing Otherwise:Race, Gender and Implicit Understanding.* University Park: Pennsylvania State University Press, 2011.

Simmons, Joy. "My White Self." *A PA Newsletter on Philosophy and the Black Experience* 6, no. 2 (Spring 2007).

Skeggs, B. "The making of class and gender through visualizing moral subject formation." *Sociology* 39, no. 5 (2005): 965–82.

Smith, L. T. *Decolonizing Methodologies: Research and Indigenous Peoples.* London: Sage, 2000.

Spelman, Elizabeth V. *Inessential Woman: Problems of Exclusion in Feminist Thought.* Boston: Beacon Press, 1988.

———. "Managing Ignorance." In *Race and Epistemologies of Ignorance*, edited by Shannon Sullivan and Nancy Tuana. Albany: State University of New York Press, 2007.

Stanley, Fred L., and Louis H. Pratt, eds. *Conversations with James Baldwin.* Jackson: University Press of Mississippi, 1989.

Stilson, Jeff. *Good Hair.* Roadside Attractions, 2009.

Stubblefield, Anna. "Meditations on Postsupremacist Philosophy." In *White on White Black on Black*, edited by George Yancy.

———. *Ethics Along the Color Line.* Ithaca: Cornell University Press, 2005.

Sullivan, S., and N. Tuana. *Race and Epistemologies of Ignorance.* State University of New York Press, 2007.

Sullivan, Shannon. *Good White People: The Problem with Middle-Class White Anti-Racism.* New York: SUNY Press, 2014.

———. *Revealing Whiteness: The Unconscious Habits of Racial Privilege.* Bloomington, Indiana: University of Indiana Press, 2006.

Takaki, Ronald. *A Different Mirror: A History of Multicultural America, revised edition.* New York: Little, Brown, 2008.

Tatum, Beverly D. *Why Are All The Black Kids Sitting Together in the Cafeteria? And Other Conversations About Race.* New York: Basic Books, 1997.

Teel, Karen. "What Jesus wouldn't do: a white theologian engages whiteness." In *Christology and Whiteness: What Would Jesus Do?*, edited by George Yancy. London and New York: Routledge, 2012. 19–35.

Thompson, Audrey. "Entertaining Doubts: Enjoyment and Ambiguity in White, Antiracist Classrooms." In *Passion and Pedagogy: Relation, Creation, and Transformation in Teaching*, edited by Elijah Mirochick and Debora C. Sherman. New York: Peter Lang, 2002. 431–52.

———. "Not the Color Purple: Black Feminist Lessons for Educational Caring." *Harvard Educational Review* 68, no. 4 (1998): 522–54.

———. "'Tiffany, friend of people of color': White investments in antiracism." *International Journal of Qualitative Studies in Education* 16, no. 1 (2003): 7–29.

Thomson, Patricia. "Field." In *Pierre Bourdieu: Key Concepts*, edited by Michael Grenfell. Durham, UK: Acumen, 2008.

Thorsen, Karen, dir. *James Baldwin: The Price of the Ticket.* San Francisco: California Newsreel, 1990.

Three Rivers, Amoja. *Cultural Etiquette: A Guide for the Well Intentioned.* Indian Valley, VA: Market Wimmin, 1990

Townes, Emilie M. *Womanist Ethics and the Cultural Production of Evil.* New York: Palgrave Macmillan, 2006.

Truth and Reconciliation Commission. "Truth and Reconciliantion Commission of Canada: Interim Report," 2012.

Tuana, Nancy. "The Speculum of Ignorance: The Women's Health Movement and Epistemologies of Ignorance." *Hypatia* 21, no. 3 (2006): 1–19.

TuSmith, Bonnie. "Out on a Limb: Race and the Evaluation of Frontline Teaching." In *Race in the College Classroom*, edited by Bonnie TuSmith and Maureen T. Reddy. New Brunswick, NJ: Rutgers University Press, 2002. 112–25.

United for a Fair Economy. "State of the Dream 2012: The Emerging Majority." http://faireconomy.org/sites/default/files/State_of_the_Dream_2012.pdf.

Van Jordan, A. *Quantum Lyrics: Poems.* New York: W. W. Norton & Company, 2009.

Vice, S. "How Do I Live in This Strange Place?" *Journal of Social Philosophy* 41, no. 3 (2010): 323–42.

Walker, Alice. *In Search of Our Mothers' Gardens: Womanist Prose.* Orlando: Harcourt, 1983.

Wallerstein, Immanuel. *The Uncertainties of Knowledge.* Philadelphia: Temple University Press, 2004.

Warren, John. *Performing Purity: Whiteness, Pedagogy, and the Reconstitution of Power.* New York: Peter Lang, 2003.

Willett, Cynthia. "Book Review: Black Bodies, White Gazes." *APA Newsletter, on Philosophy and the Black Experience* 9, no. 1 (2009): 26.

Williams, Christine, L. "The Glass Escalator: Hidden Advantages for Men in the 'Female' Professions." *Social Problems* 39, no. 3 (1992): 253–67.

Wise, Tim. *White Like Me: Reflections on Race from a Privileged Son*, revised and updated. Brooklyn, NY: Soft Skull, 2008.

———.*Colorblind: The Rise of Post-Racial Politics and the Retreat from Racial Equity.* San Francisco: City Lights, 2010.

Yancy, George, E. Ethelbert Miller, and Charles Johnson. "Interpretative Profiles on Charles Johnson's Reflections on Trayvon Martin: A Dialogue between George Yancy, E. Ethelbert Miller, and Charles Johnson." *The Western Journal of Black Studies* 38, no. 1 (2014): 3–14.

Yancy, George. "Fragments of a Social Ontology of Whiteness." In *What White Looks Like: African American Philosophers on the Whiteness Question.* New York: Routledge, 2004. 1–25.

———. *Black Bodies, White Gazes: The Continuing Significance of Race.* Lanham, MD: Rowman & Littlefield, 2008.

———. "Introduction: framing the problem." In *Christology and Whiteness: What Would Jesus Do?*, edited by George Yancy. London and New York: Routledge, 2012. 1–18.

———. *Look, A White!: Philosophical Essays on Whiteness.* Philadelphia: Temple University Press, 2012.

———. *The Center Must Not Hold: White Women Philosophers on the Whiteness of Philosophy.* Lanham, MD: Lexington Books, 2010.

——— (ed). *White on White, Black on Black.* Lanham, MD: Rowman & Littlefield, 2005.

Young, Iris Marian. *Justice and the Politics of Difference.* Princeton: Princeton University Press, 1990.

Young, Iris. *On Female Body Experience: "Throwing Like a Girl" and Other Essays.* New York: Oxford University Press, 2005.

Zinn, Howard. *A People's History of the United States*. New York: Harper, 2005.

Index

abolitionism, 185n11, 186n24
Aboriginal peoples, 63, 67n8. *See also* indigenous peoples
Ackah, William, 198–199
An Act of Terror (Brink), 57
affirmative action, 90, 177; repeal of, 178
African Americans. *See* people of color
Afrofuturism, 220
Ahmed, Sara, 5–6, 222–223; politics of disorientation, 212–213, 219–221, 226n52, 226n53
Alexander, Michelle, 168
Allen, David G., 106
"Almost Black, part 1" (Chance), 218
alterity, xix, xx–xxi
ambush, xiii; arrival, processes of, xiv; dispossession, xiv; relational white self, xiv
American Dream, 124, 127–128
Anderson, Viv, 192
antiracism, 29–30, 164, 165
antiwar movement, 172
Apology (Plato), 134
Applebaum, Barbara, xxvn7, 37, 44, 47, 54n21, 127
apprehension, 13–14, 16
Arapahoe people, 60
Armstrong, Lance, 117–118
Australasia, 195
Ayvazian, Andrea, 136
Azaransky, Sarah, 35n29

Bailey, Alison, 125, 133, 136; "whitely scripts," 135
Baker, Clarence, 208n4
Ball, Tom, xxiii–xxiv
Baldwin, James, xv, xvi, xxv, 37–38, 46, 49, 54n26, 85–86, 87–88, 96, 97, 98, 102; as bearing witness, 97–98; white guilt, 102–103
Bartky, Sandra Lee, 34n14, 155, 157
Batson, Brendan, 192
Bay, Mia, 102
Belgian Congo, 74
Beloved (Morrison), 207
Bennett, Lerone, 39
Bierce, Ambrose, 117
Black Bodies, White Gazes: The Continuing Significance of Race (Yancy), xiii, 7, 144
blackness, xx–xxi; black-on-black crime, xvii–xviii; black power, 174; burdens of, 39
Blueford, Alan, 173
Bonila-Silva, Eduardo, 4
Boulder (Colorado), 58–59, 60–61, 67n3
Bourdieu, Pierre, 162; theory of practice, 161, 164
Braden, Anne, 158
Brink, Andre, 57
Britain, 195, 197, 201, 203, 205; National Front party, 191; otherness in, 190–191; radio stations, diversity of, 192. *See*

About the Editor and Contributors

George Yancy is professor of philosophy at Duquesne University. He received his BA (with honors) in philosophy from the University of Pittsburgh, his first master's degree from Yale University in philosophy, and his second master's degree in Africana Studies from NYU, where he received a distinguished fellowship. His PhD (with distinction) is in philosophy from Duquesne University. His work focuses primarily in the areas of critical philosophy of race, critical whiteness studies, and philosophy of the black experience. He has authored, edited, or co-edited seventeen books and many academic articles and book chapters. Yancy's work has been cited as far as South Africa, Australia, Turkey, and Sweden. His first authored book received an honorable mention from the Gustavus Myers Center for the Study of Bigotry and Human Rights, and three of his edited books have received *CHOICE* outstanding academic book awards. He is co-editor of the *American Philosophical Association Newsletter on Philosophy and the Black Experience*, and is an ex-officio member of the American Philosophical Association Committee on Blacks in Philosophy. He has also recently become the editor of the Philosophy of Race series at Lexington Books. He has twice won the Duquesne University McAnulty College and Graduate School of Liberal Arts Faculty Award for Excellence in Scholarship. He is currently working on two edited books and a new authored book.

* * *

Rebecca Aanerud is associate dean of the graduate school and senior lecturer of gender, women, and sexuality studies at the University of Washington. Her research and publications have followed two separate but related lines of inquiry: issues of racism, whiteness, and feminist theory; and issues associated with graduate education and career paths of doctoral recipients. Most recently, her work has taken up wisdom. She explores the role of wisdom for social justice movements, feminist practice and pedagogy, and higher education. She is the author of "Fictions of Whiteness: Speaking the Names of Whiteness in US Literature," in *Displacing Whiteness: Essays in Social and Cultural Criticism*, edited by Ruth Frankenberg; "Now More than Ever: James Baldwin and the Critique of White Liberalism" in *James Baldwin Now*, edited by Dwight McBride; "Thinking Again: *This Bridge Called My Back* and the Challenge to Whiteness" in *This Bridge We Call Home*, edited by AnaLouise Keating and Gloria Anzaldua; and "The Legacy of White Supremacy and the Challenge of White Antiracist Mothering" in *Hypatia.*

Barbara Applebaum is associate professor in cultural foundations of education at Syracuse University. She is the author of *Being White, Being Good: White Complicity, White Moral Responsibility, and Social Justice Pedagogy* (Lanham, MD: Lexington Books, 2010). She has published in *Educational Theory, Teachers College Record*, the *Journal of Moral Education*, and *Educational Foundations*. Her current research projects focus on the relationship between agency and complicity, rearticulating white moral responsibility, and what she refers to as "white complicity pedagogy."

Alison Bailey is professor of philosophy at Illinois State University where she also directs the Women's and Gender Studies Program. Her scholarship engages broadly with questions in feminist ethics, with a focus on applied issues related to social privilege, intersectionality, reproductive justice, and epistemologies of ignorance. She has co-edited a special issue of *Hypatia* on "The Reproduction of Whiteness: Race and the Regulation of the Gendered Body," with Jacquelyn N. Zita (2007), and *The Feminist Philosophy Reader* (2008) with Chris J. Cuomo. Her scholarship appears in *Hypatia, The Journal of Social Philosophy, The Journal of Peace and Justice Studies, South African Journal of Philosophy*, and in collections such as *Race and Epistemologies of Ignorance (2007) and The Center Must Not Hold: White Women Philosophers on the Whiteness of Philosophy* (2010). Her two recent research projects address the need to reframe the moral dimensions of transnational surrogacy, and the epistemological and moral underpinnings of intersectionality.

Steve Garner is senior lecturer in sociology at Aston University, Birmingham, UK. He is the coauthor (with Simon Clarke) of *White Identities: A Critical Sociological Perspective* (Pluto Press, 2010), *Racisms* (Sage, 2009), and *Whiteness: An Introduction* (Routledge, 2007) among others. He has published in *Sociology, Ethnic and Racial Studies, Patterns of Prejudice and Ethnicities*, as well as carrying out projects for local authorities and NGOs.

His current research projects focus on the discourse around skin whitening; naturalization and obtaining citizenship as an excluding process in Europe; and the phenomenon of Islamophobia.

Robin James is an associate professor in the Philosophy Department at UNC Charlotte, where she is also affiliated with the Women's and Gender Studies Program and the Center for Professional and Applied Ethics. James's theoretical and creative research bridges philosophy, gender/sexuality studies, critical race theory, musicology, popular music studies, and sound studies. Her writing has appeared in venues such as *The New Inquiry*, *Hypatia*, *The Journal of Popular Music Studies*, *Contemporary Aesthetics*, *PhaenEx*, *Philosophy Compass*, and the anthology *Convergences: Black Feminism and Continental Philosophy*. Her book, *The Conjectural Body: Gender, Race, and the Philosophy of Music*, was published in 2010 by Lexington Books. Her creative research uses music, sound art, and digital technology to examine the role of sound in contemporary forms of knowledge, value, pleasure, embodiment, and capital.

Robert Jensen is a professor in the School of Journalism at the University of Texas at Austin and board member of the Third Coast Activist Resource Center in Austin. He is the author of several books, including *Arguing for Our Lives: A User's Guide to Constructive Dialogue* (City Lights, 2013) and *The Heart of Whiteness: Confronting Race, Racism and White Privilege* (City Lights, 2005). He also is co-producer of the documentary film *Abe Osheroff: One Foot in the Grave, the Other Still Dancing* (Media Education Foundation, 2009), which chronicles the life and philosophy of the longtime radical activist.

Crista Lebens is associate professor of philosophy in the Philosophy and Religious Studies Department at the University of Wisconsin-Whitewater. She has published in *An Anthology of Philosophical Studies* and *International Studies in Philosophy*. Her current research projects include an exploration of gender identity through the framework of Maria Lugones's Logic of Curdling.

Steve Martinot is a retired lecturer from San Francisco State University. He had worked for years as a machinist and a truck driver during the 1960s and 1970s and organized labor unions and community associations in New York City and Akron, Ohio. He has published eight books in philosophy, historical analysis, and cultural analysis. Among these are *The Rule of Racialization* (2003), and *The Machinery of Whiteness* (2009), both from Temple University Press. His latest publication is a pamphlet on "The Need to Abolish the

Prison System," self-published to the Occupy and prison abolition movements.

Nancy McHugh is professor of philosophy and department chair at Wittenberg University. She is the author of *What Can We Do?: Pragmatist Feminism and Transactionally Situated Knowing* (2015), *Feminist Philosophies A–Z* (2007), and articles in feminist epistemology and philosophy of science. Nancy is one of the founding members of FEMMSS (Feminist Epistemology, Metaphysics, Methodology and Sciences Studies). She also teaches as part of the Inside-Out Prison Exchange Program, which brings traditional college students and people who are incarcerated together to learn in a prison classroom.

Bridget M. Newell, PhD, is the associate provost for diversity at Bucknell University, Lewisburg, Pennsylvania. Prior to her arrival at Bucknell in the fall of 2012, Newell served as associate provost for diversity and global learning and professor of philosophy and gender studies at Westminster College, Salt Lake City, UT, where she served as a mentor for the Ronald E. McNair Scholars Program and chair of the Diversity Council, among others. Courses she has taught include Science, Power and Diversity, Philosophy and Diversity, and Feminist Issues in Philosophy.

David S. Owen is associate professor of philosophy and director of Diversity Programs for the College of Arts and Sciences at the University of Louisville. His research interests are in philosophy of race, social philosophy, philosophy of diversity, and the Frankfurt School. He has previously published *Between Reason and History: Habermas and the Idea of Progress* (SUNY, 2002) and is currently developing a critical theory of whiteness.

Crispin Sartwell is associate professor of art and art history at Dickinson College in Carlisle, Pennsylvania. He is the author of *Act Like You Know: African-American Autobiography and White Identity* (University of Chicago, 1998), *Against the State* (SUNY 2008), and *Political Aesthetics* (Cornell, 2010), among other books.

Alexis Shotwell is an associate professor at Carleton University. She is the author of *Knowing Otherwise: Race, Gender, and Implicit Understanding* (University Park, PA: Penn State Press, 2011). She has published in *Signs*, *Hypatia*, and *Sociological Theory*. Her academic work addresses racial formation, unspeakable and unspoken knowledge, sexuality, gender, and political transformation.

Karen Teel is associate professor in the Department of Theology and Religious Studies at the University of San Diego. She is the author of *Racism and the Image of God* (Palgrave Macmillan, 2010). Her primary research, including a chapter titled "What Jesus Wouldn't Do: A White Theologian Engages Whiteness" in a previous volume edited by George Yancy (*Christology and Whiteness*, Routledge, 2012), investigates whiteness as a Christian theological problem. In her current book project, she aims to expose dominant white ways of believing in Jesus as central to the development and perpetuation of whiteness.